Greenhouse and Nursery Management Practices To Protect Water Quality

TECHNICAL EDITOR JULIE NEWMAN

To order or obtain ANR publications and other products, visit the ANR Communication Services online catalog at http://anrcatalog.ucdavis.edu or phone 1-800-994-8849. You can also place orders by mail or FAX, or request a printed catalog of our products from

University of California
Agriculture and Natural Resources
Communication Services
6701 San Pablo Avenue, 2nd Floor
Oakland, California 94608-1239

Telephone 1-800-994-8849
(510) 642-2431
FAX (510) 643-5470
E-mail: danrcs@ucdavis.edu

Publication 3508
ISBN-13: 978-1-60107-571-0
Library of Congress Control Number: 2008907868

Photo credits are given in the captions. Front cover photos, top to bottom: D. Haver, J. K. Clark, J. Newman, and D. Zurawski; background photo: J. K. Clark. Back cover photo: T. Harter, from *Watersheds, Groundwater, and Drinking Water: A Practical Guide* (ANR Publication 3497, 2008), p. 139. Cover design by Robin Walton.

Agriculture and Natural Resources, 1111 Franklin Street, 6th Floor, Oakland, CA 94607-5201, (510) 987-0096. For information about ordering this publication visit anrcatalog.ucdavis.edu or telephone 1-800-994-8849.

To simplify information, trade names of products have been used. No endorsement of named or illustrated products is intended, nor is criticism implied of similar products that are not mentioned or illustrated.

 This publication has been anonymously peer reviewed for technical accuracy by University of California scientists and other qualified professionals. This review process was managed by the ANR Associate Editor for Land, Air, and Water Sciences.

Printed in Canada on recycled paper.

1.5m-pr-12/08-SB/RW

WARNING ON THE USE OF CHEMICALS

Pesticides are poisonous. Always read and carefully follow all precautions and safety recommendations given on the container label. Store all chemicals in their original labeled containers in a locked cabinet or shed, away from foods or feeds, and out of the reach of children, unauthorized persons, pets, and livestock.

Recommendations are based on the best information currently available, and treatments based on them should not leave residues exceeding the tolerance established for any particular chemical. Confine chemicals to the area being treated. THE GROWER IS LEGALLY RESPONSIBLE for residues on the grower's crops as well as for problems caused by drift from the grower's property to other properties or crops.

Consult your county agricultural commissioner for correct methods of disposing of leftover spray materials and empty containers. Never burn pesticide containers.

PHYTOTOXICITY: Certain chemicals may cause plant injury if used at the wrong stage of plant development or when temperatures are too high. Injury may also result from excessive amounts or the wrong formulation or from mixing incompatible materials. Inert ingredients, such as wetters, spreaders, emulsifiers, diluents, and solvents, can cause plant injury. Since formulations are often changed by manufacturers, it is possible that plant injury may occur, even though no injury was noted in previous seasons.

◖◗ CONTENTS

◖◗ AUTHORS

RICHARD EVANS, University of California Cooperative Extension Environmental Horticulture Specialist, UC Davis

BEN FABER, University of California Cooperative Extension Farm Advisor, Ventura County

JAY GAN, Water Quality Specialist, UC Riverside

DARREN HAVER, University of California Cooperative Extension Farm Advisor, Orange County

JIANHANG LU, Assistant Project Scientist, Department of Environmental Sciences, UC Riverside

VALERIE MELLANO, University of California Cooperative Extension Farm Advisor, San Diego County

DONALD J. MERHAUT, University of California Cooperative Extension Nursery and Floriculture Crops Specialist, Department of Botany and Plant Sciences, UC Riverside

JULIE NEWMAN, University of California Cooperative Extension Farm Advisor, Ventura County

KAREN ROBB, University of California Cooperative Extension Farm Advisor, Mariposa County

LARRY SCHWANKL, University of California Cooperative Extension Irrigation Specialist, Kearney Agricultural Center

CHERYL WILEN, University of California IPM Advisor, San Diego County

LAOSHENG WU, University of California Cooperative Extension Water Management Specialist, Department of Environmental Sciences, UC Riverside

◖◖◔ ACKNOWLEDGMENTS

Funding for developing this publication was provided in part through a contract with the State Water Resources Control Board (SWRCB) pursuant to the Costa-Machado Act of 2000 (Proposition 13) and any amendments thereto for the implementation of California's Nonpoint Source Pollution Control Program. The contents of this document do not necessarily reflect the views and policies of the SWRCB, nor does mention of trade names or commercial products constitute endorsement or recommendation for use.

It is not recommended that the suggested management practices in this publication ever be used as a basis for law. We understand that every operation is unique and requires a site-specific assessment of whether there is a need to implement further management practices, and whether recommended practices are in fact appropriate to a site. Not all the information needed to implement these measures is contained in this publication.

The technical editor and authors would like to acknowledge the following organizations without whose assistance this publication could not have been produced: the State Water Resources Control Board, the Los Angeles Regional Water Quality Control Board, the California Cut Flower Commission, the Channel Islands Chapter of the California Association of Nurseries and Garden Centers, and the Natural Resources Conservation District, Somis. We also thank all the nursery growers who participated in the University of California water quality program in Ventura and Los Angeles Counties and provided assistance in the development of this manual. Finally, this publication could not have been completed without the dedicated efforts in project management, copy production and coordination of photographic efforts by Kristine Gilbert, Dale Zurawski, and Amy Ellis (research associates, UC Cooperative Extension, Ventura County); the assistance in copy editing provided by Salvatore Mangiafico (Postdoctoral Researcher, Department of Environmental Sciences, UC Riverside); and the vision inspired by the Farm Water Quality Project Team Leader Mary Bianchi (UC Cooperative Extension Farm Advisor, San Luis Obispo County).

Greenhouse and Nursery Management Practices To Protect Water Quality

Protecting Water Quality

Julie Newman, University of California Cooperative Extension Farm Advisor, Ventura County

Why We Need to Protect Our Watersheds

Overview

Watersheds warrant protection because they are where we live, work, and play. We depend on water for drinking, irrigating plants, and industrial use. Our streams and lakes are valued for their beauty and for recreation, including fishing, swimming, and boating. Wildlife depends on the watershed for survival. The health of our watersheds directly contributes to our economy.

A watershed is a land area that drains water into a particular stream, river, or lake. Each watershed is a catchment area divided from the next watershed by topographic features such as ridge tops. All land is part of a watershed. Everywhere you go, you are in a watershed that is shedding its water to larger bodies of water.

Our activities affect the health of the watershed. As precipitation falls and flows down slopes, pollutants and sediments that are generated from our activities attach to the water molecules. These pollutants are then carried with the moving water. Infiltration occurs when precipitation seeps into the ground. Infiltration depends on permeability, which is a measure of how

easily something flows through a substance. The more permeable the soil, the more precipitation is able to seep into the ground. If precipitation occurs faster than it can infiltrate the ground, it becomes runoff. Runoff remains on the surface and flows into streams, rivers, and eventually large water bodies, such as lakes or the ocean. Infiltrated groundwater recharges rivers and also flows toward large bodies of water.

Pollutants originating from a single source, as from a pipe or disposal site, are referred to as point source pollution. These point sources include industry and wastewater treatment plants that now operate under permit systems. Sources of point source pollution are currently less of a problem than they have been in the past. Nonpoint source pollution is water pollution that comes from a multitude of sources, including human activities such as agriculture and nonhuman sources such as bird feces in coastal lagoons. Nationwide, nonpoint source pollution is the major contributor to water quality problems and is receiving increased attention from regulators. These sources are often difficult to identify and measure.

Nonpoint source pollution from human sources can come from a variety of activities. Oil from cars, household chemicals, erosion from construction sites, stormwater runoff from urban areas, and failing septic systems all contribute to nonpoint source pollution. Even air pollutants such as automobile exhaust and pesticide-laden dust particles that are dissipated into the atmosphere can fall back to the earth as contaminants in rainwater.

Agriculture is one of several industries that have been identified as contributing to nonpoint source pollution. Certain growing practices such as using pesticides and fertilizers contribute to nonpoint source pollution. We all contribute to nonpoint source pollution. Although we may be small contributors individually, the cumulative impact from everyone in a watershed has a tremendous effect. The best way to protect a watershed is to work together to prevent pollution. This is easier and cheaper than trying to clean up a watershed.

Increasing Regulations for Agriculture

Another reason that you as a grower should strive to protect our watersheds is that it is a legal obligation. A number of federal and state laws have been enacted to protect water quality. In addition to California, states such as Maryland have passed strict laws to protect water quality, while many states rely on federal regulations and voluntary compliance.

Following are short descriptions of selected federal and state laws that provide the State of California with the authority to regulate point and nonpoint sources of pollution, including pollution from agriculture. For more information about these laws and other regulations, refer to *Water Pollution Control Legislation* (Jones et al. 2003).

Federal Laws

Clean Water Act
The Federal Water Pollution Control Act Amendments of 1972 and 1977, known as the Clean Water Act, are the principal federal statutes for water quality protection. In California, the State Water Resources Control Board (SWRCB) and the nine regional water quality control boards administer many of the Clean

Water Act's provisions. This law addresses water pollution and water quality of surface water, including lakes, rivers, streams, estuaries, and wetlands. It includes sections addressing both point and nonpoint sources of pollution. It also establishes beneficial uses of water and water quality criteria to protect those uses. Some cities in San Diego County have been sued in recent years for not enforcing the Clean Water Act. As a result, nursery and greenhouse activities in these areas have been heavily regulated by city and county governments. Not complying with regulations can lead to increased enforcement of regulations for an entire agricultural community.

Section 303(d) of the Clean Water Act requires states to make a list of impaired water bodies and develop total maximum daily loads (TMDLs) for them. Water bodies are considered impaired when they are too polluted or otherwise degraded to support their designated and existing uses. A TMDL is the calculation of the maximum amount of a pollutant a water body can receive daily and still meet water quality standards. TMDLs affecting agricultural activities have been established and implemented for impaired water bodies in various areas throughout the state.

Safe Drinking Water Act
Under the Safe Drinking Water Act of 1974 (SDWA), the U.S. Environmental Protection Agency (EPA) identifies contaminants that may adversely affect public health and sets national drinking water standards. SDWA was amended in 1996 to require that each state assess drinking water sources such as rivers, lakes, and groundwater wells. California is implementing these requirements as part of the Drinking Water Source Assessment and Protection Program (DWSAP). This implementation includes delineating the source area of the water in wells or other drinking water source area. All potential contaminating activities within the source area must be identified. Agricultural activities, especially using fertilizers and pesticides, are listed as possible contaminating activities.

State Laws

Porter-Cologne Act

The Porter-Cologne Act of 1969 is the principal law governing water quality in California. It establishes a comprehensive program to protect water quality and the beneficial uses of water. Unlike the Clean Water Act, Porter-Cologne applies to surface water and groundwater. Porter-Cologne established the State Water Resources Control Board as the statewide water quality planning agency. It also gave authority to the nine regional water quality control boards (regional water boards) that were established 20 years earlier by the Dickey Water Pollution Act. The Porter-Cologne Act requires the adoption of water quality control plans (basin plans) by the regional water boards for watersheds within their regions.

Senate Bill 390

The California Water Code authorizes the state and regional water boards to conditionally waive waste discharge requirements (WDRs) if this is in the public interest. Although waivers are always conditional, waivers in the past had few conditions. In general, waivers required that discharges not cause violations of water quality objectives but did not require water quality monitoring. Senate Bill 390 (SB 390), signed into law on October 6, 1999, required the regional water boards to review their existing waivers and to renew them or replace them with WDRs. Under SB 390, waivers not reissued automatically expired on January 1, 2003. To comply with SB 390, the regional water boards adopted revised waivers. These included the controversial waivers for irrigated agriculture. The Central Coast, Central Valley, and Los Angeles Water Boards have adopted conditional waivers for agricultural discharges. The agricultural waivers use different regulatory models in each region, are conditional, and comply with SB 390. Eventually, regional water quality control boards in other regions will adopt conditional waivers for agricultural discharges or will issue waste discharge requirements in order to address nonpoint source pollution from agriculture. If your nursery operation is in one of the regions that have adopted revised waivers, you have mandatory monitoring and educational requirements. You should contact your regional water board if you are not already familiar with the requirements.

What Are the Nursery Pollutants?

Nursery runoff often contains fertilizers, pesticides, and sediment in quantities that exceed federal and state water quality standards. These pollutants degrade our coastal waters and other water bodies in our watersheds, causing impairment.

Fertilizers

Fertilizers in surface runoff are harmful to water bodies when levels are high enough to promote growth of algae and aquatic vegetation beyond what is naturally sustainable. This growth reduces water clarity. When growth is unchecked it can cover the entire surface of a pond or lake. Such a "bloom" of algae depletes oxygen, killing fish. Fertilizer nitrogen can also contaminate drinking water supplies. This is particularly a problem in groundwater.

Pesticides

Pesticides are designed to control specific pests, such as weeds, insects, mites, fungi, nematodes, and vertebrates. Pesticides differ greatly in their degree of toxicity. In general, insecticides that contaminate water bodies have high toxicity to fish and other aquatic organisms, even at the trace amounts commonly found in California streams. In addition, some herbicides have high toxicity to aquatic plants. Contamination of groundwater by pesticides is of human health concern, as groundwater is an important source for drinking water in California. It is critical for pesticide users to understand why and how pesticides contaminate water and what can be done to reduce pesticide runoff.

Other Chemicals

In addition to chemicals for controlling pests, other agricultural and household chemicals used in nursery production can contaminate water. These include postharvest chemical treatments, growth regulators (which are classified as pesticides), exterior shading compounds, and household cleaning and disinfectant products. Large quantities of these materials could be damaging if spilled into a small stream or a sanitary sewage treatment system, or if allowed to percolate into groundwater.

Care is needed when disposing of agricultural chemicals, especially the antiethylene postharvest treatment silver thiosulfate (STS). Silver is a heavy metal that persists in soil and water and may pollute drinking water. STS is highly toxic to aquatic organisms. When absorbed by the body, heavy metals accumulate and at toxic levels affect the nervous system.

Greenhouse shading compounds also require careful use and disposal. Most exterior shading compounds contain latex paint, which is toxic to marine life. They may contain ethylene glycol, which can also be hazardous to humans. Some greenhouse shading compounds contain sodium hydroxide, which is strongly alkaline. These products must be disposed of properly because high-pH substances can be toxic to fish.

Sediment

Sediment consists of loose particles of clay, silt, and sand mobilized by water or air. It eventually enters a body of water and settles to the bottom. It is the most common nonpoint source pollutant. Sediment is a natural component of a watershed, but in excessive amounts it has harmful effects. Water-induced erosion is the process by which the surface of the soil gets worn down by water. It begins when rain or irrigation water loosens soil or potting mix particles. Erosion produces excess sediment that can clog streams and creeks, often causing flooding.

Sediment runoff has serious implications for the health of the aquatic environment. Suspended sediment clouds the water, preventing light from penetrating to aquatic plants, including underwater grasses, submerged aquatic vegetation, and phytoplankton (microscopic algae). Reduced light affects the ability of these plants to produce food through photosynthesis. This results in fewer plants to serve as food for other aquatic organisms. In this manner, sediment disrupts the food chain. Sediment also interferes with the physiological function, feeding, and reproduction of fish and aquatic organisms. Sediment is of special concern because of its role as a carrier of other pollutants such as phosphorus and pesticides.

The Challenge for Greenhouse and Nursery Production

Generally, growing high-quality ornamental flowers and plants requires large amounts of water, fertilizer, and pesticides. The challenge for you as a grower is to manage these inputs properly so as to minimize the potential for both surface water and groundwater pollution from your operation.

Water

Many ornamental crop producers apply more water than plants need. This is partly due to untrained staff who are often charged with the responsibility of irrigating crops. In their zeal to produce rapidly growing, high-quality plants that are not water stressed, they overcompensate and apply too much water.

Another factor is inefficient irrigation systems with poor irrigation distribution. To illustrate, if one side of an irrigation system is applying half the amount of water that the other side is applying, the system must be run twice as long to ensure that the plants on the low-application side are being adequately watered. This leads to overirrigation on the high-application side, resulting in runoff water that is not used by the crop.

Excessive irrigation generates runoff. This is especially a problem in woody container nurseries, where runoff discharges from large nurseries have been documented to be as much as 4,000,000 gallons per month. Runoff also accelerates erosion, leading to excess sediment that clogs pipes and ditches, causing flooding. Sediment that leaves the nursery makes its way into nearby streams, where it impacts the health of aquatic ecosystems.

Growers who use irrigation water of marginal quality must take steps to avoid negative effects on crops. The standard industry practice is to leach to prevent accumulation of salts in the root zone. Excessive leaching leads to greater runoff volumes. Nutrients and pesticides carried by leached water can be a source of groundwater and surface water contamination.

Fertilizer

Fertilizer use on ornamental plants is very intensive due to the high demand for nitrogen by greenhouse and nursery crops. A recent survey conducted at the University of California, Davis, found that more than 60 percent of California greenhouses have more than 450 pounds of nitrogen per acre in the root zone at any given time. Some nurseries have more than three-quarters of a ton of fertilizer nitrogen per acre. In many cases, over half of the fertilizer nitrogen applied to ornamental crops is lost to leaching. The potential for fertilizer leaching is compounded when growers overwater.

Leaching of fertilizer nitrogen is especially problematic in woody container nurseries. This is due to limited root systems in container-grown plants with relatively large shoot canopies. It is also due to using porous, quick-draining plant media. Frequent fertilization is required to provide sufficient nutrients. Consequently, nitrogen usage per acre by the woody container nursery industry is often more than usage by any other horticultural or agronomic crop. Fertilizer runoff from many nurseries still exceeds the federal drinking water standard of 10 parts per million nitrate–nitrogen (10 ppm NO_3^-–N).

Pesticides

Pesticide use on ornamental crops is usually more intensive than on most other agricultural crops. This is because ornamental crops are valued for their aesthetic beauty. Consumer demand requires little tolerance for disease blemishes and insect damage. In addition,

quarantine restrictions of exotic pests mandate using pesticides known to be harmful to aquatic organisms.

Another factor that contributes to the high use of chemicals is that many of the major pests attacking ornamental crops are known to be resistant to one or more pesticides. The result is a vicious cycle of ever-expanding pesticide use in spite of stricter regulations governing pesticide use and runoff from operations.

According to the pesticide use reports submitted to the California Department of Pesticide Regulation (DPR), the greatest pesticide use at nurseries occurs in the outdoor container nurseries and field-grown plants. This heavy pesticide use, when coupled with the intensive irrigation regime used by many nurseries, poses significant risks for pesticides to contaminate surface and groundwater.

Many pesticides used by nurseries are organophosphate and synthetic pyrethroid insecticides. These pesticides have high toxicities to fish and other aquatic organisms. The presence of these pesticides in streams can cause adverse impacts on aquatic ecosystems.

This eco-toxicological consideration drives the regulation of pesticide runoff, including at sites such as commercial nurseries. There are currently a number of TMDLs in force for pesticides in California, and more pesticide TMDLs are expected in the near future.

So, What's the Solution?

How do you balance the requirements of your crops with the moral and legal obligations to protect the watershed, and still make a profit? The easiest way is to implement management practices that protect against runoff and leaching of fertilizers, pesticides, and other agricultural chemicals used in producing your crops. Helping you do this is the objective of this manual. Our goal is to provide you with the information and tools you need to understand these water quality management practices so you can more easily implement them.

Management Goals and Management Practices to Protect Water Quality

In chapter 2 you will find management goals and management practices that can help you prevent runoff or leachate from leaving your property. A management goal (MG) is an economically achievable technology or process for effectively limiting runoff and groundwater leaching. A management practice (MP) is a specific practice for accomplishing a management goal. Management practices have been referred to as "best management practices" (BMPs), but since the "best" practices vary with on-site specifications, this term is no longer used as frequently as in the past.

The first step in preventing pollution is to understand how pollution is generated in your operation and what interrelated water quality management practices can be combined to manage it. The second step involves developing a plan for protecting water quality by determining which management practices to adopt in each phase of your operation.

A. Irrigation Management Goals

Irrigation management involves matching the amount of applied water precisely to plant needs. You can reduce water use and water pollution by adjusting irrigation frequency through careful scheduling and irrigation application efficiency. We have identified five management goals that growers can implement to limit runoff and leaching:

A.1. Design or retrofit your irrigation system for improved irrigation uniformity and efficiency to reduce runoff and leaching.

A.2. Regularly maintain your irrigation system so that it continues to operate efficiently.

A.3. Regularly manage crops, crop areas, and irrigation systems to avoid applying water to noncropped areas or applying irrigation when not needed.

A.4. Use appropriate irrigation rates and scheduling.

A.5. Provide appropriate training for personnel involved in irrigating in a language that personnel clearly understand, and maintain records documenting training.

B. Nutrient Management Goals

Optimizing fertility means providing nutrients in the right quantities at the right times and at the right locations. Providing the correct balance of nutrients requires research and planning. Leaching programs must be implemented that do not contribute to nitrate runoff. We have developed four nutrient management goals:

B.1. Evaluate irrigation water, soils, growing media, and plant tissue for nutrient constituents to optimize plant growth and avoid overfertilization.

B.2. Conduct efficient fertilizer and leaching practices, including calibrating fertilizer injectors, using controlled-release fertilizers, and carefully managed leaching programs.

B.3. Avoid fertilizer material spills during all phases of transport, storage, and application.

B.4. Provide organized training sessions for personnel handling fertilizers in a language that personnel clearly understand, and maintain records documenting training.

C. Pest and Agricultural Chemicals Management Goals

Reducing the quantity of pesticides and other chemicals used should be a top priority. This can be done by adopting integrated pest management (IPM) practices and by improving pesticide application techniques. Even though agricultural chemicals are typically used in commercial IPM programs, they must be carefully selected. They should be handled in a safe manner that protects the applicator and the environment. We have developed nine pest and agricultural chemicals management goals:

C.1.   Establish an IPM program to reduce pesticide use.

C.2.   Use good sanitation and other preventive control techniques to avoid pest problems and maintain a healthy production environment.

C.3.   Where feasible and appropriate, use nonchemical control tactics to reduce overall pesticide use.

C.4.   When chemical pest control is necessary, select reduced-risk pesticides to prevent contamination of groundwater or surface water with toxic chemicals.

C.5.   Apply pesticides in a safe manner to reduce pesticide loads and potential runoff. This includes applying pesticides according to the label, following environmental hazard instructions, and checking equipment for leaks and malfunctions.

C.6.   Avoid pesticide spills and leakage during all phases of transport, storage, and application.

C.7.   In addition to pesticides, ensure that the use of other agricultural chemicals and household cleaning and disinfectant products potentially toxic to the environment do not contribute to runoff.

C.8.   Ensure that runoff and sediment containing pesticide and other agricultural chemical residues remain on the nursery property and do not move off-site in water or by wind.

C.9.   Provide organized training sessions for personnel handling pesticides in a language that personnel clearly understand, and maintain records documenting training.

D. Erosion and Runoff Management Goals

The goal for greenhouse and nursery operators should be to allow no irrigation water or sediment to leave their property. Specific strategies may vary from site to site. Nurseries that generate large volumes of runoff must respond vigorously to this issue by adopting technologies such as those available for water capture and reuse. Many nurseries that generate lower runoff levels, especially small operations that are constrained by cost, can turn to simpler and less capital-intensive solutions for erosion and runoff management. These include implementing improved irrigation, fertilizer, and pest management practices to further reduce the amount of runoff that must be managed. We have developed eight erosion and runoff management goals:

D.1.   Evaluate the quality of irrigation water and storm runoff to ensure that it complies with water regulations and determine options for reuse or treatment.

D.2.   Use practices that improve soil and media infiltration and water-holding capacity to reduce soil erosion, runoff, and excessive leaching.

D.3.   Use practices that retard movement of runoff water and sediment and keep it on the property, such as vegetative buffer strips, grass-lined channels, grass swales, and constructed wetlands.

D.4.   Manage hilly, sloped areas to prevent soil erosion and increased runoff volume and velocity. This includes practices such as using terraces, mulch, and cover crops.

D.5.   Design and manage nursery roads to prevent erosion and contaminated runoff.

D.6. Collect excess irrigation and storm water runoff and sediment in basins or ponds that can also be used for recycling.

D.7. Manage greenhouse roof runoff from storms to reduce pollution and erosion, prevent flooding, and improve drainage.

D.8. Provide organized training sessions for personnel in runoff management in a language that personnel clearly understand, and maintain records documenting training.

E. Management Goals for Nonproduction Areas

Growers may not recognize the importance of good housekeeping in nonproduction areas. Nonproduction areas that can serve as pollution sources include walkways, loading areas, packing sheds, maintenance and storage areas, offices, and grounds areas. They also include restrooms and portable toilets. Pollution can come from waste, debris, sewage, fuel, and vehicle fluids if these areas are not properly managed. We have developed six management goals for nonproduction areas:

E.1. Ensure that all nonproduction areas where nursery-related activities occur do not contribute to dry- or wet-weather runoff. Walkways, driveways, packing areas, loading areas, and parking areas should be periodically cleaned in a manner that ensures that runoff remains on the property.

E.2. Maintain vehicles, trucks, and tractors and their storage areas so that these areas do not leak fluids into groundwater or surface water.

E.3. Locate and maintain fuel tanks so that they do not leak, spill, overflow, or leach into groundwater or surface water.

E.4. Keep the nursery property free of debris and trash, which can clog storm drains and create an unsightly mess in waterways and on beaches.

E.5. Maintain restrooms to avoid spills and leakage of human waste into the municipal storm water system.

E.6. Provide organized training sessions in waste, sanitation, and spill management for all personnel in a language that they clearly understand, and maintain records documenting training.

How to Use This Manual

The first step is to read the management goals and management practices outlined in chapter 2. This is an "at a glance" list that was prepared so you can find most goals and practices for preventing nursery runoff and leaching in one convenient location.

The second step is to read chapters 3 through 8 to become more familiar with how pollution occurs in nurseries and the methods that can be used for protecting water quality. Topics covered are irrigation management (chapter 3), nutrient management (chapter 4), integrated pest management (chapter 5), management of pesticides and other agricultural chemicals (chapter 6), erosion and runoff management (chapter 7), and water recycling (chapter 8).

The third step is to take the environmental audit located in chapter 9. This audit can be photocopied for easy use. Conducting the audit will help you identify environmental problems before they become serious and explore options for solving them. The completed audit can help establish an environmental record that can be used in documenting good management practices for regulatory or public agencies.

The last step is to develop a comprehensive water quality plan to mitigate runoff and leaching, using the audit results as a basis. Work with managerial staff in determining which environmental problems you need to address in the coming year. Then come up with a plan for the management practices that will be implemented to address these problems. Finally, adopt your water plan and use the tips in this manual to ensure a cleaner environment.

References

Cabrera, R. I., and R. Y. Evans. 2001. Inorganic nitrogen loading and distribution in soil profiles beneath rose greenhouses. Acta Horticulturae 547:227–233.

Cabrera, R. I., R. Y. Evans, and J. L. Paul. 1993. Leaching losses of N from container-grown roses. Scientia Horticulturae 53:333–345.

Fallon, A., and M. D. Smolen. 1998. Water quality. In Water quality handbook for nurseries. Stillwater: Oklahoma Cooperative Extension Service, Division of Agricultural Sciences and Natural Resources and Oklahoma State University, Circular E-95. 1–3. OSU CE Web site, http://osuextra.okstate.edu/pdfs/e-951.pdf.

Harter, T., and L. Rollins, eds. 2008. Watersheds, groundwater, and drinking water: A practical guide. Oakland: University of California Division of Agriculture and Natural Resources Publication 3497.

Jones, A., T. Harter, M. Bianchi, and J. Harper. 2003. Water pollution legislation. Oakland: University of California Division of Agriculture and Natural Resources Publication 8088. ANR CS Web site, http://anrcatalog.ucdavis.edu/pdf/8088.pdf.

Padgett-Johnson, M., and T. Bedell. 2002. Watershed function. Oakland: University of California Division of Agriculture and Natural Resources Publication 8064. ANR CS Web site, http://anrcatalog.ucdavis.edu/pdf/8064.pdf.

Management Goals and Management Practices to Mitigate Runoff and Leaching

JULIE NEWMAN, University of California Cooperative Extension Farm Advisor, Ventura County

DARREN HAVER, University of California Cooperative Extension Farm Advisor, Orange County

VALERIE MELLANO, University of California Cooperative Extension Farm Advisor, San Diego County

KAREN ROBB, University of California Cooperative Extension Farm Advisor, Mariposa County

Management Goals and Management Practices

This chapter contains a list of management goals and management practices that are recommended for greenhouses and nurseries. Use this list as a guide to begin developing a plan to limit runoff and groundwater leaching from your operation, a plan known as a farm water quality plan.

For our purposes, we are defining a management goal (MG) as an economically achievable technology or process for effectively limiting runoff and groundwater leaching. Management goals are general, for example, "Establish an integrated pest management (IPM) program to reduce pesticide use." You should implement every management goal that applies to your operation. The more goals you implement, the more confident you will be that you are doing everything you can to prevent contamination of water bodies from your operation.

As used here, a management practice (MP) is a specific practice for accomplishing the management goal, for example, "Base decisions to use pesticides and other

control options on monitoring information." Growers and Cooperative Extension Farm Advisors have found these practices to be suitable for greenhouses and nurseries in California, and most are recommended practices in other areas of the country as well. Keep in mind that a management practice is not necessarily a required practice, and additional practices not on this list, or modifications to the ones on this list, may be required by regulatory agencies. Which management practices you select or plan to continue to implement depends on specific conditions unique to your nursery operation. This chapter provides MGs and MPs in five sections:

A. Irrigation MGs and MPs

B. Nutrient MGs and MPs

C. Pest MGs and MPs

D. Erosion and runoff MGs and MPs

E. MGs and MPs for nonproduction areas

Each section has a set of MGs. Under each MG there are numbered MPs. The purpose is to provide you with a quick and easy method for reviewing all the management goals and management practices in each of the five sections listed above.

In this chapter we have provided narrative explanations of some of the various management practices, but in general it is best to refer to the specific chapters that provide detailed information about these practices (chapters 3 through 8). Color photos illustrating some of the management practices are provided in a section of color plates (see page 143).

After you have reviewed the goals and practices outlined in this chapter and have referred to the supporting chapters for additional information, you will be ready to take the environmental audit in chapter 9. You will then be able to fully develop a comprehensive management plan to mitigate runoff and leaching from your nursery.

A. Irrigation Management Goals and Management Practices

MG A.1. **Design or retrofit your irrigation system for improved irrigation uniformity and efficiency to reduce runoff and leaching.**

A.1.1. Conduct an in-house irrigation audit or use professional services to determine the efficiency of the system and make appropriate adjustments. An irrigation system audit or evaluation typically includes measuring the distribution uniformity of sprinklers using the "catch can" method (plate 1) and of emitters by a representative discharge sampling, as well as pressure distribution methods for both.

A.1.2. If irrigation uniformity remains low after all practical improvements have been made, consider converting to an irrigation system with a potential for high uniformity (plate 2).

A.1.3. Use pressure regulators where appropriate (plate 3).

A.1.4. Use emitters that minimize pressure differences or pressure compensating emitters (plate 4).

A.1.5. When growing on slopes, compensate for pressure differences at the top and bottom of the slope by running the main line vertical to the slope with pressure controllers at each horizontal line junction and running each subline horizontal to the slope; include a pressure control valve.

A.1.6. When using overhead or impact systems, use flow control nozzles when pressure is too high or variable.

A.1.7. Each watering zone should have spray stakes or emitters with similar flow rates to maintain good uniformity; do not combine emitters with different flow rates in the same watering zone.

A.1.8. Place plant types and pot sizes with similar water needs in the same watering zone.

A.1.9. Correlate emitter flow rates for spray stakes and drippers with plant types, media infiltration rates, and pot sizes in each watering zone; emitters with flow rates that are too high apply water faster than plants can absorb, causing runoff.

A.1.10. Use appropriate and uniform nozzle sizes.

A.1.11. Use sprinkler heads with a high uniformity rating.

A.1.12. Use appropriate sprinkler spacing to assure proper overlap to attain optimal distribution uniformity.

MG A.2. **Regularly maintain your irrigation system so that it continues to operate efficiently.**

A.2.1. Regularly inspect for leaks in mains and laterals, in irrigation connections, and at the ends of drip tape and feeder lines. Repair any leaks found (plate 5).

A.2.2. Regularly flush and unclog lines and emitters, keeping them free of mineral deposits and biological contaminants such as algae and bacterial slimes.

A.2.3. Ensure that appropriate filtration is used and regularly clean filters.

A.2.4. Maintain appropriate pressure throughout the system (plate 6).

A.2.5. Regularly replace worn, outdated, or inefficient irrigation system components and equipment. Replace worn nozzles with like nozzles.

A.2.6. Keep maintenance records and update them regularly.

A.2.7. Have a schedule for regular audits; over time an efficient system can become inefficient if modifications are made or as clogging and wear reduce uniformity.

MG A.3. Regularly manage crops, crop areas, and irrigation systems to avoid applying water to noncropped areas and to avoid applying irrigation when not needed.

A.3.1. When using overhead or impact systems, regularly space pots or plants as closely together as possible without compromising plant quality due to reduced light. This minimizes runoff from spaces between pots and plants.

A.3.2. Manage spray stake and dripper systems to ensure that every emitter is located in a plant or pot.

A.3.3. Manage harvest operations and retail areas to avoid creating watering zones with emitters located outside of pots (plate 7).

A.3.4. Consolidate plants and shut off irrigation in unused portions, including spray stakes and other emitters that can be "turned off" when not in use (plates 8 and 9).

A.3.5. Consider using overhead emitters with check valves to prevent line drainage and drip damage (plate 10).

A.3.6. Use an on/off valve in hand-watering systems to prevent runoff (plate 11).

A.3.7. Check regularly to ensure that spray patterns of overhead irrigation systems are managed to uniformly deliver water only to plants, without creating overspray in walkways and edges (plate 12).

MG A.4. Use appropriate irrigation rates and scheduling.

A.4.1. Base irrigation scheduling and amount on environmental conditions and plant moisture requirements (plate 13). Water requirements can be determined from a reference evapotranspiration (ET) value modified with a coefficient for the specific crop. ET and coefficient values are available from the California Irrigation Management Information System (CIMIS), although coefficient values for many ornamental crops have yet to be determined. Irrigation scheduling can also be based on measured water content in the soil or plant growing media (determined with pot weight, tensiometer, electrical resistance blocks, or dielectric soil moisture sensor). For more information on these methods, see chapter 3.

A.4.2. Regularly adjust irrigation schedules to reflect changes in weather, plant needs, or measured soil moisture values.

A.4.3. Group pot sizes or plant types in watering zones according to moisture requirements.

A.4.4. Avoid irrigating overhead outdoors in windy conditions.

A.4.5. Consider pulse irrigation to split irrigation into smaller increments that can more effectively be used by plants.

A.4.6. When automatic timers are used, check regularly for accuracy and adjust to correlate scheduling with changing environmental conditions and plant growth stage.

MG A.5. Provide appropriate training for personnel involved in irrigating in a language that personnel clearly understand, and maintain records documenting training.

A.5.1. Provide training to ensure that irrigation duties are performed only by personnel who understand and practice appropriate irrigation scheduling, irrigation application practices, and crop management practices related to runoff management.

A.5.2. Ensure that appropriate personnel are trained in proper irrigation system maintenance procedures and recordkeeping related to maintenance.

A.5.3. If in-house irrigation audits are performed, ensure that personnel are trained to evaluate irrigation systems correctly and regularly.

A.5.4. Keep records of employee training, and maintain them for at least 5 years.

B. Nutrient Management Goals and Management Practices

MG B.1. Evaluate irrigation water, soils, growing media, and plant tissue to optimize plant growth and avoid overfertilization.

B.1.1. Regularly monitor the quality of your irrigation source water (plate 14). Sample seasonally (well water or surface water such as ponds or creeks) or annually (municipal water). Analyze for levels of constituents such as bicarbonates (HCO_3^-), sodium (Na), chloride (Cl^-), nitrate (NO_3^-), boron (B), soluble salts, and pH. Undesirable levels of these constituents may affect crop growth and health. Use a commercial laboratory for analysis. Soluble salts, pH, nitrate, and phosphate (PO_4^{3-}) can be analyzed on-site with instruments and kits designed for use by individual growers.

B.1.2. If well water is used on-site for human consumption, have the well water tested regularly for contamination from fertilizers.

B.1.3. Maintain records of irrigation source water quality.

B.1.4. Consider nutrients already present in your irrigation water, recovered runoff, composts, manures, and previous fertilizer applications in fertilizer management decision making. Overfertilization can result if nutrients already present in the growing environment are not taken into account.

B.1.5. Regularly test soil or growing media for nutrients, soluble salts, and pH. Along with plant tissue analysis, soil tests are your best guide to the effective use of fertilizers.

B.1.6. Test plant tissue to determine concentrations of macronutrients and micronutrients.

B.1.7. Use information and recommendations from soil, growing media, and plant tissue analyses in fertilization management.

B.1.8. When available, use nutrient recommendations for your specific crop. Use the most up-to-date recommendations from UCCE Farm Advisors and publications.

B.1.9. Regularly test fertigation water to monitor fertilizer levels and ensure injectors are properly operating.

B.1.10. Maintain records of fertilizer use. These may be required by regulatory agencies and are useful in obtaining permits or conditional waivers for agricultural discharge. Records can help you make informed decisions regarding fertilizer management.

MG B.2. Conduct efficient fertilizer and leaching practices.

B.2.1. Incorporate solid fertilizers in a manner that optimizes nutrient availability to growing roots. When mixing fertilizer into media, be sure that fertilizer is evenly distributed throughout the root zone or container at the correct rate; this provides good nutrition and avoids leaching losses of fertilizer nutrients.

B.2.2. Use composts or manures that have been thoroughly composted before application. Composts and manures that are not thoroughly composted may contribute bacteria and other contaminants to runoff.

B.2.3. Carefully apply top-dressed fertilizers to keep granules in the pot or around the plants at the correct rate (plate 15).

B.2.4. Ensure that injected fertilizers are carefully mixed and applied at correct rates. Excessive amounts of highly soluble liquid fertilizers are easily lost with leachate water.

B.2.5. Calibrate fertilizer injectors to accurately deliver liquid fertilizer through the irrigation system.

B.2.6. Use slow-release or controlled-release fertilizers to minimize leaching losses of nutrients.

B.2.7. Time fertilizer applications with environmental parameters and the growth stage of the plants. Fertilizer management that provides nutrients at appropriate growth stages yields better plant nutrition and minimizes nutrient losses to the environment.

B.2.8. Flush excess salts from root systems by using carefully managed leaching practices. Excessive leaching represents wasted water and fertilizer and creates greater runoff volumes to manage. Excess nutrients carried by leached water can be a source of groundwater and surface water contamination.

B.2.9. Use the electrical conductivity (EC) of root media or leachate water to determine leaching practices. The soluble salt level of leachate water or root media can be monitored with a portable EC meter. Different plants have different tolerances to EC. High fertilizer concentrations are not recommended as they require frequent leaching to avoid salt buildup in containers.

B.2.10. Set irrigation schedules to perform appropriate leaching, either with fertilizer injectors turned off (clear water) at specific irrigation events, or by applying the appropriate leaching fraction with fertilizer water at each irrigation.

B.2.11. Measure the amount of leaching that occurs and ensure that the appropriate fraction of applied water (the leaching fraction) runs through the container. Without actual measuring, the tendency is to underestimate leachate volumes and therefore leach excessively.

MG B.3. Avoid fertilizer material spills during all phases of transport, storage, and application.

B.3.1. Have a plan for how to deal with spills.

B.3.2. Store fertilizers in a structure that complies with local, state, and federal guidelines.

B.3.3. Locate fertilizer storage and mixing areas as far away from water conveyances (streams, creeks, and storm drains) as possible.

B.3.4. Include a concrete pad and curb to contain spills and leaks in the fertilizer storage facility. This pad area should be protected from rainfall and irrigation to prevent fertilizer residues from washing into surface water bodies.

B.3.5. Equip fertilizer tanks with secondary containment to contain spills and leaks.

B.3.6. Conduct fertilizer mixing and loading operations on an impermeable surface such as a concrete floor in areas where potential for runoff is low.

B.3.7. Perform fertilizer operations at least 100 feet downslope of a well or other water supply (plate 16).

B.3.8. Verify regularly that fertigation equipment is properly calibrated and fertilizer solution tanks are free of leaks.

B.3.9. When transporting fertilizer, do not overfill trailers or tanks. Cover loads properly and display appropriate placards on vehicles.

B.3.10. When transferring fertilizer into storage or into a fertilizer applicator, do not allow materials to spill.

B.3.11. Immediately clean up fertilizer spills according to a predetermined protocol.

B.3.12. Use check valves on application equipment.

B.3.13. When applying fertilizer from a tractor or rig in a field, shut off the fertilizer applicators during turns.

B.3.14. Whenever you are injecting fertilizer into irrigation water, install backflow prevention devices and check them at least once a year, recording the date and result of this check.

B.3.15. Do not allow backflow into wells or other water sources.

B.3.16. Dispose of fertilizer bags in trash bins with lids to prevent trash with fertilizer residues from blowing into nearby waterways.

MG B.4. Provide organized training sessions for personnel handling fertilizers in a language that personnel clearly understand, and maintain records documenting training.

B.4.1. Provide training to ensure that appropriate personnel understand how and when to use fertilizers (plate 17).

B.4.2. Provide training to ensure that appropriate personnel understand how and when to leach.

B.4.3. Provide training to ensure that appropriate personnel understand safe fertilizer transport, storage, and disposal practices.

B.4.4. Provide training for all personnel on what to do in case of a fertilizer spill.

B.4.5. Keep records of personnel training provided, and maintain for at least 5 years.

C. Pest and Agricultural Chemicals Management Goals and Pest and Agricultural Chemicals Management Practices

MG C.1. **Establish an integrated pest management (IPM) program to reduce pesticide use and the potential contamination of groundwater and surface water with pesticides.**

C.1.1. Regularly monitor (scout) your crop for insects and mites and other pests such as snails and slugs. Look for pests and pest damage. Monitoring methods for these types of pests on ornamental crops include regularly inspecting plants for pest presence and damage symptoms, using sweep nets for making pest counts, beat counts, and assessing numbers and types of adult insect pests trapped on sticky cards (plate 18).

C.1.2. Regularly inspect crop and noncrop areas for weeds.

C.1.3. Regularly inspect crop and noncrop areas for vertebrate pests.

C.1.4. Ensure that all personnel who monitor pests and diseases are trained to identify disease symptoms and all pests (insects, mites, weeds, vertebrates) commonly found in your nursery, and ensure that they are familiar with pest and pathogen life cycles.

C.1.5. Update training as new pests and diseases are introduced.

C.1.6. Train other employees who handle or walk the crop, such as irrigators and flower harvesters, to recognize common pests and diseases so they can communicate problems they see to the scout.

C.1.7. Use diagnostic laboratory services or other professional assistance to identify unknown pathogens, pests, or growth problems before implementing a control measure. If you diagnose your problem incorrectly you may apply an ineffective treatment; if the symptoms are related to environmental conditions or to nutrient or water stress, you cannot remedy the problem with pesticides.

C.1.8. Monitor environmental parameters to help predict the growth of pest and pathogen populations.

C.1.9. When applicable, use degree-days to predict insect development and timing of pesticide applications, or use computer modeling programs for disease forecasting.

C.1.10. Keep records of pest counts, degree of injury, and other data needed to determine pest pressure and pest population trends.

C.1.11. Summarize data collected by graphing to illustrate pest population trends or by comparing current data with the previous collection period.

C.1.12. Base decisions to use pesticides and other control options on monitoring information. Evaluating pest populations on a regular basis helps determine the actual need for chemical control, rather than making regularly scheduled chemical applications.

C.1.13. Use economic thresholds in deciding when and whether chemical pesticides should be used. Sometimes a certain level pest damage can be tolerated, such as damage on lower leaves of cut flowers that are removed before flowers are sold to the final consumer. The benefit of controlling a pest with chemicals must be weighed against the cost of pesticide application and the potential hazards.

C.1.14. Use monitoring and threshold data to select the most appropriate control strategies (cultural, environmental, biological, chemical).

C.1.15. Use techniques to reduce pesticide use such as spot spraying (focusing pesticide applications in infested areas rather than spraying the entire crop), direct spraying (directing spray toward the part of the canopy where the pest resides), applying pesticides at the lowest recommended rate on the label, and using adjuvants (products that cause the pesticide to better spread, stick, or penetrate the plant material) (plate 19). Reducing amounts of pesticides used in the nursery reduces pesticide loads in the environment. It also enhances control by natural enemies, which reduces pesticide need.

C.1.16. Rotate classes of pesticides. When pests become pesticide-resistant, pesticides become less effective in controlling pests, and chemical use often escalates.

C.1.17. To ensure that your control tactics are effective, use the most recent IPM recommendations for crops. Consult with your UCCE Farm Advisor, pest control adviser, and relevant sources, such as the *UC IPM Pest Management Guidelines for Floriculture and Ornamental Nurseries* at the UC IPM Web site (see the Resources at the end of this chapter).

MG C.2. Use good sanitation and other preventive control techniques to avoid pest problems and maintain a healthy production environment.

C.2.1. Inspect plant material brought into the nursery, including plants, plugs, cuttings, and transplants, to ensure that they are free of pests and diseases.

C2.2. Treat or discard infected plant materials promptly before introducing into the growing area to prevent other plants from becoming infected by the discarded material.

C.2.3. Inspect propagation areas and treat or discard infected plants before they are introduced into the growing area.

C.2.4. Quarantine new plants before introducing them into growing areas (plate 20).

C.2.5. Eliminate weeds in the growing environment and in noncropped areas. Weeds harbor pests and diseases that can infect the crop.

C.2.6. Fumigate, heat-steam, or chemically treat planting areas and recycled media before establishing new crops to eliminate pest problems from previous crops (plate 21).

C.2.7. Select plants that are tolerant of or resistant to pests and diseases whenever possible to prevent problems and reduce pesticide use.

C.2.8. Use certified or culture-indexed stock where available and feasible. Culture-indexed plants are vegetatively propagated and tested to confirm that they are free of specific bacterial, fungal, or viral pathogens.

C.2.9. Keep irrigation hose nozzles off the ground to avoid contaminating plants (plate 22).

C.2.10. Avoid standing water in the growing environment to eliminate breeding areas for pests and spread of disease.

C.2.11. Eliminate pathogen reservoirs by removing diseased plants, destroying them, or treating them in an isolated area.

C.2.12. Use hand dispensers and footbaths at production house entrances and in propagation facilities to disinfect hands and shoes that can become contaminated when working with diseased plants. Ensure that appropriate employees use them regularly.

MG C.3. Where feasible and appropriate, use nonchemical controls to reduce overall pesticide use.

C.3.1. Incorporate cultural controls into your IPM program. These are modifications of normal plant care activities that reduce or prevent pests, such as separating new plantings from older, possibly infested plantings to prevent movement of pests and pathogens to newer crops.

C.3.2. Incorporate mechanical control tactics into your IPM program, which reduce pest abundance using methods such as hand-picking, physical barriers, and machinery. Examples include hand-pulling weeds and installing screens to exclude flying insects.

C.3.3. Use environmental (physical) control methods where feasible to reduce pests and prevent damage by manipulating the environment. For example, many greenhouse foliar pathogens can be controlled by altering humidity and temperature, increasing ventilation, or applying heat.

C.3.4. Become familiar with the beneficial insects and mites that naturally occur in your growing area.

C.3.5. Monitor populations of beneficial insects and mites.

C.3.6. Consider the effects of pesticides when making pest control decisions to reduce overall pesticide use. Use compatible pesticides whenever possible when beneficial insects are present.

C.3.7. When possible, use control strategies that conserve beneficial insects and mites, such as direct spraying, spot spraying, and reduced pesticide rates.

C.3.8. Consider incorporating commercially available beneficial organisms into your IPM program on crops where their use has been demonstrated to be effective.

C.3.9. Manage ants to prevent their disruption of natural enemies.

MG C.4. When chemical pest control is necessary, select reduced-risk pesticides to prevent contamination of groundwater or surface water with toxic chemicals.

C.4.1. Consider site conditions, pesticide labels, and hazard warnings of migration risk when selecting pesticides. Use databases such as the UC PesticideWise Web site to provide information on the product's potential for contaminating groundwater or surface water. The water-related risks of pesticide active ingredients can be compared at the UC IPM Pest Management Guidelines Web site and can be customized by application and site conditions by clicking the blue "Water Quality Compare Treatments" button at the top of the list of treatments.

C.4.2. Select pesticides that do not potentially contaminate groundwater (e.g. imidacloprid, metalaxyl) whenever possible.

C.4.3. Avoid using groundwater-risk pesticides in rainy weather, in areas of shallow water tables, or where soils are sandy or have low organic matter content.

C.4.4. Whenever possible, select pesticides that will not potentially contaminate surface water. Many pesticides are hazardous to aquatic life and disrupt food chains. These include organophosphate insecticides (such as chlorpyrifos and diazinon); carbamate insecticides (such as carbaryl); and synthetic pyrethroids (such as cyfluthrin, permethrin, and bifenthrin).

C.4.5.   Choose pesticides that are the most selective for the target pest species, avoiding the use of broad-spectrum pesticides whenever possible. This enhances natural population control mechanisms and reduces pesticide need.

MG C.5.   Apply pesticides in a safe manner to reduce pesticide loads and potential runoff.

C.5.1.   Accurately measure pesticides to assure that you are within the label rate and to eliminate disposal problems associated with excess spray mix.

C.5.2.   Know the exact location of the area to be treated, as well as the potential hazard of spray drift or subsequent pesticide movement to the surrounding areas.

C.5.3.   Apply pesticides according to the label and follow environmental hazard instructions.

C.5.4.   Calibrate pesticide spray equipment to ensure the best coverage and efficacy and accurate application rates (plate 23).

C.5.5.   Check equipment for leaks and malfunctions. Replace worn nozzles and screens, cracked hoses, and faulty gauges.

C.5.6.   Avoid spraying pesticides when wind could move them off target as drift.

C.5.7.   Avoid applying pesticides when rain or scheduled irrigation will move pesticides in runoff and ground percolation.

C.5.8.   Maintain records of the amount and type or pesticides applied. Monthly reports to your county agricultural commissioner's office on all pesticide treatments are a legal requirement. Use these records to plan future pest control measures and limit pesticide accumulation.

C.5.9.   Maintain irrigation systems with uniform distribution and use proper irrigation scheduling and timing to reduce surface water and groundwater pollution.

MG C.6.   Avoid pesticide spills and leakage during all phases of transport, storage, and application.

C.6.1.   Store pesticides in a structure that complies with local, state, and federal guidelines.

C.6.2.   Locate pesticide storage and mixing areas as far away from water conveyances (streams, creeks, and storm drains) as possible, and at least 100 feet from a well or other water supply.

C.6.3.   Include a concrete pad and curb to contain spills and leaks in the pesticide storage facility. This pad area should be protected from rainfall and irrigation to prevent pesticide residues from washing into surface water bodies.

C.6.4.   Conduct pesticide mixing and loading operations on an impermeable surface such as a concrete floor in areas where potential for runoff is low.

C.6.5.   Perform operations involving pesticides in areas at least 100 feet downslope of a well or other water supply.

C.6.6.   Verify regularly that pesticide solution tanks are free of leaks.

C.6.7.   When transporting pesticides, ensure that pesticides do not spill. Do not overfill trailers or tanks; cover loads properly.

C.6.8.   Pesticides should be transported in the back of a truck, and all containers should be secured to prevent breaking or spilling.

C.6.9. Never leave pesticides unattended in a vehicle unless they are in a locked container.

C.6.10. When transferring pesticides into storage or into pesticide application equipment, do not allow materials to spill.

C.6.11. Use check valves on application equipment. When applying pesticides from a tractor or rig in a field, shut off the nozzles during turns.

C.6.12. Whenever you are injecting pesticides into irrigation water, do not allow backflow into wells or other water sources.

C.6.13. Install backflow prevention devices and check them at least once a year, recording the date and result of this check.

C.6.14. Clean up any spilled potting media that contains pesticide residues.

C.6.15. If pesticides are mixed into potting media before potting, use concrete curbs or sandbags to isolate these areas so that the potting mix does not get washed away in the runoff.

C.6.16. Keep a spill kit available at the pesticide storage facility and at any other sites where pesticides are used.

C.6.17. Immediately clean up pesticide spills according to a predetermined protocol. Always refer to the pesticide product material safety data sheet (MSDS) for information on cleaning up and decontaminating small spill sites.

C.6.18. Immediately report all leaks or spills of pesticides to the county agricultural commissioner as soon as possible.

C.6.19. Distribute rinse water from pesticide application equipment evenly over the crop. This reduces pesticide contamination in nontarget areas during the cleanup process following application.

C.6.20. Dispose of pesticides and pesticide containers according to label instructions and in an environmentally safe manner. Take empty, triple-rinsed, punctured plastic pesticide containers to pesticide container recycling facilities. Alternatively, take them to sanitary landfills or have them disposed of by licensed disposers of hazardous waste.

MG C.7. **In addition to pesticides, ensure that the use of other agricultural chemicals potentially toxic to the environment (such as postharvest treatments containing STS and greenhouse shading compounds) and household cleaning and disinfectant products do not contribute to runoff.**

C.7.1. When using silver thiosulfate (STS, e.g., Chrysal AVB) for treatment of ethylene-sensitive cut flowers, do not allow the product to reach groundwater, surface waterways or sewage systems. Residuals should be neutralized before disposal following manufacturer instructions.

C.7.2. Where 1-methylcyclopropene (1-MCP, e.g., EthylBloc) is an effective treatment for your ethylene-sensitive crop, select it as an alternative to STS. There are no expected risks to the environment associated with using 1-MCP because it is approved only in indoor, enclosed spaces.

C.7.3. Plant growth regulators used for postharvest (e.g., 1-MCP and STS) and growth regulators used to control plant height are technically classified as pesticides and should be treated accordingly.

C.7.4. Select exterior greenhouse shading compounds for temperature control that are relatively nontoxic, or select interior shade fabric or reflective covers. Most exterior shading compounds contain latex paint, which is toxic to marine life, and they may also contain ethylene glycol, which can be hazardous to humans. "Environmentally friendly" shading compounds may contain sodium hydroxide, which is strongly alkaline and must be disposed of properly because high-pH water can be toxic to fish.

C.7.5. Apply and remove exterior shading compounds so that they produce minimal runoff and remain on the property. Do not allow runoff to enter the municipal storm water or sewer system.

C.7.6. Use care when disposing of household products used in greenhouses and nurseries such as cleaning products and disinfectants when these can be damaging to streams and sewage treatment systems.

MG C.8.   Ensure that runoff and sediment containing pesticide and other agricultural chemical residues remain on the nursery property and do not move off-site in water or by wind.

C.8.1. Install and maintain a capturing basin to collect runoff and sediment that may potentially contain pesticides.

C.8.2. When construction of a basin is not feasible, use sand bags and berms to curtail runoff and trap sediments.

C.8.3. Use sediment traps to slow flow and drop out sediment. Clean out the trapped sediment before the rain season.

C.8.4. Consider using fiber or activated charcoal filters in recycling systems for filtration of pollutants such as pesticides by adsorptive removal.

C.8.5. Establish vegetation to filter sediment that may contain pesticides.

C.8.6. Consider using polyacrylamide (PAM) to adsorb pesticides. UC has conducted studies on commercially available polyacrylamides that demonstrate that they can be effective in reducing pesticide transport to water bodies. This is because they cause flocculation and precipitation of suspended sediments, which may hold adsorbed pesticides.

MG C.9.   Provide organized training sessions for personnel handling pesticides in a language that personnel clearly understand, and maintain records documenting training.

C.9.1. Provide training to ensure that appropriate personnel understand how and when to use pesticides in a safe manner.

C.9.2. Provide training to ensure that appropriate personnel understand safe pesticide transport, storage, and disposal practices.

C.9.3. Provide training for all personnel on what to do in case of a pesticide spill.

C.9.4. Keep records of personnel training provided and maintain for at least 5 years.

D. Erosion and Runoff Management Goals and Management Practices

MG D.1.   Evaluate the quality of irrigation water and storm runoff to comply with water regulations and determine options for reuse or treatment.

D.1.1. Inventory chemicals used in your operation, especially those likely to be present in runoff such as pesticides, fertilizers, and shading compounds.

D.1.2. Regularly sample runoff water, as there will likely be seasonal variations in the analyses (plate 24). Runoff should not exit property, but if it does, it is especially important to sample this water to determine what is leaving the property. Follow commercial lab instructions for taking and handling samples, as this greatly affects the results.

D.1.3. Conduct analyses on runoff water samples to determine what is in it and at what levels (plate 24). Parameters to test for include pH, electrical conductivity (EC), nitrate (NO_3^-), and phosphate (PO_4^{-3}), which can be analyzed on-site with instruments and kits designed for use by growers. Alternatively, water samples can be sent to commercial labs. In addition, it is recommended to use a good commercial lab to test for other contaminants according to the products used, such as specific pesticides that you suspect may be present in runoff. The lab should use EPA standards and be certified for good laboratory practices (GLP).

D.1.4. Compare water analyses against local and state water quality standards and regulations (plate 25).

D.1.5. Maintain water quality runoff records for at least 5 years.

MG D.2. Use practices that improve soil and media infiltration and water-holding capacity to reduce soil erosion, runoff, and excessive leaching.

D.2.1. Incorporate organic amendments into sandy soil to improve water-holding capacity and prevent excessive leaching.

D.2.2. Incorporate amendments on clay soil to improve infiltration and reduce runoff.

D.2.3. Use mulches or cover crops on bare soil to reduce runoff (plate 26).

D.2.4. Test media used in containers and select media for high water-holding capacity as well as good drainage.

D.2.5. Consider using wetting agents in container media to increase water absorption, allow quicker wetting, and reduce channeling down the sides of pots. Wetting agents should not be overused, as they can be toxic to plants and a contaminant in runoff.

MG D.3. Use practices that retard movement of runoff water and sediment and keep it on the property.

D.3.1. Determine where and how much erosion and runoff is generated and whether runoff exits the property. All dry-weather runoff and sediment is prohibited from entering street gutters, rivers, creeks, or other conveyances that drain to public waters (plate 27). Discharging dry-weather runoff and sediment onto neighboring properties is also illegal, unless done with consent.

D.3.2. Establish engineered barriers or buffers between production areas and ditches, creeks, ponds, lakes, or wetlands (plate 28). Examples of plant buffers include vegetated buffer strips, grass-lined channels, grass swales, and constructed wetlands. Buffer vegetation can help absorb both dry- and wet-weather-contaminated runoff if properly located. Engineered barriers such as berms and containment structures can regulate runoff flow and contain it. For example, detention basins can temporarily hold excess storm water (plate 29); the basin will slowly drain as the collected water infiltrates into permeable soil or evaporates. For information about barriers and buffers, see chapter 7.

D.3.3. Wherever possible, convert paved or bare soil areas to vegetation that retards runoff and takes up nutrients, pesticides, and other pollutants (plate 30).

D.3.4. Consider using polyacrylamide (PAM) to remove sediment from runoff water (plate 31).

D.3.5. Use windbreaks or shelterbelts in areas prone to wind erosion (plate 32).

D.3.6. If your property is affected by discharge sediment or runoff from upslope or upstream properties, use practices to contain this sediment or runoff, such as diversions, filter strips, sediment basins, and underground outlets.

D.3.7. Implement and maintain a record-keeping system for documenting management practices addressing runoff management. Record-keeping may be required by some regulating authorities.

MG D.4. Manage hilly, sloped areas to prevent soil erosion and increased runoff volume and velocity. This includes hilly production areas and sloped nonproduction areas.

D.4.1. Use terraces where appropriate to control soil erosion and runoff (plate 33).

D.4.2. Use mulches where appropriate to control soil erosion and runoff (plate 33).

D.4.3. Use vegetation (cover crops, buffer strips, grassed swales, etc.) to control soil erosion and runoff.

D.4.4. Use berms to control soil erosion and runoff.

D.4.5. Use proper irrigation management in hilly production areas and in hilly landscaped nonproduction areas to avoid runoff and soil erosion.

D.4.6. Use proper pest and nutrition management practices in hilly production areas and in hilly landscaped nonproduction areas to avoid pesticide and fertilizer runoff.

MG D.5. Design and manage nursery roads to prevent erosion and contaminated runoff.

D.5.1. Ensure that all new roads are properly designed and permitted to avoid erosion. This may require submitting an engineering plan, specifications, and an environmental assessment. Soils should be evaluated for erodibility and excessive slopes should be avoided.

D.5.2. Use waterbreaks (waterbars) on nursery roads with gradients exceeding 8 percent. These should be properly sized and placed only where water flow has an outlet and diverted water does not flow into septic fields or waterways.

D.5.3. Use filter strips between roads and waterways to absorb runoff from roads and to trap sediment.

D.5.4. Inspect culverts and clean them out during winter rains so that water drains freely.

D.5.5. Prevent contaminant-laden dust from traffic and wind erosion by sealing or watering unpaved roads. This also helps control mites. Ensure that water applied for dust control does not create runoff.

MG D.6. Collect excess irrigation and storm water runoff and sediment.

D.6.1. Use retention basins to store excess irrigation runoff and storm water (plate 34). Basin capacity should be designed on the basis of probable storm events and to prevent seepage and groundwater contamination. Use qualified engineers for design and implementation.

D.6.2. Use captured water to irrigate noncrop areas, thereby preventing overflow.

D.6.3. Recycle captured water onto crops, treating or blending with fresh water as necessary, avoiding basin overflow during both dry and wet weather (plate 35).

MG D.7. Manage greenhouse roof runoff to reduce pollution and erosion, prevent flooding, and improve drainage (plate 36).

D.7.1. Direct roof runoff to avoid flow across areas where contaminants will be washed into the municipal storm water, sewer system, or agricultural drainage system. Roof runoff may contain pollutants such as toxic sediments and shading compounds.

D.7.2. Direct roof runoff into pervious areas such as gravel, vegetation, paving material, self-contained tail water system, or retention ponds.

D.7.3. Reuse collected roof runoff to irrigate noncrop or crop areas.

MG D.8. Provide organized training sessions for personnel in runoff management in a language that personnel clearly understand, and maintain records documenting training.

D.8.1. Ensure that all appropriate employees receive training in runoff management and all applicable regulations. All growing operation employees must understand and implement the required practices for runoff management to be effective.

D.8.2. Train staff so that they know the location of all drainage conduits and ditches on the property and know where they drain.

D.8.3. Ensure that all municipal storm water or sewer system conduits and ditches are stenciled or designated with signs, and that there are no illicit connections to the municipal storm water or sewer system.

D.8.4. Keep documentation and records of employee training for at least 5 years. Documentation can include written instructions, posted signs (e.g., "No Dumping"), and information received at meetings.

E. Management Goals and Management Practices for Nonproduction Areas

MG E.1. Ensure that all nonproduction areas where nursery-related activities occur do not contribute to dry- or wet-weather runoff. These include walkways, driveways, packing areas, loading areas, and parking areas.

E.1.1. Clean indoor walkways, loading areas, and packing areas using only dry methods (such as sweeping or dry absorbents; see plate 37); if wet-cleaned, ensure that runoff remains on the property. These areas may contain fertilizers, pesticides, and vehicle fluids that could contaminate surface or groundwater.

E.1.2. Periodically clean outdoor driveways, walkways, parking areas, loading areas, and packing areas to remove debris, vehicle residues, and other contaminants and prevent them from washing off during wet weather. Use only dry methods (such as sweeping or dry absorbents); if wet-cleaned, ensure that runoff remains on the property.

MG E.2. Maintain vehicles, trucks, and tractors and their storage areas so that fluids do not leak into groundwater or surface water.

E.2.1. Regularly maintain vehicles, trucks, and tractors used in the nursery to detect and prevent fluid leaks that are very toxic to the environment.

E.2.2. Ensure that wash runoff from vehicles, trucks, and tractors remains on the property and does not drain into the municipal storm water or sewer system, or leach into groundwater.

E.2.3. Properly dispose of collected fluids.

E.2.4. Drain fluids and properly dispose of them from vehicles, equipment, or storage tanks that are no longer used on the property.

E.2.5. Locate maintenance and storage areas for vehicles, trucks, and tractors where wet weather will not wash fluids into surface water or cause fluids to percolate into groundwater.

E.2.6. Clean maintenance and storage areas to avoid oil and grease buildup.

E.2.7. Immediately and properly clean up spills from vehicles, trucks, and tractors.

MG E.3. Locate and maintain fuel tanks so that they do not leak, spill, overflow, or leach into groundwater or surface water.

E.3.1. Locate fuel tanks where wet weather will not wash fluids into surface water or cause fluids to percolate into groundwater (plate 38).

E.3.2. Check and maintain fuel tanks to prevent leaks.

E.3.3. Perform fueling activities carefully to avoid overflow and spills.

E.3.4. Immediately and properly clean up fuel spills.

MG E.4. Keep the nursery property free of debris and trash so that it does not clog storm drains and create an unsightly mess in waterways and on beaches.

E.4.1. Regularly maintain the entire nursery property to keep it clean and free of debris. Solid waste and debris can cause fatalities for marine life through strangulation or ingestion (plate 39).

E.4.2. Ensure that an adequate number of waste containers are available where needed and that they are regularly collected to avoid overflow.

E.4.3. Ensure that waste containers are kept in good condition and kept closed.

E.4.4. Ensure that waste containers, collection areas, storage areas, and stockpile areas are located indoors or covered when outdoors to prevent wet weather or wind from washing or blowing trash into storm drains and waterways.

MG E.5. Maintain restrooms to avoid spills and leakage of fecal coliform from human waste into the municipal storm water system. Fecal coliform at high levels causes beach closures and poses serious human and animal health hazards.

E.5.1. Ensure that adequate restrooms and portable toilets are available where needed.

E.5.2. Ensure that toilets, floor, and sink drains in restrooms are properly hooked up to the sanitary sewer system.

E.5.3. Ensure that portable toilets are located where wet weather will not wash waste into the municipal storm water system.

E.5.4. Ensure that restrooms and portable toilets are regularly maintained to prevent sewage and human waste from entering the municipal storm water systems.

MG E.6. **Provide organized training sessions in waste, sanitation, and spill management for all personnel in a language that they clearly understand, and maintain records documenting training.**

E.6.1. Ensure that all employees receive training in proper waste disposal and the use of restrooms and mobile toilets.

E.6.2. Train all employees on what to do in the event of a spill.

E.6.3. Educate and require your employees to recycle all the waste that you can from your nursery operation, such as metal, oil, paper, and plastic.

E.6.4. Educate employees in the proper disposal of batteries, paints, and other potentially hazardous materials used in the nursery.

E.6.5. Document and maintain records of employee training for at least 5 years. Record-keeping helps to document waste, sanitation, and spill management practices and is required by some regulating authorities.

Resources

Bianchi, M., D. Mountjoy, and A. Jones. 2008. Farm water quality plan. Oakland: University of California Agriculture and Natural Resources Publication 8332. ANR CS Web site, http://anrcatalog.ucdavis.edu/pdf/8332.pdf.

UC IPM Pest management guidelines for floriculture and ornamental nurseries, UC IPM Web site, http://www.ipm.ucdavis.edu/PMG/selectnewpest.floriculture.html.

UC PesticideWise Web site, www.pw.ucr.edu.

Irrigation Management Practices in Nurseries

LARRY SCHWANKL, University of California Cooperative Extension Irrigation Specialist, Kearney Agricultural Center

RICHARD EVANS, University of California Cooperative Extension Environmental Horticulture Specialist, UC Davis

BEN FABER, University of California Cooperative Extension Farm Advisor, Ventura County

Overview of Irrigation Systems

Many irrigation systems are available for nursery applications. These range from hand-watering to complex sprinkler systems and from irrigating many plants at a time with a single sprinkler to using drip systems with a single dripper per plant. More sophisticated drip systems provide a higher level of irrigation control at the price of increasingly complex maintenance and operation.

Sprinkler Irrigation Systems

Various kinds of "overhead" sprinkler systems apply water over the top of plants, covering a wide area and irrigating many plants at a time. These sprinklers are most commonly impact sprinklers, but other application methods are also used. The impact sprinkler head discharge rate is in the gallons per minute range. Other sprinkler types, especially those used in enclosed nurseries, may have lower discharge rates, with each head covering a smaller area. As the discharge rate of sprinklers decreases, their discharge rate is measured in gallons per hour, and they begin to be categorized as a microirrigation system emission device. In this chapter, the discussion of sprinkler systems emphasizes impact sprinklers due to their common use.

Microirrigation Systems

Microirrigation systems using emitters are often referred to as drip irrigation. These emitters may be built into the drip tubing (in-line emitter), a spray-stake, an individual emitter with a weight or stake holding it in place, or some other modification. A low discharge rate is a common trait among these drip emission devices, ranging from as low as 0.5 gallons per hour (gph) for an individual drip emitter to nearly 20 gallons per hour for spray-stake emitters designed for large potted plants.

Certain microirrigation devices (microsprinklers or misters) spray water over a wider area. Their discharge rate may be as high as 20 to 30 gallons per hour, and they often irrigate multiple plants at a time.

Microirrigation system emission devices are characterized by small flow passageways that allow controlled low discharge rates but increase the danger of emitter clogging. Drip system maintenance requirements are high but are necessary to maintain a high level of performance.

Irrigation System Performance

Good irrigation requires applying the correct amount of water to only the locations desired. Two irrigation system performance measures are used to characterize irrigation: irrigation efficiency and irrigation uniformity.

Irrigation Efficiency

Irrigation efficiency is a measure of how much of the applied irrigation water is "beneficially" used. Satisfying plant water needs is the primary beneficial use. In formula form, irrigation efficiency is

> irrigation efficiency (%) = (beneficially used water ÷ total water applied) × 100

Note that two important factors must be known in order to determine irrigation efficiency. First, the amount of water required by the plant must be known. This is usually determined using irrigation scheduling techniques, such as weighing pots or using evapotranspiration values. Second, the irrigation application amount must be known. This requires measuring the applied irrigation water. Using a flow meter installed in the irrigation pipeline is the easiest and most accurate way to measure the application amount. Multiple flow meters should be used when multiple, widely spaced sections of an irrigation system are operated.

Irrigation Uniformity

A sprinkler or microirrigation system must apply water uniformly in an irrigation zone. In other words, all the sprinklers or emission devices in the zone should have the same discharge rate. For sprinklers, uniform irrigation also requires that the sprinkler spacing be the same within the zone.

Irrigation uniformity in a zone is quantified by comparing the minimum amount of water applied to the average amount. Sprinkler system uniformity is measured by placing collection containers (catch cans) in the irrigated area, operating the system, and measuring the water collected in the containers. The results are quantified using the measure distribution uniformity (DU), where

> distribution uniformity (%) = (average of the low 25% of catch cans ÷ average of all catch cans) × 100

Measure the water collected in a catch can either as a volume or as a depth. Both work in the above equation.

Microirrigation system irrigation uniformity is quantified using emission uniformity, which is similar to DU, where

> emission uniformity (%) = (average of the low 25% of emitter discharges ÷ average of all emitter discharges) × 100

To use the above equation, collect the discharge from a sampling of emission devices in an irrigation zone. Commonly, 30 or 60 seconds of discharge from multiple emission devices is measured in milliliters (mL).

Ideally, the discharge from similar sprinklers or emission devices should be the same. This is seldom the case, since pressure differences and manufacturing or maintenance issues often yield different discharge rates. The causes of irrigation nonuniformity are discussed in greater detail later in this chapter.

Irrigation Scheduling

Growers can improve irrigation water use efficiency and reduce runoff by proper irrigation frequency and duration. All that is needed is knowledge of daily crop water use (evapotranspiration), the water-holding capacity of the soil or container mix in which the crop is growing, and the rate of irrigation water delivery.

Crop Water Use

Plant water use in container nurseries can be measured directly by weighing plant containers. The weight change in grams over a 24-hour period, with no intervening irrigation, represents the milliliters of water lost from the container during that time (1 milliliter of water weighs 1 gram). As with the other methods described here, it is important to select representative plants when measuring water use. Large plants tend to use more water than small ones, and those on the borders of fields, benches, or nursery blocks tend to use more than those in the interior. Since accurate scales can be purchased for less than $100, this method provides a fast, accurate, inexpensive way to monitor plant water use.

Estimates of evapotranspiration for field-grown crops can be made using evaporation pans, atmometers, or automated weather stations, all of which can provide estimates of the amount of water loss in a given surface area. Evapotranspiration values are expressed in units of inches per day or centimeters per day. This value reflects the change in the depth of a pool of water that would occur during a day due to evaporation and transpiration. To calculate the equivalent volume of evapotranspiration, multiply this value by the area affected. Because an evaporation pan provides a measure of water loss from standing water, it can give only a rough approximation of plant water use. Atmometers measure the amount of water that evaporates from a porous surface designed to represent a leaf surface. Weather stations estimate evapotranspiration from calculations that use measurements of sunlight, wind speed, relative humidity, and temperature. (For more information on using weather-based irrigation scheduling, see the California Department of Water Resources CIMIS Web site in the references at the end of this chapter.) Regardless of which indirect method is used to estimate evapotranspiration, the values obtained must be corrected for the size and type of crop being grown. In addition, since the results are only estimates of evapotranspiration, growers should check soil moisture in the field to verify the accuracy of water use estimations.

Direct measurement of soil moisture in the root zone of a crop can be made using moisture-sensing instruments such as tensiometers, resistance blocks, capacitance probes, and time domain reflectance sensors. Capacitance probes and time domain reflectance sensors measure actual soil water content; tensiometers and resistance blocks measure soil suction, which indicates the relative ease with which plants can remove soil moisture. These instruments can be used to measure moisture in field soils or in container media, but resistance blocks do not perform well in coarse-textured media. The sensors should be placed in the root zone of plants selected to represent all of those in the irrigated area. Factors to consider when selecting representative plants include plant size and location. These moisture-sensing instruments can be connected to computers or data loggers so that data can be collected continuously and irrigation valves can be set to operate based on the measured soil moisture values.

Available Water

Water in the root zone that a plant can easily extract is known as the available water. The amount of available water can be easily determined for potted crops. Irrigate some plants thoroughly and wait for drainage to stop for up to 1 hour. Weigh the pots, then withhold irrigation until the plants show the first signs of wilting. Weigh the pots again. Subtract this weight from the weight just after irrigation. The difference (in grams) is equal to the volume of water (in milliliters) that is available to plants. You can think of this as measuring the plant's "gas tank," the amount it can hold from one fill-up to the next. In field soils, available water is defined as the difference between the amount of water at field capacity and the amount at the wilting point. It is usually expressed as the volume fraction, percentage, or inches of water in a given amount of soil (see table 3.1). For example, a soil with an available water fraction of 0.2 has 2.4 inches of available water per foot of soil depth.

Table 3.1. Approximate available water contents of some typical soil textures

Texture	Available water (volume fraction)
sands	less than 0.10
loamy sands, sandy loams, loams, clay loams	0.10–0.15
silty clay, clay	0.10–0.20
silt, silt loam, silty clay loam	0.15–0.25

Table 3.2. Recommended leaching fractions

EC applied (dS/m)	EC leached (dS/m)			
	3	6	9	12
0.50	0.17	0.08	0.06	0.04
0.75	0.26	0.12	0.09	0.06
1.00	0.33	0.17	0.11	0.08
1.25	0.43	0.20	0.15	0.10
1.50	0.50	0.25	0.17	0.12
1.75	0.60	0.28	0.21	0.14
2.00	0.67	0.33	0.22	0.17
2.25	—	0.36	0.27	0.18
2.50	—	0.42	0.28	0.21
3.00	—	0.50	0.33	0.25
5.00	—	—	0.56	0.42

Irrigation Frequency

In general, irrigation should take place when about half of the available water has been lost from a pot. For example, if a pot holds 500 milliliters of available water, irrigation should be scheduled when about 250 milliliters has been lost from the pot. The same rule applies to irrigation of field soils: a soil that has 2.4 inches of available water per foot should be irrigated when about 1.2 inches of evapotranspiration has occurred.

Irrigation Duration

The length of an irrigation event determines the amount of irrigation water applied. Although decisions about irrigation frequency depend only on replacing the available water that the crop has used, the amount of irrigation water required is more complicated. An irrigation event must replenish the soil water removed by the crop, leach out accumulated salts, and compensate for any lack of irrigation system uniformity.

Growers who use irrigation water of marginal quality must take steps to avoid negative effects on crops. One possibility is to treat water (usually by deionization or reverse osmosis) to improve its quality, but this approach is expensive. A practical alternative for many growers is to develop an effective leaching program to prevent excessive accumulation of salts in the root zone. Leaching is best achieved on ornamental crops by applying the proper leaching fraction. This is the ratio of the volume of water leached (for example, the water that runs out of the bottom of a pot) to the volume of water applied (for example, the total amount of water applied to a pot). The proper leaching fraction depends on the salinity of the irrigation water (including fertilizer, in a liquid feed program) and the sensitivity of the crop to salinity. In table 3.2, "EC applied" is the salinity of the irrigation water and "EC leached" is the desired value in the water that has passed through the root zone. For most ornamental crops, EC leached should be from 6 to 9 dS/m.

Applying the selected leaching fraction requires using the information known about crop water use and irrigation distribution uniformity. Table 3.3 gives the volume of irrigation water needed for several amounts of plant water use and several leaching fractions. The values for leaching fraction and water use can be rounded off to conform to the table values. For example, a potted chrysanthemum that used 240 mL of water should be irrigated with about 323 mL of water if the EC applied is 2 dS/m and the desired leachate EC is 9 dS/m (the leaching fraction is about 0.22).

The values in table 3.3 do not take into consideration the distribution uniformity of the irrigation system. To correct for that, the values in the table must be divided by the distribution uniformity value. For example, if the distribution uniformity is 0.8, the plant in the example above would require 390 mL. Table 3.4 is a worksheet that can be used to determine the proper irrigation duration.

Irrigation Audits

Irrigation system performance can be evaluated by the nursery operator, but it is often easier to have an irrigation audit done by professionals. While professional auditors may provide some irrigation efficiency information, their efforts will primarily be quantifying irrigation system uniformity. Discharge from sprinkler heads or microirrigation devices will be collected to quantify irrigation uniformity and rate. This can also help diagnose problems with clogging or maintenance. Pressure measurements will be taken at key locations in pipelines and tubings to characterize the system pressure distribution. Measuring pressure is important since it controls the discharge rate of most sprinklers and many microirrigation emission devices. Operational conditions of the irrigation components, such as valves, gauges, and filters, will also be noted.

Irrigation audits should be done on a yearly basis or whenever any major changes are made in the system. Audits are particularly important in microirrigation systems, since they may detect clogging problems at early stages when they can be more easily solved. Audits also provide information on changes that occur over time. For example, a decrease in drip emitter discharge from one year to the next may require a change in irrigation times, but it may also indicate a

Table 3.3. Volume of water (in mL) to apply to achieve desired leaching fraction

Leaching fraction	Plant water use (mL)										
	50	75	100	125	150	175	200	250	300	350	400
0.075	54	81	108	135	162	189	216	270	324	378	432
0.100	56	83	111	139	167	194	222	278	333	389	444
0.125	57	86	114	143	171	200	229	286	343	400	457
0.150	59	88	118	147	176	206	235	294	353	412	471
0.175	61	91	121	152	182	212	242	303	364	424	485
0.200	63	94	125	156	188	219	250	313	375	438	500
0.225	65	97	129	161	194	226	258	323	387	452	516
0.250	67	100	133	167	200	233	267	333	400	467	533
0.275	69	103	138	172	207	241	276	345	414	483	552
0.300	71	107	143	179	214	250	286	357	429	500	571
0.400	83	125	167	208	250	292	333	417	500	583	667
0.500	100	150	200	250	300	350	400	500	600	700	800

Table 3.4. Irrigation calculations worksheet

1. Measure distribution uniformity of irrigation system.

    A. Measure weight of empty can. Record weight in grams. _____ g

    B. Space catch cans regularly throughout irrigation block. Run irrigation system for known period of time

        (record time here: _____ min). Record weights of cans. _____ g

    C. Calculate amount of water in cans. Subtract **1.A** from **1.B** for each can. _____ g

    D. Calculate average amount in each can (1 g = 1 mL). _____ mL

    E. Calculate average amount in lowest one-quarter of the cans. _____ mL

    F. Calculate distribution uniformity. Divide **1.E** by **1.D**. _____

2. Calculate flow rate of irrigation system.

    A. Record length of irrigation in step **1.B** (in minutes). _____ minutes

    B. Calculate flow rate in mL per minute. Divide **1.D** by **2.A**. _____ mL/minute

    C. For overhead irrigation systems, you must correct the value in **2.B** for pot size.

        Use the following calculations or the table that follows this worksheet.

        i. Record the radius of the catch cans by measuring the diameter (in centimeters) and dividing it by 2. _____ cm

        ii. Take the square of **2.C.i** (multiply the value times itself). _____ cm^2

        iii. Repeat steps **2.C.i** and **2.C.ii** for finding the square of the radius of the plant container at the rim. _____ cm^2

        iv. Calculate the correction factor. Divide **2.C.iii** by **2.C.ii**. Enter the value in the space to the right. _____

        v. Apply the correction factor. Multiply **2.B** by **2.C**. _____

        iv. The result is the rate at which the overhead irrigation system applies water

            to the plant containers. _____ mL/minute

3. Measure electrical conductivity of irrigation water.

    A. Use meter to measure electrical conductivity (EC) of irrigation water.

        Record value in decisiemens per meter (dS/m). _____ dS/m

4. Select desired leaching fraction.

    A. Choose desired leachate EC (lower value for more salt-sensitive crops). _____ dS/m

    B. Use table of recommended leaching fractions to select suitable value. _____

5. Determine plant water use.

    A. Weigh container with plant after irrigation and drainage. Record weight in grams. _____ g

    B. Weigh container with plant 24 hours after **5.A**, with no intervening irrigation. Record weight in grams. _____ g

    C. Calculate daily plant water use. Subtract weight in **5.B** from weight in **5.A**.

        Record value as the volume in mL (1 g = 1 mL). _____ mL

6. Calculate appropriate irrigation volume.

    A. Enter amount needed to replace plant water use (use the value in **5.C**). _____ mL

    B. Correct for leaching fraction. Use Table 3.3.

        Record the value in mL. _____ mL

    C. Correct for distribution uniformity to calculate the total volume of water to apply to each pot.

        Divide **6.B** by value in **1.F**. Record the value in mL. _____ mL

7. Calculate appropriate length of irrigation.

    A. Divide irrigation volume (value in **6.C**) by irrigation flow rate value in **2.B** (or in **2.C.v** for overhead irrigation).

        Record value in minutes. _____ minutes

8. Irrigate crop and monitor results.

    A. Run irrigation system for appropriate time and catch leachate.

    B. Measure leachate EC. Record value in dS/m. _____ dS/m

    C. Measure volume of leachate. Record value in mL. _____ mL

    D. Calculate actual leaching fraction. Divide leachate volume (**8.C**) by volume of water applied (**6.C**). _____

        Record value and compare to desired leaching fraction (**4.B**). _____

Overhead irrigation correction factor for different catch can and pot sizes (multiply the measured flow rate in step **2.B** by this factor to correct for the different diameters of catch cans and pots)

Catch can diameter		Pot size		
cm	inches	4"	6"	1 gal
7.8	3 ¹/₁₆	1.6	3.7	4.0
10.2	4	0.9	2.2	2.4
12.7	5	0.6	1.4	1.5
15.2	6	0.4	1.0	1.0
20.3	8	0.2	0.5	0.6
25.4	10	0.1	0.3	0.4
30.5	12	0.1	0.2	0.3

drop in system pressure or an emitter clogging problem. Additional irrigation audit information should be gathered to explain the emitter discharge decrease and to point to steps to correct the problem.

Improving Nursery Irrigation Management Practices

The following irrigation management improvements can be made in any nursery, whether hand-watering, sprinkler irrigation, or drip irrigation is used.

Pulse Irrigations

Applying water in short, "pulsed" irrigation durations can significantly reduce runoff and improve irrigation efficiency. Pots hold only a certain volume of water, and any irrigation in excess of that amount simply runs through or off the pots. Multiple pulsed irrigations during the day can prevent runoff while satisfying plant needs. Determining how often and how long to irrigate is best done by observing the irrigation and noting the operating time at which runoff begins. Setting irrigation durations to this amount of time or less minimizes irrigation runoff. This pulsed irrigation time varies with irrigation systems, plant types, and pot sizes.

A consideration with pulsed irrigations is the filling and draining of the irrigation system during each irrigation event. The lowest elevation point in an irrigation system receives the water draining out of the system after shutdown. This draining water can lead to runoff and sometimes to plant damage. Low-pressure check valves can be installed to minimize this drainage.

Irrigation Zones

Establishing zones in which irrigation is constant and can be controlled improves irrigation water management. It allows a nursery manager to operate only those zones needing irrigation for only the time needed.

Irrigation zones can be controlled using either a manual or an electronically controlled valve. Having more irrigation zones increases operational flexibility. It is often possible to retrofit an existing irrigation system to create irrigation zones. New or expansion irrigation systems should include as many irrigation zones as will be needed in the future.

Group Plants with Similar Water Needs

Placing plants with similar irrigation needs together in an irrigation zone allows efficient irrigation water management. This prevents a situation in which the plants with the greatest water needs dictate the watering schedule, which can cause other plants to be overwatered. Overwatering can lead to runoff or groundwater contamination, as well as plant disease.

Avoid Irrigating Where There Are No Plants

Avoiding applying water where there are no plants seems like common sense, but it can be difficult to accomplish. It is made easier where increased irrigation control is provided by numerous irrigation zones, each of which can be controlled separately.

As plants are sold, group remaining plants that have similar water needs together to improve irrigation efficiency and reduce runoff. Moving plants is labor-intensive, but it can reduce water applications and minimize impacts on water quality.

Automation

Irrigation automation can improve water management, but it should be used in conjunction with good human management. In automated irrigation, a controller operates solenoid-equipped valves at specified times and durations. While the controller may remember to turn the irrigation system on and off, it takes human management to determine whether there is too much runoff or few or no plants in an irrigation zone being irrigated. Automation is a tool to help the operator improve water management, not a substitute for human judgment.

Sprinkler Irrigation Systems

System Components and Operation

Sprinkler heads consist of a small orifice, round being the most common shape, through which pressurized water jets. To improve the water distribution, the water stream is broken up by mechanical means. In an impact sprinkler, a spring-mounted sprinkler spoon repeatedly breaks up the water stream. Some water drops thus travel the maximum distance while others fall at various distances from the sprinkler head.

A single sprinkler head does not distribute water uniformly over the area it waters. Sprinkler heads are therefore spaced to provide overlap of the wetting patterns, increasing the irrigation uniformity. Closer sprinkler spacing increases irrigation uniformity, but it also increases the water application rate. An increased application rate can lead to runoff in some soil situations, but in container plants, with their highly permeable soil media, this is less of a concern. It remains important to know the application rate in order to apply the desired amount of irrigation water.

The sprinkler application rate, usually measured in inches per hour (in/hr), is determined from the sprinkler discharge rate and the spacing of the sprinklers. The discharge rate, usually measured in gallons per minute (gpm), of a sprinkler is controlled by the sprinkler nozzle size and the sprinkler operating pressure.

Table 3.5 lists the sprinkler discharge rate (in gpm) for various nozzle sizes and operating pressures. The greater the nozzle size operated at a given pressure, the greater the sprinkler discharge rate. The nozzle size is frequently engraved on the side of the nozzle, but it can also be determined by testing the nozzle opening using drill bits of a known size. The operating pressure can be determined by placing a pressure gauge fitted with a pitot tube, available at most irrigation supply stores, into the water stream just outside the nozzle opening.

Table 3.5. Sprinkler discharge (gpm) for various nozzle sizes (in) and pressures (psi)

	Nozzle size (in)										
psi	3/32	7/64	1/8	9/64	5/32	11/64	3/16	13/64	7/32	15/64	1/4
20	1.17	1.60	2.09	2.65	3.26	3.92	4.69	5.51	6.37	7.32	8.34
25	1.31	1.78	2.34	2.96	3.64	4.38	5.25	6.16	7.13	8.19	9.32
30	1.44	1.95	2.56	3.26	4.01	4.83	5.75	6.80	7.86	8.97	10.21
35	1.55	2.11	2.77	3.50	4.31	5.18	6.21	7.30	8.43	9.69	11.03
40	1.66	2.26	2.96	3.74	4.61	5.54	6.64	7.80	9.02	10.35	11.79
45	1.76	2.39	3.13	3.99	4.91	5.91	7.03	8.30	9.60	10.99	12.50
50	1.85	2.52	3.30	4.18	5.15	6.19	7.41	8.71	10.10	11.58	13.18
55	1.94	2.64	3.46	4.37	5.39	6.48	7.77	9.12	10.50	12.15	13.82
60	2.03	2.76	3.62	4.50	5.65	6.80	8.12	9.56	11.05	12.68	14.44
65	2.11	2.88	3.77	4.76	5.87	7.06	8.45	9.92	11.45	13.21	15.03
70	2.19	2.99	3.91	4.96	6.10	7.34	8.78	10.32	11.95	13.70	15.59
75	2.27	3.09	4.05	5.12	6.30	7.58	9.08	10.66	12.32	14.19	16.14

The sprinkler discharge rate can also be determined by using a short length of garden hose (approximately 4 feet), a 5-gallon bucket, and a stopwatch. Determine the discharge rate from the sprinkler by placing the hose over the sprinkler nozzle, directing the water into the bucket, and timing how long it takes water to fill the bucket. Use the following formula to calculate the discharge rate (the value of 300 in the equation is a unit conversion constant):

sprinkler discharge rate (gpm) = 300 ÷ time to fill a 5-gallon bucket (sec)

Measurements should be taken at various locations within the nursery since sprinkler discharge rates vary with the pressure differences.

The sprinkler application rate (in/hr) can be determined, once the discharge rate of the sprinkler (gpm) and the sprinkler spacing (ft) are known, using the following equation:

application rate (in/hr) = [96.3 × sprinkler discharge rate (gpm)] ÷ [sprinkler spacing along row (ft) × sprinkler spacing across row (ft)]

Table 3.6 can also be used to determine the sprinkler system application rate. The sprinkler area in square feet (ft^2) is determined by multiplying the sprinkler spacing along the row (ft) by the sprinkler spacing between rows (ft).

Pipeline Flow and Uniformity

Pipelines supply the sprinklers with pressurized water. Ideally, the pressure at each sprinkler head should be the same, facilitating uniform application. This seldom occurs, since the pressure changes within a sprinkler system due to elevation changes and frictional pressure losses. A pressurized line running uphill experiences a decrease in pressure once water has been "lifted" to the higher elevation. Conversely, a line running downhill gains pressure. Converting elevation changes to system pressure can be done using the following relationship:

1 psi = 2.31 feet of elevation change

Pressure is also lost as water flows through pipelines, fittings, valves, and other devices in a sprinkler system. The amount of pressure loss is determined by the volume of flow and the characteristics of the pipe or line. For pipelines, pressure loss (or friction loss) is determined by the pipeline size and material (plastic, metal, etc.) and by the flow volume. For example, a large volume of water flowing in a small pipe loses more pressure than the same volume flowing in a larger pipe.

The implications of these pressure changes are important when making changes in a sprinkler system.

- Adding sprinklers to an existing system often decreases sprinkler pressure, since more water flows through the pipe and the size of the pipe does not change.

- Using small pipe in a sprinkler system does not increase pressure; rather, it increases frictional losses and decreases pressure.

- The longer the pipeline, the more pressure that is lost. Pressure loss tables usually present pressure losses per 100 feet of pipe.

- Changing nozzles in sprinkler heads affects pressure. Increasing the nozzle size increases the nozzle discharge rate and decreases pressure. Decreasing nozzle size often increases pressure.

Determining pressure losses in sprinkler systems is not difficult. Friction loss tables for pipelines are readily available from irrigation dealers, and friction loss "calculators" are available on the Web. Pressure losses through devices such as valve or flow meters are provided by their manufacturer.

Improving Sprinkler Irrigation Systems and Management

Sprinklers on Slopes

Sloping ground provides a number of sprinkler irrigation challenges. First, as mentioned previously, pressure varies with elevation change (1 psi = 2.31 feet of elevation change), which in turn affects sprinkler discharge and application uniformity. If the pipeline runs downhill, increasing pressure, flow control nozzles limiting the nozzle discharge rate may be beneficial.

Second, runoff is greater and occurs more quickly on sloping ground. All techniques to minimize runoff described in this chapter are even more important when irrigating on sloping ground.

Third, an irrigation sprinkler system on sloping ground often tends to drain from the lowest point following shutdown. This can lead to runoff, especially when pulsed (short and frequent) irrigations are used. Check valves, which close at low pressure and also prevent reverse flow (backflow), can prevent some of this drainage. The loss of pressure when using a check valve should be considered, however.

Table 3.6. Average application rate (in/hr) for various sprinkler discharge rates (gpm) and areas of coverage (ft²)

Sprinkler area (ft²)	Sprinkler discharge rate (gpm)							
	0.75	1.00	1.25	1.50	1.75	2.00	2.25	2.50
500	0.14	0.19	0.24	0.29	0.34	0.39	0.43	0.48
550	0.13	0.18	0.22	0.26	0.31	0.35	0.39	0.44
600	0.12	0.60	0.20	0.24	0.28	0.32	0.36	0.40
650	0.11	0.15	0.19	0.22	0.26	0.30	0.33	0.37
700	0.10	0.40	0.17	0.21	0.24	0.28	0.31	0.34
750	0.10	0.13	0.16	0.19	0.22	0.26	0.29	0.32
800	0.09	0.12	0.15	0.18	0.21	0.24	0.27	0.30
850	0.08	0.11	0.14	0.17	0.20	0.23	0.25	0.28
900	0.08	0.11	0.13	0.16	0.19	0.21	0.24	0.27
950	0.08	0.10	0.13	0.15	0.18	0.20	0.23	0.25
1000	0.07	0.10	0.12	0.14	0.17	0.19	0.22	0.24
1050	0.07	0.09	0.11	0.14	0.16	0.18	0.21	0.23
1100	0.07	0.09	0.11	0.13	0.15	0.18	0.20	0.22
1150	0.06	0.08	0.10	0.13	0.15	0.17	0.19	0.21
1200	0.06	0.08	0.10	0.12	0.14	0.16	0.18	0.20
1250	0.06	0.08	0.10	0.12	0.13	0.15	0.17	0.19
1300	0.06	0.07	0.09	0.11	0.13	0.15	0.17	0.19
1350	0.05	0.07	0.09	0.11	0.12	0.14	0.16	0.18
1400	0.05	0.07	0.09	0.10	0.12	0.14	0.15	0.17
1450	0.05	0.07	0.08	0.10	0.12	0.13	0.15	0.17
1500	0.05	0.06	0.08	0.10	0.11	0.13	0.14	0.16
1550	0.05	0.06	0.08	0.09	0.11	0.12	0.14	0.16
1600	0.05	0.06	0.08	0.09	0.11	0.12	0.14	0.15

Container Spacing

When using overhead sprinkler systems, containers should be spaced as close together as possible while still maintaining adequate light for the plants. This minimizes the "empty" area where water does not land in a pot. Irrigation water that is not applied to a plant is inefficient water application and is more likely to contribute to runoff.

Overspray

Adjustable sprinkler heads that irrigate only part of a circle should be used on the edges of irrigated areas to prevent water from landing on bare areas adjacent to plants during irrigation. In addition to being an inefficient water use, water applications to these low-permeability areas can lead to significant runoff.

Adjust sprinkler heads to apply water only to the plant area. Adjustable sprinkler heads that turn only a portion of a circle have an increased application rate. For example, a sprinkler irrigating a half-circle has double the application rate of a similar sprinkler head irrigating a full circle. To compensate for this, place smaller nozzles in edge sprinklers. This works well in permanent sprinkler systems, but if portable pipe is used, it can be difficult to keep track of which sprinklers have which nozzle size.

Using Sprinkler Nozzles of Different Sizes

Mixing sprinkler nozzles of different sizes should be done only following the recommendation of an irrigation professional. It is difficult to predict what the consequences will be for the application rate when using nozzles of different sizes. If different sizes are used, an irrigation audit should be done to determine the application rate and distribution uniformity.

Avoid the unintentional mixing of different-sized sprinkler nozzles. This can easily happen during maintenance and repairs. Check impact sprinkler nozzles using standard drill bits rather than trying to read the size stamped on the side of the nozzles.

Periodically check all sprinkler heads that are supposed to have the same nozzles to ensure that that is the case.

Vertical Risers

Sprinklers providing overhead irrigation are often located on pipe risers. Ensure that these risers are vertical. The distribution pattern of sprinklers on nonvertical risers is distorted, resulting in lower sprinkler application uniformity. Ensuring that risers are vertical is an "attention to detail" task that can improve irrigation management and reduce runoff.

Wind

Wind distorts the sprinkler application pattern and leads to lower application uniformity. Some plants may be underirrigated and runoff may increase when irrigating under windy conditions. Avoid irrigating under windy conditions if at all possible.

Routine Maintenance

Detecting leaks and checking sprinkler nozzle wear are two critical sprinkler system maintenance tasks. Leaks are usually obvious and should be fixed immediately, since even a small leak can quickly lead to runoff and erosion.

Water often contains fine particles that can wear a sprinkler nozzle, enlarging it and leaving wear marks. Brass nozzles are particularly susceptible to this. Use the appropriate drill bit to check the size of the nozzle opening for unacceptable wear. Compare the drill bit fit in a used nozzle to that in a new one to get a "feel" for unacceptable wear.

Sprinkler head bearings also wear with use, and the sprinkler will not turn properly if the bearings need replacement. Sprinkler heads can often be rebuilt for much less than the price of a new head.

Microirrigation Systems

System Components and Understanding How They Work

Microirrigation systems (fig. 3.1) use drip emitters, spray stakes, misters, or microsprinklers as emission devices. A microirrigation system in a nursery may have a combination of emission devices tailored to fit the mix of plants and containers.

Emission devices are usually connected to polyethylene drip tubing, often in various diameters, customized to fit the plants being irrigated. Barbed and compression fittings allow easy assembly and modification of the system.

The polyethylene tubing is frequently connected to PVC pipelines, often installed below ground. These PVC pipelines, referred to as submains and mainlines, carry clean, pressurized water from a pump and filter station that often can also inject nutrients and chemicals.

Filtration of water used for microirrigation is very important to prevent emitter clogging. Microirrigation emission device passageways are small and can be clogged even by very small particles. Screen, disk, or sand media filters can provide the level of filtration suggested by the emission device manufacturer. The choice of filter is influenced by the water quality and the clogging hazard. Groundwater sources, which tend to be clean, can often be filtered using screen or disk filters. Water supplies from open canals, ponds, or reservoirs can contain organic contaminants and are best filtered with sand media. Screen or disk filters remove organic matter but must be cleaned frequently, a maintenance headache.

The following sections discuss a number of irrigation management issues unique to microirrigation systems.

Emission Device Selection

Choosing a microirrigation emission device is usually based on the desired discharge rate and coverage. For example, a large container plant with a high water

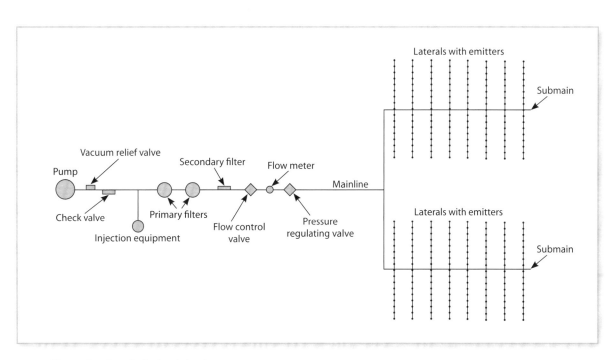

Figure 3.1. A typical microirrigation system.

demand requires an emission device that wets most of the pot area and has a high discharge rate. In general, the higher-discharge emission devices have larger flow passageways and are less susceptible to clogging. Another consideration in choosing an emission device is ease of inspection for clogging.

If drainage from emitters after system shutdown is a problem, drip emitters are available that have a built-in check valve that closes at low pressure. Drip systems that are pulse irrigated—multiple, short irrigations per day—may benefit from these specialty drippers.

Pressure Compensating Emission Devices

The discharge rate of standard drip emitters and microsprinklers is related to the operating pressure (fig. 3.2). As pressure changes, the discharge also changes. Pressure changes due to elevation differences and friction losses are common in a microirrigation system. Pressure changes that result in varying emitter discharge rates reduce the system's emission uniformity. This can lead to overirrigation of some plants and lower irrigation efficiency.

Pressure compensating (PC) emission devices maintain a constant discharge under a range of pressures (fig. 3.3). They can be an advantage in maintaining high emission uniformity, especially in systems with variable pressures such as facilities on sloping ground.

Pressure Control and Regulation

Maintaining constant pressure in a microirrigation system facilitates high application uniformity. Adjustable pressure regulating valves and pressure regulators preset to a pressure (for example, 35 psi) are available. These valves are actually pressure reducing valves since they can reduce their inlet pressure only to a constant downstream pressure.

Pressure regulating valves may be placed at various locations in a microirrigation system. Commonly, one is placed at the head of the system, downstream of the pump and filter station. Other designs place them throughout the system to maintain constant pressure. Using multiple pressure regulators (for example, one

at the head of each drip lateral) is more common in systems on sloping ground where pressure differences due to elevation changes must be compensated for.

Mixing Drip Emitters

Care should be taken when using drip emitters with different sizes or manufacturers in the same system. Mixing emitters makes it extremely difficult to maintain high application uniformity. Mixing different sized emitters from a single manufacturer may make it difficult to tell what emitters are being used, since discharge rates (such as 0.5 gph, 1 gph, etc.) may look similar. Mixing emitters of the same size from various manufacturers leads to poor irrigation uniformity: seldom is the emitter discharge-pressure relationship the same for emitters from various manufacturers. For example, a 1 gph dripper from Manufacturer A discharges 1 gph at 15 psi, while a 1 gph dripper from Manufacturer B discharges 1 gph at 12 psi and 1.1 gph at 15 psi. Avoid mixing emitters from different manufacturers in the same irrigation zone unless there is a good reason to do so.

Monitoring and Audits

Microirrigation systems should be monitored to detect clogging or other maintenance issues and to check the volume of applied water for irrigation scheduling purposes. Pressure gauges and flow meters are excellent monitoring tools. Readings from pressure gauges on the downstream and upstream sides of filters can detect when a filter is dirty and needs to be cleaned. Monitoring and keeping flow meter records can detect clogging in emitters, since the flow rate drops as the emitters clog.

The best health check on a microirrigation system is a system audit. An audit measures the discharge from a sampling of emitters to determine the system's emission uniformity and pressure, and it also gives a general assessment of the system's condition. Microirrigation systems should be audited on a yearly basis, and the audit reports should be kept so that any year-to-year changes can be detected.

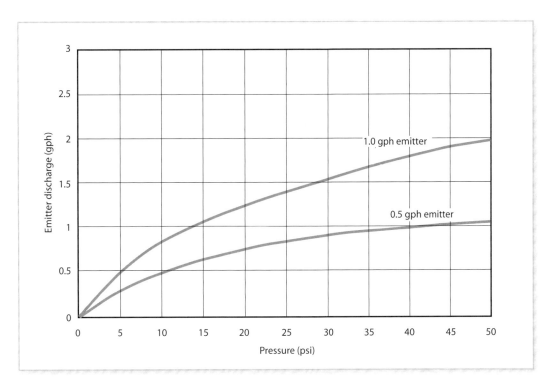

Figure 3.2. Discharge-pressure relationship for a non-pressure-compensating drip emitter.

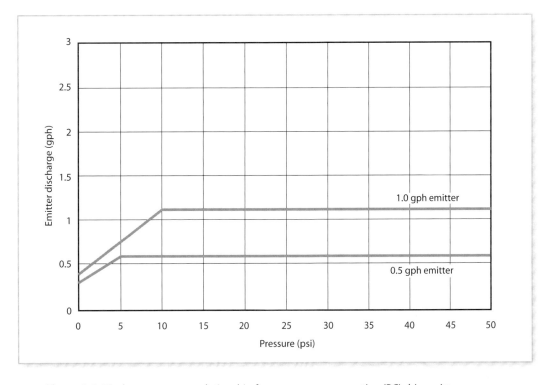

Figure 3.3. Discharge-pressure relationship for pressure compensating (PC) drip emitters.

Emission Device Clogging

Emitter clogging can be caused by particulate matter such as sand, chemical precipitates such as lime or iron, or biological growths such as algae or bacterial slime.

Good filtration is a major factor in solving all clogging problems. Particulate matter clogging can usually be solved simply with good filtration. Preventing biological clogging requires good filtration, usually sand media, along with periodic use of a biocide, such as chlorine, injected into the irrigation water.

Lime (calcium carbonate) precipitate clogging requires the addition of acid materials to lower the water pH and dissolve the lime deposits. Lime clogging can often be handled with periodic pH adjustment or adjustment only for the last portion of each irrigation, but serious lime clogging may require continuous pH adjustment. Iron precipitate clogging is difficult to solve. The most common solution is to place water in a pond or reservoir and allow the iron precipitate to settle out before using the water for irrigation.

Flushing

Microirrigation systems should be flushed on a regular basis, every 2 weeks or at least monthly. Silt and clay particles in water are very small and may pass through filters to settle in the pipelines, particularly in the lateral lines where they can clog emitters. Flush valves installed on the pipelines should be opened and the water should be allowed to flush clean. The lateral line ends should be opened and allowed to flush clean. If little material is evident at flushing, increase the flushing interval. Very dirty lines should be flushed more frequently.

References

ASABE (American Society of Agricultural and Biological Engineers). 2007. ASABE standards. St. Joseph, MI: ASABE.

Burt, C. M., A. J. Clemmens, R. Bliesner, and J. L. Merriam. 2000. Selection of irrigation methods for agriculture. Reston, VA: American Society of Civil Engineers.

Davidson, H., C. Peterson, and R. Mecklenburg. 2000. Irrigation of nursery crops. In H. Davidson, ed., Nursery management: Administration and culture. 4th ed. Upper Saddle River, NJ: Prentice-Hall.

Hanson, B., L. Schwankl, and A. Fulton. 1999. Irrigation scheduling: When and how much. Oakland: University of California Agriculture and Natural Resources Publication 3396.

Israelsen, O. W., and V. E. Hansen. 1962. Irrigation principles and practices. New York: Wiley.

Jensen, M. E., ed. 1980. Design and operation of farm irrigation systems. St. Joseph, MI: ASAE Monograph No. 3.

Merriam, J. L., and J. Keller. 1978. Farm irrigation system evaluation: A guide for management. Logan: Utah State University.

Pair, C. H., ed. 1983. Irrigation. Silver Spring, MD: The Irrigation Association.

Schwab, G. O., R. K. Frevert, T. W. Edminster, and K. K. Barnes. 1981. Soil and water conservation engineering. 3rd ed. New York: Wiley.

SCS (USDA Soil Conservation Service). 1982. Florida irrigation guide. Gainesville, FL: SCS.

———. 1987. Farm irrigation rating method. Gainesville, FL: SCS Engineering Technical Note FL-17.

Smajstrla, A. G., B. J. Boman, G. A. Clark, D. Z. Haman, D. S. Harrison, F. T. Izuno, D. J. Pitts, and F. S. Zazueta. 1991. Efficiencies of Florida agricultural irrigation systems. Gainesville, FL: University of Florida, Florida Cooperative Extension Service.

Resources

California Department of Water Resources CIMIS Web site, http://www.cimis.water.ca.gov/cimis/welcome.jsp.

Nutrient Management Goals

RICHARD EVANS, University of California Cooperative Extension
Environmental Horticulture Specialist, UC Davis

Nutrient Management

Fertilizer application is essential to commercial floriculture and nursery production, but it also can be an environmental issue. Inefficient fertilizer use can be a significant source of two nutrients, nitrogen (N) and phosphorus (P), that can harm water quality. It is important for growers to understand and implement practices that minimize the loading of these nutrients into surface water and groundwater. Successful implementation of these management practices depends on growers' knowledge of the chemical properties of their irrigation water and growing medium, nutritional requirements of their crops, and proper application and storage of fertilizers.

Irrigation Water Quality

For agriculture, the salts in water are the main determinants of water quality. Water picks up salts from the geologic materials it comes in contact with. Table 4.1 lists major and minor constituents of water in

Table 4.1. Common constituents of water in California

| | Cations | | Anions | | |
	Element	Symbol	Element	Ion	Symbol
MAJOR			carbon	bicarbonate	HCO_3^-
	calcium	Ca^{2+}	carbon	carbonate	CO_3^{2-}
	magnesium	Mg^{2+}	chlorine	chloride	Cl^-
	sodium	Na^+	sulfur	sulfate	SO_4^{2-}
MINOR	potassium	K^+	boron	borate	$B(OH)_3$
			fluorine	fluoride	F^-
			nitrogen	nitrate	NO_3^-
			phosphorus	phosphate	HPO_4^{2-}
			silicon	silicate	$Si(OH)_4$

California, depending on the geologic materials through which the water passes.

In reports from laboratories, these constituents are usually reported in either milligrams per liter (mg/L) or milliequivalents per liter (meq/L). An older unit, parts per million (ppm), is equivalent to mg/L.

Water quality is important in ornamental crop production for several reasons. First, salt accumulation in soil or container media can decrease yield and crop quality. Most irrigation water, especially from wells, contains dissolved salts. Plants exclude some of these salts as they take up water, resulting in salt accumulation in the root zone. Over time, the accumulated salts reduce the amount of water available to plants. A high amount of dissolved salts reduces yield and crop quality.

The salinity of water is usually measured by its electrical conductivity (EC). EC was formerly reported as millimhos per centimeter (mmho/cm), but now the common unit is decisiemens per meter (dS/m). The values are the same for both units. EC is related to total dissolved solids (TDS):

$$EC \times 640 = TDS \ (mg/L)$$

Irrigation water with an EC greater than 1.5 dS/m is regarded as having a high salinity hazard.

Water quality also affects soil pH. The addition to soil of bicarbonate from irrigation water causes soil pH to increase gradually. The pH rise can result in micronutrient unavailability (for example, iron chlorosis), particularly for permanent or long-cycle crops. If the bicarbonate concentration is from 2 to 4 meq/L, the soil pH can be managed by increasing the use of ammonium fertilizers. If the bicarbonate concentration exceeds 4 meq/L, it may be necessary to acidify the water. This should be done through consultation with a laboratory familiar with acid injection.

In addition to monitoring the salinity hazard of irrigation water, growers should have water tested for constituents that become toxic to plants if they accumulate. Boron (B), chloride (Cl^-), and sodium (Na) are the most important problems for California ornamental crop producers. Boron is toxic to plants at concentrations as low as 0.5 mg/L. It is absorbed by plant roots and transported to the leaves, where it accumulates and causes browning along the leaf tips and margins. Chloride also moves through the plant and accumulates in the leaves. Some crops tolerate chloride, but others (such as roses, camellias, azaleas, and rhododendrons) develop marginal burning or leaf drop. Overhead irrigation with water high in chloride (greater than 3 meq/L) results in foliar uptake, which can also cause leaf scorch or leaf drop. Plants irrigated with water high in sodium (greater than 3 meq/L) may develop symptoms similar to those from chloride. In mineral soils, high levels of sodium cause poor infiltration of water. However, this is rarely a problem in soilless container media.

Irrigation water can be a significant source of three elements that plants require in large amounts: calcium (Ca), magnesium (Mg), and sulfur (S). In addition, some water sources contain enough nitrogen to be a significant fertilizer source. For example, water containing the maximum amount of nitrogen allowed in potable water can supply nearly half the nitrogen required by some nursery crops. Therefore, growers should consider the contribution of irrigation water to crop nutrition when deciding on fertilizers and rates of addition.

Growers who use irrigation water of marginal quality must treat the water (usually by deionization or reverse osmosis) or implement a leaching program. Leaching is described in chapter 3.

Soil Testing

It is generally recommended that the chemical properties of container media be tested whenever a new formulation of a mix is used, as well as at regular intervals during crop production. The interval varies, but a good practice is to have tests conducted approximately once per month. It is important to obtain representative soil media samples in order to make valid decisions after testing. Most laboratories can provide instructions and containers in which to place samples. In general, samples should be taken midway between fertilizer applications. Approximately 8 to 10 samples should be taken from each greenhouse, more if the container media or crops within a greenhouse differ. Sampling should be done by inserting a soil probe and withdrawing a sample that represents the profile from the surface to the bottom of the container. Samples should be marked clearly with labels. Guidelines for analyses depend greatly on the analytical methods used by the soil testing laboratory. Figure 4.1 gives some general guidelines.

Electrical Conductivity (ECe)

Electrical conductivity is an index of soil salt content, expressed as dS/m, determined from a saturated paste extract. Potential effects of ECe values are

- < 2: no salinity problem

- 2 to 4: restricted growth of salt-sensitive crops

- 4 to 8: restricted growth of most crops

- 8 to 12: large yield reductions in most crops

- Over 12: only salt-tolerant plants survive

Table 4.2 gives the effect of salinity, as measured by EC_e, on selected floricultural crops.

Saturation Percentage

Some laboratories report the saturation percentage, which expresses the grams of water required to saturate 100 grams of soil. The saturation percentage is more relevant for mineral soils than for soilless media. It is related to soil texture:

- < 20: sand or loamy sand

- 20 to 35: sandy loam

- 35 to 50: loam or silt loam

- 50 to 65: clay loam

- 65 to 135: clay (some clays reach 150)

- > 135: usually organic (peat or muck)

The water-holding capacity of field soil when irrigated and drained is approximately half of the saturation percentage. About half of the water-holding capacity (or one-quarter of the saturation percentage) is available to plants.

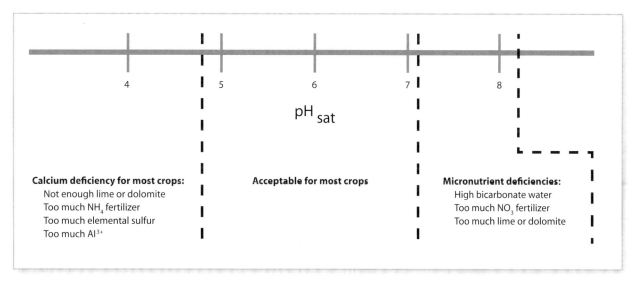

Figure 4.1. The pH of a saturated paste of the medium provides an indication of some potential nutrient deficiencies.

Elemental Analysis

It is usually best to follow the guidelines of the laboratory performing an elemental analysis because values depend on the method of extraction. Commonly used guidelines are presented in tables 4.3 and 4.4.

Foliar Analysis

Plant tissue testing of ornamental crops is less common than soil testing, but it is a useful tool for diagnosing nutrient deficiencies and monitoring fertilizer practices. The mineral composition of a leaf blade depends on many factors, such as its stage of development, climatic conditions, availability of mineral elements in the soil, root distribution and activity, irrigation, water status, and so on. The plant integrates all of these factors, and the composition of the blade reflects this integration.

Plants of the same species that receive the same cultural practices can be sampled as a single group: one to three composite samples of 20 to 30 recently matured leaves each is sufficient under these conditions, even for large production areas. The most recently matured leaves should be taken at random from plants within the growing area. The samples can be placed in paper bags and sent to a laboratory testing service for analysis. Some laboratories may advise to wash and dry leaves before sending the samples.

The nutritional requirements of most ornamental crops are not well defined. General guidelines for selected crops are given in table 4.5.

Nitrogen Application

Nitrogen is often applied in excessive amounts to ornamental crops. Although certain crops, particularly herbaceous ones, take up some excess nitrogen, most of the unneeded nitrogen is wasted. Nitrogen that is not taken up by plants has six possible fates:

- **Leached below the root zone.** Nitrate moves readily with water that percolates through the root zone. Much of the excess applied nitrogen leaches out of the root zone and becomes a potential contaminant of groundwater.

- **Soilborne erosion losses.** Nitrogen present in soil and container media can be moved by water or wind. Nitrogen present as either ammonium or nitrate will move with sediments.

- **Denitrification.** Soil microbes can convert ammonium or nitrate to nitrogen gas, which is lost to the atmosphere. This denitrification occurs to some extent in all soils when oxygen levels are low, for example, after irrigation or rainfall when the soil is saturated and has no air. In heavy clay soils with poor drainage, in soils with restrictive layers that prevent drainage, or in container media with low air-filled porosity, nitrogen losses through denitrification may be 15 to 50 percent of the amount applied in fertilizer. In general, only a small percentage of applied nitrogen is lost through denitrification.

- **Immobilization and mineralization.** Applied nitrogen may be tied up (immobilized) in soil organic matter or in the biomass of soil microbes as they work to decompose crop residues. Large amounts of applied nitrogen can be temporarily

Table 4.2. Effect of salinity on selected floricultural crops

Crop	EC$_e$ for 10% yield drop
African violet	1.5
azalea 'Mrs. Fred Saunders'	1.0
azalea 'Sweetheart Supreme'	1.0
carnation (flower quality of 'Sim')	2.5
carnation (flower yield of 'Sim')	3.0
China aster 'King'	2.0
chrysanthemum 'Albatross'	2.0
chrysanthemum 'Bronze Kramer'	6.0
gardenia	1.0
geranium (cutting production of 3 cultivars)	2.0
gladiolus (spike length of 2 cultivars)	2.0
gladiolus (spike weight of 2 cultivars)	2.0
lily (height)	2.0
poinsettia (bract size of 'Barbara Ecke Supreme')	4.0
poinsettia (leaf drop of 'Barbara Ecke Supreme')	2.5
rose 'Better Times'	3.5
stock (height response of 6 cultivars)	4.0

Table 4.3. General standards for nutrients in greenhouse soils

Nutrient	Sodium acetate extraction (ppm of dry soil)		Spurway (ppm of extract solution)	
	Low optimum	High optimum	Low optimum	High optimum
NO_3^--N	25	60	25	100
NH_4^--N	0	25	—	—
P	25	50	4	6
K	75	175	30	50
Ca	2,000	4,000	200	200+
Mg	100	500	—	—
SO4	25	50	—	—
B	1	2.5	—	—
Zn	1.5	2.5	—	—
Cu	0.8	1.2	—	—
Mn	8	12	—	—
Fe	10	20	—	—

Table 4.4. Standard values for nutrient levels (mg/L) in saturated media extracts of container mixes

Nutrient	Low	Acceptable	Optimum	High	Very high
NO3–N	0–39	40–99	100–199	200–299	>300
P	0–2	3–5	6–10	11–18	>19
K	0–59	60–149	150–249	250–349	>350
Ca	0–79	80–199	200+	—	—
Mg	0–29	30–69	70+	—	—
Fe	15	—	—	—	—
Mn	15	—	—	—	—
Zn	15	—	—	—	—
B	0.7	—	—	—	—
Cu	0.3–10	—	—	—	—

Table 4.5. Desirable foliar levels of macronutrients for selected ornamental crops (% by weight of dry tissue)

Crop	N	P	K	Ca	Mg
azalea	2.0–2.3	0.3–0.5	0.8–1.0	0.2–0.3	0.17–0.33
carnation	3.0–5.0	0.25–0.45	2.5–4.0	1.0–2.0	0.2 0.5
chrysanthemum	3.5–5.0	0.35–0.60	4.0–6.0	1.0–1.5	0.45–0.60
geranium	3.3–4.8	0.40–0.65	2.5–4.3	0.80–1.20	0.20–0.52
philodendron	2.0–3.5	0.20–0.35	3.0–4.5	0.35–1.0	0.25–0.50
poinsettia	4.5	0.9	2.8	0.75	0.57
rose	3.2–4.5	0.20–0.30	1.8–3.0	1.0–1.5	0.25–0.35
sansevieria	1.5–3.0	0.15–0.30	2.0–3.5	0.75–1.25	0.25–0.50

immobilized into organic nitrogen by soil microbes when plant material containing a high carbon to nitrogen ratio is incorporated into the soil. This is the phenomenon commonly known as "nitrogen draft." Organic nitrogen is continuously converted to plant-available nitrogen at a slow rate by the process of mineralization. The loss of soil organic matter reduces the capacity of the soil to retain applied nitrogen.

- **Residual soil nitrogen.** Nitrogen may remain in soil, available for subsequent season uptake. This soil-residual nitrogen usually accumulates over time, as long as irrigation is controlled to minimize leaching loss. However, winter rainfall in most of coastal California leaches most of the residual nitrate from the root zone.

- **Ammonium volatilization.** When animal manure, urea, or ammonium-containing fertilizers are left on the surface of the soil, nitrogen can be lost to the air as gaseous ammonia. This loss can be significant when the pH of soils or container media reaches values of 8 or higher. If manure or fertilizers are incorporated within a few hours after application, this loss is negligible.

Nitrate is the predominant form of fertilizer nitrogen used by nurseries and greenhouses. It may also be applied as urea or ammonium. Urea is rapidly converted to ammonium in the soil. Although ammonium is readily taken up by plants, it accounts for only a small percentage of crop nitrogen uptake. The microbial process of nitrification rapidly converts ammonium to nitrate in warm, moist soils. The majority of nitrogen taken up by plants is typically in the form of nitrate. Also, since ammonium is bound to soil particles by its positive charge, it is less easily leached than nitrate. For these reasons, the focus of nitrogen management strategies is nitrate.

Liquid feeding (fertigation) is widely used by nurseries and greenhouses. It is less expensive than controlled-release fertilizers, after initial capital costs for injectors,

and it is well suited to the production of large areas of uniform crops because fertilizer concentrations can be varied according to crop needs: for example, decreasing the nitrogen supply late in a chrysanthemum crop. The appropriate concentration of nitrogen in nutrient solutions depends on the crop being produced. Although exceptions exist, most herbaceous crops require nitrogen concentrations of 100 to 150 mg/L in continuous liquid feeds. For most woody nursery crops, 50 mg/L is sufficient. The major disadvantages of liquid feeding are its inefficiency in putting nitrogen into the root zone and its susceptibility to leaching losses of nitrogen from excessive irrigation.

Controlled-release fertilizers can greatly reduce nitrogen losses if they are applied correctly. Nutrient release rates are controlled by the properties of the capsule walls and by temperature and moisture, not by plant needs. This restricts nitrogen leaching losses from overirrigation to the small amount released since the previous irrigation. However, application of nutrients cannot easily be varied according to crop needs. For example, an amount of controlled-release fertilizer that releases enough nitrogen to feed a rapidly growing plant (for example, a 40-day-old chrysanthemum that takes up 30 mg of nitrogen per day) would be far more than the amount needed for a young plant or one that is no longer taking up much nitrogen (for example, a 70-day-old chrysanthemum). The excess nitrogen that is released can be lost to leaching if plants are overirrigated.

The likelihood of nitrogen leaching losses from controlled-release fertilizers is greatest in the first few weeks after planting, when plant root systems are limited, nutrient demand is low, and plants are consuming relatively small amounts of water. It is best to apply controlled-release fertilizers just below the plant roots at the time of planting ("dibbling") or to broadcast it on the soil surface.

Plant requirements for nitrogen vary according to growth rate and stage of development. For example, the rate of nitrogen uptake by potted chrysanthemums increases during vegetative growth, then decreases sharply after flower buds form. Poinsettias behave in a similar fashion. Roses and certain other woody species exhibit a cyclical pattern of nitrogen uptake that is related to episodes of shoot growth and pruning or dormancy. Depending on the method of applying nitrogen, it may be possible for growers to adapt the fertilizer program to match changes in plant nitrogen demand.

Phosphorus Application

Phosphorus is present in the soil in a number of chemical forms. Soil water contains a very low concentration of soluble inorganic phosphorus. Larger amounts of phosphorus are usually present in less soluble forms in chemical precipitates, as a constituent of organic matter, or adsorbed onto soil particles. These different phosphorus sources often establish an equilibrium in the soil, so that as plants remove soluble phosphorus, the other forms replenish the soluble phosphorus supply. In mineral soils, phosphorus solubility is low, and most phosphorus is present in chemical precipitates that are relatively immobile. These forms of phosphorus are not usually transported off-site unless rainfall or irrigation moves sediment containing phosphorus. In contrast, the solubility of phosphorus in soilless container media is relatively high, especially in acidic media. This soluble phosphorus can be leached out of containers by rainfall or excessive irrigation. Leaching losses of 30 to 60 percent of fertilizer phosphorus are common, even when it has been added as treble superphosphate. These leaching losses can be reduced significantly, with little or no decreases in crop yields, by incorporating ferrous sulfate into the medium at a rate of 4.8 pounds per cubic yard. In addition, phosphorus bound to particles of soilless media that have been spilled or washed out of containers can move off-site in irrigation or rainwater. The movement of phosphorus into streams and lakes can lead to algal blooms and fish kills.

Common laboratory soil test procedures provide an estimate of the amount of phosphorus in the soil that is available to plants. Unlike soil nitrate testing, which measures the actual amount of nitrate present, soil testing for phosphorus, as carried out by most laboratories, gives an index value or ranking of the relative phosphorus supply. Researchers over many years have calibrated these soil test procedures in greenhouse and field trials so that the results can be used to predict whether a crop is likely to respond to additional phosphorus fertilization. For most ornamental crops, plant demand for phosphorus is about 5 to 15 milligrams per day. For field-grown woody nursery plants, the typical recommendation is to supplement existing soil phosphorus with fertilizer to provide a total of 44 pounds of actual phosphorus (100 pounds when expressed as P_2O_5) per acre. For container-grown crops, phosphorus is usually added to the growing medium as treble superphosphate (1 pound per cubic yard) before planting. Alternatively, phosphorus can be added as a component of a complete controlled-release fertilizer.

It is not normally necessary to supplement the preplant addition with a liquid feed source of phosphorus unless the crop will be grown for more than 3 to 6 months. In that case, injection of phosphorus into the irrigation water at a rate of 15 to 20 mg/L is effective. However, liquid feeding with phosphorus is subject to the same problems that are associated with liquid feeding with nitrogen.

The best way to prevent phosphorus from moving off-site is to reduce runoff. Evaluate your property so that you know the surface drainage patterns and take action to prevent runoff from reaching surface water bodies. Filter strips, grassed waterways, sediment basins, nutrient management, or other Natural Resources Conservation Service (NRCS) practices should be used in conjunction with soil testing to be effective at addressing the phosphorus runoff issue.

Fertilizer Injection

Fertilizer proportioners are used in liquid feeding systems to eliminate the need for immense stock solution tanks. They allow for the measured injection of highly concentrated fertilizer solutions. Several types of proportioners are available, and the choice of a proportioner depends on factors such as the size of the production area, need for mobility, need for multiple injector heads, and desired stock solution concentration. An understanding of the principles of operation of proportioners, as well as their limitations and maintenance needs, is important in making the best choice.

Size of Production Area

Proportioners that have a low flow rate or a low injection ratio are not well suited for use in large nurseries. The low flow rate limits the area that can be irrigated at a given time, and the low injection ratio requires a relatively large stock tank in relation to the volume of irrigation water to be applied.

Injection Ratio

The choice of the dilution ratio between the fertilizer stock solution and the final concentration to be applied to plants depends on the volume of water to be applied and the composition of the fertilizer stock solution. A highly concentrated stock solution permits using a relatively small stock tank. However, some fertilizers are incompatible at high concentrations. Typically, a ratio of 1:100 is convenient.

Multiple Injector Heads

Multiple injector heads allow for greater flexibility in the delivery of fertilizers and also help to overcome the problem of incompatibility of fertilizers in highly concentrated stock solutions by relegating incompatible fertilizers to separate stock tanks.

Proportioner Types

The venturi type of proportioner is the simplest. The principle of operation is the same as that for the carburetor on a gasoline engine. The venturi proportioner employs a venturi tube, which places a constriction in the flow of irrigation water. To maintain the volume of flow through the constriction, the water moves faster. This causes the water pressure at the end of the constriction to be lower than at the beginning. An inlet tube inserted at that point allows a fertilizer stock solution to flow in

because the pressure in the stock tank is higher than in the venturi. In essence, a suction in the venturi draws in the stock solution. The basic models of this type of proportioner are inexpensive and mobile, but the maximum flow rate is low and the injection ratio is low. Thus the stock solution cannot be highly concentrated. These are suitable for a small greenhouse operation. Venturi proportioners are also subject to variation in dilution ratio when water pressure in the mainlines fluctuates. Some of the drawbacks of the venturi proportioner are overcome by introducing a pressurized stock tank, which allows for higher injection ratios.

Positive displacement pump proportioners are more expensive, but they can accommodate a wide range of flow rates and operating pressures. They have chambers of a specific size, usually at a fixed ratio set by the manufacturer, for the incoming irrigation water and the stock solution. After each of the chambers is filled, pistons driven by a hydraulic or electric pump force the water and stock solution into the outlet line in a fixed ratio.

More recently, manufacturers have developed proportioners that base the injection of fertilizer on the electrical conductivity and the pH of the output solution. These proportioners are effective for almost all fertilizers except urea, which is not a salt and does not conduct electricity. They are particularly well suited to operations that recirculate the drainage after irrigation.

Management of Injection Systems

A reliable proportioner makes liquid feeding of crops a simple procedure, but the output from the proportioner must be monitored, and the chemicals in the stock solution must be compatible and mixed properly.

The ingredients in the fertilizer stock solution must be readily soluble in water to be used effectively with a proportioner. Technical grade chemicals are preferable to fertilizer grade ones, despite their higher cost, because they have fewer impurities that can decrease solubility. Some chemicals are not compatible in highly concentrated stock solutions because they form a solid precipitate. The most common problems occur when fertilizers containing calcium are mixed with fertilizers containing sulfate or phosphate, or if iron compounds are mixed with compounds containing phosphate, especially if the proportioner operates at an injection ratio of 1:200 or higher. If you formulate a new fertilizer stock solution, first test for incompatibility by scaling down the recipe to fit in a small volume, then mixing the chemical ingredients in a glass jar. Wait for a couple of hours and then check for cloudiness or a fine film on the bottom of the jar, either of which indicates the presence of a precipitate. If precipitation occurs, the formulation must be changed.

In some cases, precipitation can be avoided by heating the stock solution during mixing. Fertilizers usually dissolve more readily in hot water (water at approximately 150°F works well). However, it is wise to follow the edict "When in doubt, leave it out." The alternative is to use multiple injector heads that have separate tanks to hold incompatible stock solutions.

It is very important to monitor injector function. Just as carburetors in cars can develop problems, so can proportioners. A simple and useful practice is to incorporate a water-soluble dye into the stock solution as a visual indicator that the injector is working. However, it is also important to check the proportioner at least once a month to ensure that it is operating accurately. One method is to measure the volume of stock solution uptake in relation to that of the delivered irrigation solution. The ratio of these volumes should equal the intended injection ratio. An easier method for monitoring the proportioner is to measure the electrical conductivity of the output solution or to install an EC meter in the irrigation line beyond the proportioner. The EC should equal the sum of the raw irrigation water EC plus the EC imparted by the fertilizers.

Backflow Prevention

Backflow prevention devices are required when chemicals are applied through irrigation water. An air gap—a physical break between the irrigation water supply line and the open end of the line—is the most reliable form of protection against backflow contamination. The gap must be at least twice the diameter of the supply pipe and not less than 1 inch in diameter. Although air gaps are highly effective, they have the disadvantage that water at the receiving end is no longer pressurized.

For systems in which fertilizers are injected, one practice is to install a check valve with an atmospheric vacuum breaker between the water supply and the injector to prevent water movement back toward the water source. A low-pressure drain must be installed upstream of the check valve, usually below the vacuum breaker. Alternatively, a gooseneck pipe loop can be installed in the main line between the pump and the injectors. The gooseneck assembly must have a vacuum relief valve at the top of the loop, and it must rise at least 24 inches above the highest outlet in the irrigation system. The injector port must be at least 6 inches below the bottom of the pipe at the loop in the gooseneck. In the injection line, a typical backflow prevention system employs a spring-loaded check valve with an opening pressure of at least 10 psi installed where the injection line joins the main irrigation line. This prevents stock from draining from the tank into the irrigation line when the system is not pressurized, and it also keeps water from flowing back into the stock tank if the injection pump fails. In addition, a normally closed solenoid valve should be installed between the stock tank and the injection pump to prevent unwanted flow into or out of the stock tank.

Backflow prevention devices should be tested annually, and the date and results of the tests should be recorded and saved.

Fertilizer Storage

Fertilizers should be stored in a manner that prevents their direct entry into groundwater or surface water. They should be placed in covered and secure locations to prevent direct contact with water from rainfall or irrigation and should be kept as far as possible from wells or surface water. The storage area should provide secondary containment to prevent movement of fertilizers in the event of a spill. Secondary containment should include an impermeable floor, as well as waterproof curbs around the storage area. If liquid fertilizer is stored, the secondary containment should be able to contain at least 110 percent of the volume of fertilizer stored.

In the event of a spill, sweep up dry fertilizer and return it to the storage container or place it in a properly labeled sealable container. Liquid spills can be recovered by pumping the solution into tanks labeled for reuse.

References

Bunt, A. C. 1988. Media and mixes for container-grown plants. London, UK: Unwin-Hyman.

Handreck, K., and N. Black. 2002. Growing media for ornamental plants and turf. Sydney: University of South Wales Press.

Mills, H. A., and J. Benton Jones Jr. 1996. Plant analysis handbook II. Athens, GA: MicroMacro Publishing.

Using Integrated Pest Management to Prevent Pesticide Runoff

Julie Newman, University of California Cooperative Extension Farm Advisor, Ventura County
Karen Robb, University of California Cooperative Extension Farm Advisor, Mariposa County
Cheryl Wilen, University of California Area IPM Advisor, Southern California

Greenhouse and nursery growers face one of the most difficult challenges of all agricultural producers: using pesticides while upholding water quality. In California, data gleaned from pesticide use reports have documented that in general, ornamental crops receive significantly more pesticides per acre than other agricultural crops such as cotton. Weekly pesticide applications in greenhouses and nurseries are not uncommon.

One reason chemical use is so prevalent in ornamentals is that growers strive to produce the aesthetically perfect crops that are demanded by consumers. Another reason is that growers are legally mandated to use pesticides to meet quarantine requirements when exotic pests are detected. In recent years pesticide use in nursery regulation programs has accelerated with the increased number of introduced exotic pests, including glassy-winged sharpshooter, Diaprepes root weevil, *Puccinia horiana* (causing chrysanthemum white rust), and red imported fire ant.

Many of the major pests that attack ornamental crops have become resistant to one or more pesticides, and this also has contributed to chemical dependency. Pesticide resistance leads to increased pesticide application rates in an effort to obtain control previously achieved at lower rates. The overall result of chemical dependency is a cycle of expanding pesticide use in spite of stricter regulations governing pesticide use and runoff from nursery and greenhouse operations (for more information on management practices to avoid pesticide runoff, see chapter 6).

Recent monitoring by state regulatory agencies in California showed that a number of pesticides consistently appear in nursery runoff and adjacent creeks. A concern is that pollution-laden runoff from coastal nurseries can eventually contaminate ocean estuaries. Pesticides found include organophosphate and synthetic pyrethroid insecticides that have high toxicities to fish and other aquatic organisms. Some of the pesticides detected, such as pyrethroids, are required in quarantine programs or shipping protocols, so eliminating these pesticides from growers' arsenals is not possible.

Many growers have mitigated pesticide runoff and leaching through the implementation of sound integrated pest management (IPM) practices. In this chapter we examine how the implementation of IPM programs, including using monitoring data and threshold levels to determine appropriate timing of control measures, can reduce pesticide loads generated by nursery and greenhouse operations. Preventive measures, nonchemical control practices, and pesticide application techniques that reduce pesticide loads are also discussed. For more information on selection of environmentally friendly pesticides, safe pesticide handling, and practices to avoid pesticide runoff, see chapter 6.

Basic Concepts of IPM

Pests

When organisms found in nurseries cause economic or aesthetic damage to crops, they become pests. Examples include insects, mites, fungi, bacteria, viruses, nematodes, snails and slugs, and weeds. Pests can directly affect crop quality by damaging plant parts or by reducing plant growth. Insect pests and weeds can also indirectly cause injury as vectors of plant pathogens (pests that are the causal agents of plant diseases). Pests must be controlled in greenhouses and nurseries in order to meet grower objectives of producing high-quality plants, obtaining a good economic return, and complying with regulatory requirements.

What Is IPM?

Integrated pest management is an ecosystem-based strategy that focuses on long-term prevention of pests or their damage through a combination of control strategies. In nursery IPM programs, these control strategies include biological control, insect exclusion, attention to cultural practices, sanitation, and conventional pesticide applications. These strategies are implemented according to established guidelines only after monitoring indicates that such treatment is appropriate. This involves knowledge of pest life cycles and an understanding of crop production. Pest control materials are selected and applied in a manner that minimizes risks to human health, beneficial and nontarget organisms, and the environment, with the goal of removing only the target organism.

Integrated pest management is key to reducing pesticide use and preventing pesticide contamination of water supplies. Using pesticides is often a last resort measure. When pesticides are applied, techniques should be used that minimize the number of applications or the amount of pesticide used. Effects on environmental quality and human health should also be considered. Reduced pesticide loads result in reduced liabilities for the grower.

Importance of Pest Identification

Before a pest can be controlled, the problem must be identified. Proper identification of the underlying cause or causes of poor plant performance is essential in making appropriate and effective IPM decisions. Pesticides and other control measures that may be effective for a given pest may not be appropriate for another pest. In addition, poor plant growth and damage is not always caused by pests. Sometimes these problems are due to environmental and cultural conditions, such as unfavorable temperatures, insufficient light, or overwatering. Symptoms related to environmental conditions or to nutrient or water stress cannot be remedied with pesticides. If problems are incorrectly diagnosed, inappropriate chemical treatments could be used that will be ineffective and add unnecessary pesticide loads to the environment.

Every employee who monitors pests and diseases should be trained to identify all stages of pests commonly found in the nursery and should be familiar with damage symptoms and pest life cycles. Training should be updated regularly, particularly as new pests and diseases are discovered in the nursery or in the state. In addition, other employees who handle or walk the crop, such as irrigators or flower harvesters, should also be trained to recognize common pests so they can be on the lookout for pests as they perform other duties.

Diagnostic laboratory services or other professional assistance should be used to identify unknown pathogens, pests, or growth problems before implementing a control measure. Disease diagnosis may require sample testing for pathogens in commercial laboratories. This may include using on-site kits such as ELISA for certain viruses and root and crown decay fungi. For more information concerning diagnostic kits see *Easy On-site Tests for Fungi and Viruses in Nurseries and Greenhouses* (Kabashima et al. 1997).

Scouting Programs

The basis of IPM is a monitoring or scouting program. Monitoring is the regular inspection of plants and surrounding areas in order to assess the status of pest and natural enemy populations and the damage induced by pests. The monitoring data assists growers in detecting troublesome pests while the pests are still manageable and before they cause major plant damage. This data is used along with the crop's tolerance for damage to make pest management decisions. A treatment is made only when a pest problem actually exists.

Benefits of Monitoring

Historically, nurseries have used pesticides on a calendar schedule. For example, a grower may have applied a pesticide every 2 weeks starting from planting, irrespective of pest presence. The problem with this approach is that it resulted in pesticide applications that missed the target pest or susceptible life stages of the target pest. It also led to needless and inefficient use of chemicals, pesticide resistance, and unnecessary exposure of workers and the environment to toxic substances.

Today, most growers no longer control insect pests and weeds using calendar schedules for treatments. However, using preventive pesticide sprays applied on a calendar schedule for control of some diseases is still prevalent. Research is currently underway to develop and refine disease models for ornamental plants. This will likely result in replacing calendar spray schedules for

controlling these diseases with environmental monitoring and scouting.

Monitoring provides many advantages. It serves as an early warning system for pest presence. This allows for the implementation of appropriate control strategies before populations escalate, as well as using slower-acting methods that are more environmentally friendly and safer for workers. Monitoring is also useful because it locates specific sites of infestation and provides an opportunity to identify the kinds of pests, stage in the life cycle, and pest numbers present. Collecting and graphing monitoring data over time can help predict future pest populations, especially when this information is correlated to weather conditions. Another benefit of regular monitoring is that it allows for the evaluation of pest management control actions, including using natural enemies.

The implementation of monitoring programs generally leads to reduced pesticide use. Benefits include fewer problems with pesticide resistance, fewer disruptions of cultural practices that occur during pesticide applications, less exposure of workers to pesticides, and reduced pesticide runoff. Monitoring programs also improve plant growth and quality by minimizing phytotoxicity (plant damage induced by overuse of toxic pesticides). Worker safety is improved and environmental risks are minimized. Because labor and materials associated with pesticide application are high production costs in greenhouses and nurseries, reduced pesticide usage results in increased profits to the grower. In unpublished studies conducted by the University of California on a wide variety of ornamental crops, scouting programs reduced pesticide use up to 50 percent and resulted in significant cost savings.

The Scout and the IPM Team

The IPM scout is the person who does the monitoring, records field data, and summarizes the information. The scout may or may not be responsible for pest control decisions. If the scout is not responsible for these decisions, he or she should meet regularly with the person who is responsible for making pest control decisions and present summarized data for the decision-making process.

Many nurseries involve a team of players in the overall pest management program. The two necessary requirements for a successful IPM program are a commitment by all members of the IPM team to base pest management decisions on monitoring data, and good communication among all team members, including the scout, grower, pest control adviser, and pesticide applicators. The IPM team should meet on a regular basis to discuss if, when, and where control actions should be taken, and to evaluate whether previous steps to mitigate pest problems have or have not been successful.

The team should also evaluate the effectiveness of the IPM program and discuss potential changes. It is a good idea for the scout to organize monitoring information and other pest management records into a notebook kept at the nursery, where the data is accessible to all involved in the IPM program for the purpose of evaluation by the team.

Scouting Activities

The scout's activities begin with gathering information concerning previous pest history in the crop and in the nursery and other potential pest problems. The scout should walk the entire nursery looking for possible trouble spots and ensure that these problems are addressed by nursery personnel. Examples of potential trouble spots are dripping hoses that could result in poor drainage and root rot, weeds that could harbor pests, and crop debris and other poor sanitation practices. Another important initial task is to develop a written monitoring plan that delineates what sampling methods are to be used and how they will be employed. It is important that the site is sampled the same way each week to make results comparable among sample dates. This method can then be used to determine whether pest populations are increasing or decreasing.

Propagation areas and incoming shipments from other nurseries should be intensely monitored to ensure that plants are free from pests and diseases when they are planted out (see the section "Preventive Control" later in this chapter). Once the propagation material is planted into the nursery, the scout begins routine inspections, monitoring crop and noncrop areas at least once a week for pests (e.g., pathogens, arthropods, snails, slugs, rodents and other vertebrates, and weeds). Monitoring and keeping records of environmental conditions such as temperature and relative humidity can also be important as these can be used to predict the growth of pest and pathogen populations.

Much of the scout's job at this point involves data collection and record keeping. The scout must keep written records of pest counts or degree of injury. This information is recorded on a data collection sheet such as the form shown in table 5.1. These records should include the date, location, name of the person sampling, pests encountered, and other important information. Additional forms should be developed and used to incorporate background information, site plans of the nursery with monitoring areas identified, and plot maps.

As mentioned in the previous section, if the scout is not the pest management decision maker, he or she will need to summarize the data and present it at least once a week to the grower and others involved in pest management decision making. Summarized information includes the type and abundance of pests, percentage of infested plants, and location of heavy infestations. From such data collected over time, the scout may prepare a graph to illustrate pest population trends or compare current data with the previous collection period. These summarized data should be presented to the grower and others involved in pest management decision making.

Scouts also need to maintain equipment and tools used for pest identification, collection, and record keeping. Essential tools for scouting are listed in table 5.2.

Table 5.1. Sample scouting form. This form, used for scouting cut roses, can be adapted to specific crops and pests found in a nursery. The percentage of plants infested or a rating scale can be substituted for actual counts of the pests.

Scouting Record:	Scouting Location: PMU#:		Date:	
Scout's Name:	Time in:		Time out:	

Number of pests									
Sample number	Aphids	Mites	White-flies	Thrips	Other insects	Rust	Powdery mildew	Botrytis	Other diseases
1									
2									
3									
4									
5									
6									
7									
8									
9									
10									
11									
12									
13									
14									
15									
16									
17									
18									
19									
20									
Pest total									
Average									

Comments (*also note any biological control or natural enemies*):

Action or Treatment Thresholds

Treatment or action thresholds are a fundamental part of IPM programs. A threshold is the level at which plant injury or pest population size is sufficient to warrant some type of control action; below this level the presence of pests and amount of damage can be tolerated. Unfortunately, very few action thresholds have been developed for ornamental crops, so another typical scouting responsibility is collecting data to develop this information. Even if published thresholds exist, use them only as a guideline; develop your own thresholds based on experience and economics.

The scout assists in establishing thresholds by monitoring plants, keeping good records, and evaluating the acceptability of the finished crop. Thresholds should be quantitative (numerical) to be useful. For example, they could be based on the average number of pests per trap each week, the percentage of plants or leaves found to be damaged or infested during visual inspection, or the number or size of weeds in a container.

Thresholds vary with crop, stage of plant development, cost of control methods, and time until harvest and market. For example, in cut flower crops damage to lower leaves may be acceptable because these leaves are removed before sale to the final consumer, whereas in potted plants damage to lower leaves may be unacceptable if these are part of the purchased commodity. Thresholds can often be higher if highly effective or quick-acting methods are available for controlling the problem. Conversely, if available controls are slow-acting or only partially effective, thresholds may be relatively low for that pest. In certain situations, regulations such as quarantines may

Table 5.2. Common tools used by scouts in greenhouses and nurseries

• beating stick and sheet or tray	• petunia indicator plants and stand
• calculator	• pheromone traps
• camera with macro lens	• plastic traps
• clipboard	• pocket knife
• clothes pins or clips to secure traps	• pocketed apron or tool belt
• disease diagnostic kits	• record-keeping forms
• dissecting microscope or field microscope	• ruler
• flagging tape and survey flags	• saran wrap
• hand lens (10–15×)	• shovel
• ice chest	• stakes
• measuring tape	• sticky traps
• mini-saw	• stop watch
• moisture-sensitive paper to evaluate spray coverage	• string soil corer
• notebook	• sweep net
• optivisor (visor-like magnifier)	• trowel
• paper (white)	• tweezers
• paper bags	• vials with alcohol (for collecting insects)
• pencils	• wire or chain to hang traps
• permanent waterproof marker	

impose zero pest tolerance even when pest populations are low and do not directly damage the marketed crop.

Economics are an important consideration in developing treatment thresholds. In fact, action thresholds are often developed based on the cost of treatment balanced against the price the grower will receive for the commodity. Growers also have to consider the hazards associated with making a pesticide application. By applying remedial action only if pest populations exceed this threshold, overall pesticide use and liabilities associated with it can be reduced.

Sampling Methodology

There is no single correct sampling method, but the methods chosen by the scout need to be appropriate to the target pests and the crop. The sampling procedure must be standardized, with the same procedure used every time the site is monitored. This way, comparisons can be made from week to week. Consistency is important, so ideally the same person should perform all the monitoring at a given site. If two or more people are involved, they should compare their methods in a preliminary sampling exercise to ensure that they are using the same methodology and recheck their methods periodically.

Growing areas are typically too large to be sampled as a single unit. Thus, the nursery should be divided into more manageable areas, or pest management units (PMUs). Each PMU is a contiguous area containing the same crop, usually at the same stage of growth. By separating a large area into smaller PMUs, scouting can be done more efficiently and pesticide use can be limited only to PMUs that need it. A PMU can be a greenhouse bench, a greenhouse range, or a section of a flower field.

If there is just one crop and the plants are of a similar age, PMUs may be arbitrarily divided. However, if several crops are growing, or if different ages of the same crop are planted, divide the area into PMUs by crop, age, or even by variety. For example, since yellow rose varieties often host more thrips than varieties of other colors, you might consider delineating PMUs by variety when monitoring roses. PMU boundaries can be delineated by greenhouse structures (e.g., by greenhouse

peaks in a greenhouse range) or by stakes and flagging tape in the field. If a crop is of very high value or is very susceptible to pests, more intensive scouting may be needed. Dividing the growing area into smaller PMUs allows for more intensive sampling and smaller treatment areas for spot treatments.

The scout must examine an adequate number of plants per unit area. This number will vary with every site, and more sampling may be necessary for high-value crops or for those that are very susceptible to pest problems; however, the number of samples should be constant over time. The number of plants examined in a given PMU often ranges from 5 to 25, depending on the size of the PMU and the value of the crop. Typically, one data sheet is used for each PMU, so if you have too much data in a PMU to fit on one data sheet, consider breaking the sampling area up into smaller PMUs. Keep in mind that pests are rarely distributed uniformly over all parts of an individual plant, and not all production areas will be infested. Sampling can help the grower determine where the infestation is located to better target sprays.

Indirect Monitoring Methods

Pests may be monitored directly or indirectly. Counting insects on plant parts or weeds in containers are examples of direct monitoring. Indirect monitoring can be accomplished in a number of ways, depending on the pest type. Examples include using sticky traps, pheromone traps, potato discs, and indicator plants. Record keeping should include plot maps and locations of traps, potato discs, or indicator plants.

Yellow Sticky Traps

Yellow sticky traps can be used to monitor adult flying insect pests, including aphids, thrips, leafminers, whiteflies, fungus gnats, and shoreflies. They can also be used to monitor adult parasitoid populations in biological control programs (see the section "Biological Control" later in this chapter). Blue sticky traps are sometimes used on crops for which western flower thrips are the only significant pest. A minimum of 1 sticky trap for every 10,000 square feet of growing area is recommended. Sticky traps should be positioned vertically just above the crop canopy and should be raised as the crop grows taller. To minimize the labor cost involved in scouting, especially when sticky traps are heavily infested, it is useful to take counts from a 1-inch central strip on both sides of the cards. Use sticky traps that are sold with grids, or make a 1-inch template to assist in the counting. A UC study showed that this rapid technique gives accurate data and can be extrapolated to whole trap data. (For example, if a 1-inch strip equals one-quarter of the card area, multiply the count by 4 to estimate insect counts on the whole trap.) Be sure to orient the strip to be counted in the same direction that it was when mounted. If the sticky card was mounted vertically in the greenhouse or nursery, orient the counting strip vertically; if the card was mounted horizontally, orient the counting strip horizontally. Counting the insects from sticky cards in the field with a hand lens usually saves time compared with counting them in indoors under a microscope, especially if the scout is less experienced in using a microscope. Counting sticky cards with a microscope requires wrapping traps in saran wrap for transporting indoors, which takes additional time. Microscope work may be necessary, however, in some situations, such as in biological control programs. Access to a microscope at the site, in a head house or office, for example, may be crucial in these instances. For more information about using sticky traps and the rapid technique, see *Sticky Trap Monitoring of Insect Pests* (Dreistadt et al. 1998).

Pheromone Traps

Pheromone-baited traps capture adults of many caterpillars that attack floricultural crops. There are also pheromone traps for some mealybugs and thrips, but these are not yet widely available for commercial use. Pheromone traps for moths typically consist of a sticky surface and a dispenser containing a pheromone. The pheromone is a sex attractant that lures adults (usually males). When the number of adult moths in the traps rises, more intensive inspection of plants is warranted because this is when females are most apt to be laying eggs. If you know how long it takes for larvae to hatch from eggs after adults are caught you can use traps to time pesticide applications. Because insect egg development is related to ambient temperature, degree-day models are useful in predicting when larvae will emerge. The timing of pesticide applications when caterpillars are young has a tremendous impact on efficacy, especially when using Bt (*Bacillus thuringiensis*), because small caterpillars are more susceptible to pesticides than are older larvae. Hang traps during the season when moths are expected. Separate each trap by at least several hundred feet. Reapply sticky material or replace the traps when they are no longer sticky. Pheromone dispensers may need to be replaced about once a month, especially in hot weather. Check with trap suppliers for specific types of pheromones available and for the appropriate use of specific traps.

Potato Discs

Larval populations of fungus gnats can be monitored during cool, moist weather conditions or in cool greenhouses by using potato cubes or discs. During periods of warm weather, potato discs may decompose too rapidly to be useful. Place discs cut approximately 1 inch in diameter and ½ inch thick with the cut surface face down. Press discs just into the soil or growing media so that the cut surface stays moist and does not dry out. Mark the area or pots with flagging tape to facilitate locating the cut potatoes for frequent inspection. Check both the growing media and underside of the potato discs for larvae. Replace during weekly scouting.

Indicator Plants

Indicator plants are used in monitoring programs because they are hypersensitive to plant pathogens and show symptoms before crop plants do. Some indicator plants show early symptoms that are easy to recognize, but the plants do not act as a reservoir for the pathogen. These types of indicator plants should be selected over those that might spread disease. For example, research done in California greenhouses has shown that petunias could be good indicator plants for tospoviruses such as tomato spotted wilt virus (TSWV) and impatiens necrotic spot virus (INSV) because these tospoviruses do not become systemic in petunias and because petunias show distinctive local lesions when thrips infected with these tospoviruses feed on them.

Direct Sampling

If indirect monitoring methods detect the presence of a pest, it does not mean that the pest has actually infested the crop. In addition, although sticky cards and pheromone traps provide information concerning adult insect populations, they cannot be used to determine the size of immature populations or to monitor disease presence. For these sorts of data, plants must be visually inspected by examining foliage and other plant parts for pests using a hand lens or optivisor (a visor with a built-in magnifying lens, similar to a jeweler's magnifying visor).

How many plants do you sample? The number can be different for each crop. More sampling is required for high-value crops or those that are very susceptible to insect or disease problems. If the crop is blooming, it is important to also sample flowers. It may be necessary to beat flowers over white paper to dislodge and count insects such as western flower thrips that may reside in the flowers. For some pests, such as the glassy-winged sharpshooter, a sweep net may be used to collect and count insects. Sweep nets are designed to quickly sample a wide variety of short (generally 4 feet or less in height) woody and herbaceous plants, such as those found in nurseries. Care must be exercised when using these nets to avoid injuring plants.

Scout the entire growing area in a consistent, uniform manner, inspecting some plants from each location. For example, a scout may travel in a serpentine pattern through the planting blocks or rows, stopping at regular intervals and evaluating three leaves from the bottom, middle, and top of the randomly selected plant. Another approach is to take many samples (such as 100) and record only whether pest species are present or absent on each sample.

Although it is important to randomly select some or most plant samples, it helps to also target "hot spots" where pests tend to be a problem. Hot spots might

include areas near vents, doors, edges of rows, susceptible cultivars, or warmer areas of the greenhouse. Be sure to examine the underside of leaves or inner plant parts where many pests prefer to reside. To avoid spreading pathogens, wash your hands after handling diseased plants or wear disposable gloves.

Record the specific location of infested plants using maps and flags so that control actions can clearly target that location. Reinspect these plants after taking action to determine whether control was effective.

Don't be limited by the sampling plan, but be alert for any sign of pest or natural enemy presence anywhere in the nursery or greenhouse while scouting. As you walk through the PMU, look for plants that are damaged by pests, adverse environmental conditions, or incorrect use of agricultural chemicals such as pesticides and fertilizers.

Injured plants should be examined for signs of the pest. For insect damage, look first at the part of the plant where the symptoms are occurring. Use a hand lens to get a better view of the pest. For plant diseases, look at plant roots, leaves, and stems. If the causal agent cannot easily be determined, it may be necessary to send plant samples to a diagnostic laboratory.

When monitoring in the nursery, make note of evidence of control from natural enemies. Look for evidence of insect parasitism, such as aphid "mummies" (parasitized aphids), darkened whitefly pupae or psyllid nymphs, and scales with exit holes of parasitoids (see the section "Biological Control" later in this chapter).

Using Degree Days to Predict Insect Growth

Unlike mammals and other warm-blooded animals, most insects cannot maintain a constant temperature, that is, the body temperature of an insect varies with the temperature of the environment. This fact makes estimating insect development difficult. Consequently, we need some way to combine time and temperature to predict insect and plant development. In other words, we need to measure physiological time. Degree days measure physiological time by combining time and temperature.

Degree days are referred to by a number of other terms such as heat units, thermal units, and growing degree days, but the concept is the same. Degree days represent the number of degrees above some minimum temperature necessary for growth multiplied by time in days. For example, 10 degrees above the minimum for 5 days represents 50 degree days, just as does 2 degrees above the minimum for 25 days. Both instances represent the same amount of physiological time: an insect would have grown the same amount under either condition. The total number of degree days can be associated with different developmental stages. For example, an insect may need 10 degree days to go from larva to pupa but 50 degree days to go from pupa to adult.

The first requirement for calculating degree days is to recognize that growth occurs only within a range of temperatures. The minimum temperature below which no growth occurs is the minimum developmental threshold or the minimum threshold. Growth increases with higher temperatures up to a maximum temperature, the maximum developmental threshold. These thresholds are determined experimentally and are different for each species. Although a minimum threshold is required for insect development, maximum thresholds often are not included since insects rarely experience temperatures near the maximum threshold during springtime development.

UC IPM operates a calculator on their Web site for determining degree days of insect pests, as well as models for other pests, such as greenhouse whitefly (see the Resources at the end of this chapter).

Starting a Scouting Program

Many nurseries prefer to start with existing employees as scouts rather than hire a professional scouting consultant or pest control adviser. Existing employees have the advantage of being on-site every day and knowing the nursery. However, if in-house employees are used, they must have extensive training in pest and natural enemy recognition and in data collection techniques. They should also have good attendance records, as scouting is an activity that must be done consistently. An important limitation of employee scouts is that their job often includes other responsibilities in addition to pest management. Therefore, during busy periods in the nursery, scouting may often be neglected in lieu of more immediate duties.

Monitoring should be conducted on a regular basis, and hiring a professional scout is recommended if you do not have in-house employees with a dedicated responsibility to regular monitoring. Because scouting programs reduce pesticide use and result in significant cost savings to the grower, the expense of hiring a professional scout can be offset. However, whether a professional is hired to do the scouting or not, it is still wise to have other nursery employees trained to recognize pests and contribute to the scouting effort. Even the best scouts cannot see everywhere. Irrigators, harvesters, and other employees can be trained to examine plant material as they irrigate, pot, or prune. A system can be developed that facilitates communication of the problems employees see in the course of day-to-day activities to the appropriate personnel, so that this information can also be used in making pest management decisions.

The success and sophistication of your scouting program depends on the experience, skill, and enthusiasm of these employees. Don't expect them to perform new tasks without encouragement and training. Additionally, it's important to share the process by involving all production personnel in the day-to-day IPM process as early as possible so that they understand and support the program.

When initiating a scouting program it is best to gain experience by starting small. Keep track of the time and labor involved in scouting. This helps you determine whether the program is cost-effective or whether you need to revise the number of samples collected. Test your methods and review your overall program regularly by evaluating records. Incorporate changes and fine-tune your program, but don't change everything at once. When the program is working successfully in one area or against one pest, expand the program to other areas or pests. Using insect identification guides and other reference materials is critical to an expanding IPM program. Be sure you have the most recent information available.

In addition to monitoring, it is important that someone be assigned the responsibility for making decisions, carrying out the pest management strategies, and evaluating the effectiveness of your program. This could be the scout, grower, PCA, or other consultants. Develop a plan to ensure that each member of the IPM team communicates with each other on a regular basis, and stick to it.

Implementing Preventive and Nonchemical Control Practices to Reduce Pesticide Runoff

Preventive Control

Many growers reduce pesticide use in the nursery and pesticide loads in the environment by practicing preventive control techniques. Prevention is the best control method and is critical to any IPM program. Methods to prevent pest development and spread include using resistant plant varieties, good sanitary practices, and proper plant culture.

Resistant Plants

Certain plant varieties, cultivars, or species have physical or biochemical characteristics that make them more resistant to pests. Some varieties may be less desirable to insects, nematodes, or plant pathogens for feeding or reproduction. Other varieties may be able to support large pest populations without suffering appreciable damage. Some plant species are better able to resist weed competition by growing faster and shading out emerging weed seedlings. Before buying plant material, especially

propagation stock, check with your supplier for resistant varieties. Keep records of plants that demonstrate good disease and insect resistance.

Good Sanitary Practices

Sanitation practices remove pathogen sources before pathogens spread and infect other plants or another part of the same plant. Use the following sanitation practices whenever possible and appropriate.

Purchase certified plant material. Certified or culture-indexed stock is available for some plant species. Culture-indexed plants are vegetatively propagated and tested to confirm that they are free of specific bacterial, fungal, or viral pathogens. Nematode-free stock for certain crops can be obtained from participants in the California Certification Nursery program. This is especially important when selecting propagation stock. Visit your plant supplier to become familiar with their sanitation program.

Inspect incoming plant material. Carefully inspect all new shipments of plants, plugs, cuttings, or transplants brought into the greenhouse or nursery; treat or dispose of infected plants promptly before introduction to the growing area. This ensures that other plants do not become infected and reduces the size of areas that require treatment. Avoid purchasing plants with weeds growing in the containers or liners since the weeds may spread in the nursery.

Quarantine plants. Because disease symptoms may not be immediately expressed, place plants in a separate greenhouse or nursery section to monitor them separately for pests before introducing them to the main production area.

Eliminate weeds in production and nonproduction areas. Many plant disease vectors proliferate on weeds, as is the case with western flower thrips infected with tospoviruses. In addition, weeds can harbor other pests (mites, aphids, whiteflies, etc.) and can increase competition for water and nutrients. Weeds can also decrease air circulation, especially near the soil line. Install weed mat barriers if floors are bare dirt or gravel and keep them maintained. Weeds removed from containers should be removed from the site and not just discarded on the ground. Pulled weeds do not die immediately after removal from the soil, and their flowers and seeds can continue to develop. In addition, weeds discarded on the ground often can reroot in the soil near the containers.

Eliminate pathogen reservoirs. Remove diseased plants; destroy them or treat them in an isolated area. Collect, bag, and remove crop residues, pruned plant material, old flowers, and unmarketable plants. Place these materials in a covered dumpster away from and downwind of healthy plants and production areas.

Treat planting areas and media before establishing new crops. This can be done by fumigating, heat steaming (at 140°F for 30 minutes) or chemically treating media. If possible, purchase planting media that has been pasteurized to kill plant pathogens and pests. All media should be stored in the original bags until use, or in covered containers or covered piles to prevent contamination by plant pathogens. You may temporarily save money by reusing untreated media, but you risk devastating losses due to plant pathogens. In addition, using untreated media may increase the need for fungicide treatment of root rots.

Disinfest hands and shoes. Hands and shoes can be readily contaminated when working with diseased plants or when coming into contact with soil and debris. Hand dispensers and foot baths should be set up at production house entrances and in propagation facilities. Ensure that employees use them regularly. Consider hand sanitizing products, which typically contain alcohol in addition to soap. Use footbaths or mats with a disinfectant at each greenhouse entry point. Change disinfectant daily and wash floor mats at least weekly. Keep feet off benches.

Keep hoses off the ground by using hose hangers. This simple practice avoids transferring pathogens from the ground to growing areas.

Treat recycled containers. Thoroughly wash containers to remove debris, soil, and plant material that cling to these items and can serve as a source of pathogens such as *Rhizoctonia* and *Pythium*. Follow with steam treatment; ideally, the containers should reach at least 140°F, but check temperature recommendations in manufacturers' guidelines to avoid heat damage. Where steam is not available, hot water can be effective if the minimum water temperature is 140°F. Treatment time can be as short as 1 minute, but longer treatment times are more reliable. Chemical disinfectants can also be used for pathogen control.

Keep refuse containers tightly closed inside and outside the greenhouse. Infested plants or potting media that are thrown into trash bins can still support all stages of whiteflies, fungus gnats, and western flower thrips. These insects can easily fly out of the container and reinfest your crop.

Proper Cultural Practices and Environmental Management

Many pest problems can be prevented by providing good growing conditions to avoid environmental stresses. Healthy plants are more likely to avoid or withstand infection or infestation by pests than are unhealthy plants. Nurseries and greenhouses have numerous microenvironments, small areas that differ in temperature, humidity, and light. Select planting sites within your production area that best match your specific crop requirements. Before planting or moving plant material into an area, check irrigation lines, heaters, and other equipment to make sure they are in proper working order. Maintain vigorous plant growth by providing plants with the proper potting mix, fertilization, irrigation, and other environmental and cultural practices that are optimal for the species.

Provide adequate fertilization. Adequate fertilization is needed to avoid nutrient deficiencies and keep plants healthy enough to resist and recover from diseases. Too much nitrogen, however, can encourage excessive growth of new shoots, which may be more susceptible to plant pathogens. It can also produce overly succulent growth, exacerbating certain insect problems such as leafminer infestations. Overfertilization can also cause an excess of soluble salts in the soil, which can lead to leaf scorch symptoms and damaged root systems.

Provide good air circulation. Use a good horizontal air flow system and provide adequate plant spacing to promote good air circulation.

Avoid prolonged leaf wetness. Wet leaves encourage the development of foliar diseases. Free moisture is necessary for the germination of many disease-causing fungal spores, including *Botrytis*. Subirrigation or the use of a drip system is recommended; avoid overhead watering during blooming. If this is the only method of irrigation available, irrigate early in the day so that the foliage can dry as rapidly as possible.

Provide good drainage and water management. Overwatering and poor drainage promulgate root rot diseases and contribute to runoff. Never allow plants to be in or around standing water, as this is particularly damaging to plant health. Pools of water spread disease or serve as breeding areas for pests such as fungus gnats and shore flies. Also avoid water stress: for example, spider mite infestations are worse on water-stressed plants.

Nonchemical Control Practices

When monitoring indicates that pest control measures are necessary, consider implementing nonchemical control strategies as an alternative to, or in addition to, chemical control. The use of nonchemical strategies, such as pest exclusion, host-free periods, crop rotation, and biological control, may reduce the need to use chemicals and slow the development of pesticide resistance. These practices can also help mitigate pesticide runoff.

Cultural Control

Cultural controls are modifications of normal plant care activities that reduce or prevent pests. Knowledge of the life histories of pest species is essential to the effective use of cultural control. Since these methods are used more to prevent pest problems than to control them, some of these methods were discussed in the section on pest prevention. Other cultural control methods include

+ adjusting planting time to avoid pest migration into the newly planted crop from a susceptible crop

+ locating susceptible varieties together in a nursery so you can intensify pest management strategies and control methods in this area

+ separating new plantings from older, possibly infested plantings to avoid pest and pathogen movement to newer crops

Mechanical Control

Mechanical control tactics reduce pest abundance using methods such as hand-picking, physical barriers, or machinery. Examples include

+ hand-pulling weeds or applying mulch for weed control

+ applying reflective plastic mulches beneath container plants and using reflective mesh plant covers to repel certain insects

+ installing screens to exclude flying insects

+ applying sticky barriers to exclude climbing insects such as ants and weevils

+ applying mesh covers for small, containerized fruit trees and other plants to keep out large insects and birds

+ using trap boards for snails, slugs, and weevils

Details concerning the use of these strategies can be found in Integrated Pest Management for Floriculture and Nurseries (Dreistadt 2001).

Environmental Control

Environmental control methods indirectly control pests and prevent damage by manipulating the physical environment. Using heat is an environmental method that can be used effectively in nurseries and greenhouses. Composting, solarization, and steam pasteurization are heat treatments that control soilborne pests. Soaking seeds in hot water can also control pathogens found on the seed coat. Altering humidity and temperature by increasing ventilation, applying heat, and changing irrigation timing and method (such as switching from sprinklers to drip irrigation) can control many foliar pathogens. Improving the drainage and aeration of planting media prevents many abiotic and pathogenic problems.

Biological Control

Biological control practices use living organisms to reduce pest populations. These practices can be highly effective in keeping pests in check and can also result in less potential pesticide runoff.

Organisms that provide biological control of pests—beneficials, natural enemies, or biological control agents—help to keep pest populations low enough to prevent significant economic damage. There are many kinds of biological control agents. The most common ones used for biological control in nurseries and greenhouses are predators, parasitoids (parasites), and pathogens.

- Predators are generally very mobile and larger than their prey (the pest species). Predators include a wide range of beneficial insects, spiders, mites, and other living organisms. A predator seizes, overpowers, or immobilizes its prey and either consumes it entirely or sucks its body fluids. General predators feed on a wide variety of pest species that attack nursery crops. In comparison, parasitoids are more host-specific.

- Parasitoids are smaller than the host pest species and spend part or all of their life cycle with their host. Insect parasitoids that attack insect pests such as aphids, scales, and whiteflies are generally tiny wasps or flies that sting their hosts to lay eggs but are too tiny to sting people. Beneficial nematodes are another parasitoid biological control agent. Insect parasitoids typically deposit one or more eggs in or on the host, and when the eggs of the parasitoid hatch, the larvae feed on or inside the host. Eventually the host dies and an adult parasitoid emerges from the host's body. Ant control is important when relying on insect parasitoids for pest control because ants often attack and kill beneficial parasitoid insects.

- Beneficial pathogens are microscopic organisms such as bacteria, viruses, and fungi that cause diseases in pest insects, mites, nematodes, or weeds.

Beneficial organisms can occur naturally in nursery environments. Often, the importance of naturally occurring biological control agents may not be appreciated until the use of a broad-spectrum pesticide aimed at primary pests kills natural enemies. The eradication of beneficial insects then allows outbreaks of pests that are no longer controlled by the natural enemies. This phenomenon is known as a secondary pest outbreak. One example might be the sudden outbreak of aphid, scale, mite, or whitefly populations throughout a nursery soon after application of a broad-spectrum insecticide.

In crop production systems, biological control practices generally fall into two categories: conservation and augmentation. In most greenhouse and nursery situations, conservation of naturally occurring biological control organisms is emphasized. Insects such as aphids are often maintained at low populations by natural enemies. Conservation is accomplished through the judicious use of pesticides and the maintenance of alternative hosts (including plants) for beneficial organisms. The most important thing you can do to encourage the activities of biological control agents is to avoid using pesticides whenever possible. Insecticides and some fungicides and soil fumigants can reduce the numbers of beneficial organisms in the environment. Learn to identify the beneficial insects and mites that naturally occur in your growing area. Monitor populations of beneficial insects and mites and consider the effects of pesticides when making pest control decisions. If chemical control is necessary, use the least disruptive materials, such as soaps, oils, and botanicals, or a pesticide that is specific to the pest you are attempting to control. When feasible, use control strategies such as direct spraying, spot spraying, and reduced pesticide rates that conserve beneficial insects and mites.

Augmentation is the periodic release or application of biological control agents into the production system. It usually involves purchasing and releasing commercially produced insect or microbial beneficial organisms. Augmentation in combination with good management practices and judicious use of pesticides has been highly successful with certain greenhouse crops such as cut roses and gerberas. More research is necessary before recommendations concerning the use of biological agents can be made for other ornamental crops. If recommendations for the crops you grow are not available and you are interested in trying augmentation, start small and evaluate the effectiveness of the agents before making large economic investments. A biological control practice that can be used on many ornamental crops is incorporating commercial preparations containing antagonistic bacteria or fungi into planting mixes to control certain root pathogens. Crown gall, a disease that affects the roots and stems of a wide range of nursery crops, can be prevented by treating exposed root systems or pruned surfaces with an antagonistic strain of *Agrobacterium*.

Chemical Application Practices That Reduce Pesticide Use

When using chemical control measures, various application tactics can be incorporated into an IPM program that minimize pesticide use. These tactics include avoiding pesticide resistance, spot spraying, direct spraying, use of adjuvants, and other practices.

Avoiding Pesticide Resistance

Pesticide resistance can occur when insects survive applications because they have genes for resistance to a given pesticide or class of pesticide. Over time, these survivor insects will breed, producing a resistant population. Using the same chemicals or class of chemicals over and over to control a particular pest promotes pesticide resistance. After a period of time, the chemical no longer effectively controls the pest at the same application rate. As resistance increases, higher rates and more frequent applications become necessary until eventually the chemical provides little or no control.

Key elements of insecticide resistance management include minimizing pesticide use, avoiding tank mixes, avoiding persistent chemicals, and using long-term rotations of pesticide from different chemical classes.

Minimize pesticide use. Minimizing pesticide use is fundamental to pesticide resistance management. IPM programs help determine the best application timing for pesticides (when they will do the most good), thus helping to reduce the number of applications.

Avoid tank mixes. Never combine two pesticides with the same mode of action in a tank mix. For example, two organophophates, such as acephate and chlorpyrifos, should not be used together. Such a "super dose" often increases the chances for the establishment of resistant pest individuals. Long-term use of two-class pesticide mixes should also be avoided, even in situations where the tank mix provides superior pest control. Two-class tank mixes can give rise to pesticide resistance if resistance mechanisms to both pesticides arise together in some individuals of the pest population. Continued use of the mixture may result in a pest population that is resistant to both pesticides (multiple-pesticide-resistant pests).

Vary formulations. Use different formulations when multiple pesticides are required for control. For example, insect growth regulators (IGRs) control only the immature stages of insects. If the adult stage must also be controlled, it will be necessary to apply another insecticide. Rather than applying an adulticide in the same manner as the IGR, choose a formulation that requires a different type of application. For instance, if the IGR is applied as a spray, it would be preferable for the adulticide to be applied as an aerosol or smoke to kill the adults rapidly and leave little residual pesticide that might lead to resistance in surviving immatures.

Avoid persistent chemicals. An ideal pesticide quickly disappears from the environment, leaving no residual active pesticide to encourage the development of resistant pest populations. When persistent chemicals must be used, consider where they can be used in a rotation scheme to provide the control needed with a minimum length of exposure.

Use long-term rotations for insects. Resistance management strategies for insects, weeds, and fungal pathogens include rotating classes of pesticides. For example, classes of insecticides include pyrethroids, organophosphates, and carbamates, among others. However, the strategies used in rotations differ. For example, with fungicides, it is suggested that classes be rotated every application. With insecticides, it is suggested that long-term rotations be used. This means that a class would be used for at least 6 to 8 weeks, depending on the target pest, before rotating to a new class of materials. If insecticides are switched with every application, the same individual insects will be exposed to both classes of pesticides, encouraging the development of resistance to both classes. Short-term rotations of insecticides basically function as a tank mix. If only one chemical is effective against a pest and other available products are only marginally effective, a good strategy to follow is to use the marginally effective materials when pest pressure is less severe and reserve the more effective material for when control is needed quickly. Reversal of some resistance can occur by allowing time between applications of a class of pesticide to permit resistant populations to become diluted by pesticide-susceptible individuals.

Other Methods to Reduce Pesticide Use

A number of practices typically used in IPM programs reduce pesticide use in the nursery and pesticide loads in the environment.

Spot spraying. Monitoring can identify areas in the nursery and plant parts where pests reside. Focusing pesticide applications in these areas rather than spraying the entire crop can significantly reduce overall pesticide use. Although spot spraying can be more labor intensive, it still results in significant economic savings for the grower due to reduced material costs. In UC demonstrations, monitoring and spot spraying reduced pesticide use by as much as 50 percent.

Direct spraying. Certain pests may be found primarily in certain parts of the crop plant. For example, western flower thrips typically reside in the top third of the crop, in the flowers and buds. Conversely, spider mites are typically found in the lower two-thirds of the crop. Directing spray toward the part of the plant where the pest resides can reduce the overall amount of pesticide applied.

Use the lowest label rate. Always start with the lowest recommended rate and use the lowest effective application frequency to reduce pesticide resistance.

Use pesticide adjuvants where appropriate. Pesticide adjuvants enhance the performance of pesticide applications. In general, they cause the pesticide to spread, stick to, or penetrate the plant material, resulting in more effective pest control. Using adjuvants can allow for reduced pesticide use by providing more uniform coverage. Wetting agents or surfactants reduce the surface tension of water in the pesticide spray, allowing it to spread more easily over the leaf. Stickers increase the chemical attraction of the pesticide to the plant surface. They increase the length of time the pesticide stays in contact with the pest by resisting being washed off by rain or irrigation and reducing evaporation and volatilization. There are also extenders, which work like stickers, and plant penetrants, which work like surfactants. Before using an adjuvant, read the label. Some manufacturers produce adjuvants that are most compatible with their own products. If an adjuvant is needed, information on what and how much to use can be found on the label. Some manufacturers add adjuvants to their pesticide products so no additional adjuvants are needed in these formulations. Be sure to read the product label for information about the appropriate types of adjuvant, if needed, for the pesticide you are using.

Use current IPM recommendations. To ensure that your control tactics are effective, use the most recent IPM recommendations for crops. Consult with your UCCE Farm Advisor, pest control adviser, and relevant publications such as *UC IPM Pest Management Guidelines for Floriculture and Ornamental Nurseries*, as well as the UC IPM Web sites listed in the Resources.

References

California Pesticide Information Portal (CalPIP) Pesticide Use Reporting Data Source Web site, calpip.cdpr.ca.gov/cfdocs/calpip/prod/infodocs/aboutpur.cfm.

Dreistadt, S. H. 2001. Integrated pest management for floriculture and nurseries. Oakland: University of California Agriculture and Natural Resources Publication 3402.

Dreistadt, S. H., J. P. Newman, and K. L. Robb. 1998. Sticky trap monitoring of insect pests. Oakland: University of California Agriculture and Natural Resources Publication 21572.

Ferrentino, G., J. Grant, M. Heinmiller, J. Sanderson, and M. Daughtery. 1993. IPM for poinsettias in New York: A scouting pest management guide. Ithaca: Cornell University Cooperative Extension, New York State IPM Program Publication 403.

Flint, M. L., and P. Gouveia. 2001. IPM in practice: Principles and methods of integrated pest management. Oakland: University of California Agriculture and Natural Resources Publication 3418.

Flint, M. L., and S. H. Dreistadt. 1998. Natural enemies handbook: The illustrated guide to biological pest control. Oakland: University of California Agriculture and Natural Resources Publication 3386.

Kabashima, J. N., J. D. MacDonald, S. H. Dreistadt, and D. E. Ullman. 1997. Easy on-site tests for fungi and viruses in nurseries and greenhouses. Oakland: University of California Agriculture and Natural Resources Publication 8002. ANR CS Web site, http://anrcatalog.ucdavis.edu/pdf/8002.pdf.

Robb, K. L., and M. P. Parrella. 1995. Integrated pest management of western flower thrips. In B. L. Parker, M. Skinner, and T. Lewis, eds., Proceedings of the 1993 International Conference on Thysanoptera: Towards Understanding Thrips Management. New York: Plenum. 365–370.

Robb, K. L., C. Casey, A. Whitfield, L. Campbell, J. Newman, and D. Ullman. N.d. Using petunia indicator plants to monitor tospoviruses in ornamental plants. UC Cooperative Extension San Diego County Web site, http://commserv.ucdavis.edu/CESanDiego/petunia.pdf.

Robb, K. L., J. P. Newman, J. Virzi, and M. P. Parrella. 1995. Pesticide resistance of the western flower thrips *Frankliniella occidentalis* (Pergande). In B. L. Parker, M. Skinner, and T. Lewis, eds., Proceedings of the 1993 International Conference on Thysanoptera: Towards Understanding Thrips Management. New York: Plenum. 341–346.

Resources

UC IPM models: Insects, mites, diseases, plants, and beneficials. UC IPM Web site, http://ipm.ucdavis.edu/MODELS/index.html.

UC IPM Pest management guidelines for floriculture and nurseries, UC IPM Web site, http://www.ipm.ucdavis.edu/PMG/selectnewpest.floriculture.html.

UC IPM run models and calculate degree-days, UC IPM Web site, http://www.ipm.ucdavis.edu/WEATHER/ddretrieve.html.

Pesticide Use and Water Quality Protection

Jay Gan, Water Quality Specialist, University of California, Riverside
Darren Haver, University of California Cooperative Extension Farm Advisor, Orange County
Julie Newman, University of California Cooperative Extension Farm Advisor, Ventura County

Pesticides are often found in surface streams and estuaries as well as in groundwater aquifers in California. The levels of pesticides present in surface streams are usually very low, so pesticide contamination to surface water is generally not a human health concern. However, even at trace levels, some pesticides may cause adverse effects to aquatic organisms. More often than not, the ecological risk drives the regulation of nonpoint source pesticide runoff, including at sites such as commercial nurseries. There are currently a number of total maximum daily loads (TMDLs) in force for pesticides in California, and more pesticide TMDLs are expected in the near future.

Contamination of groundwater by pesticides is of human health concern, as groundwater is the main source for drinking water in California. In contrast to contamination of runoff, groundwater contamination is more of a localized issue and is of significance mostly in the Central Valley, particularly in counties such as Tulare, Fresno, and Kern. It is critical for pesticide users to understand why and how pesticides contaminate surface water and groundwater, and what may be done to reduce the potential risk.

Commercial nurseries in California are heavy users of a great number of pesticides. According to the pesticide use reports submitted to the California Department of Pesticide Regulation (DPR), the most pesticide use at nurseries occurs in outdoor production. Although summer use of pesticides is relatively heavy compared to that in winter months (November through March), substantial use also occurs during the winter. Heavy pesticide use, coupled with the intensive irrigation regime used by many nurseries, poses significant risks for pesticides to contaminate surface water through runoff or groundwater through leaching. The actual risk closely depends on the environmental settings and management practices of the specific nursery. This chapter takes a brief look at factors that may affect the potential for a pesticide to move in runoff or leach to groundwater and discusses practices that may be easily implemented to reduce the runoff risk and groundwater risk at nursery sites.

Factors Affecting Pesticide Runoff

Pesticide Properties

The likelihood that a pesticide will move in irrigation or storm water runoff from the site of application depends in large part on the chemical properties of the active ingredient. Important properties to consider include pesticide adsorption, persistence, and water solubility.

Pesticide Adsorption

Pesticide adsorption refers to how well a pesticide adheres to soil particles moving in solution. The soil adsorption coefficient for the pesticide, K_{oc}, is pesticide-specific; the larger the K_{oc} value, the more strongly the pesticide adsorbs to soil. Typically, as pesticide solubility in water increases, adsorption in soil decreases, since water-soluble pesticides tend to stay in the soil solution. A pesticide with a low K_{oc} (that is, weak adsorption) and high solubility moves in the dissolved form, while a pesticide with a high K_{oc} (that is, strong adsorption) moves primarily by associating itself with eroded soil or sediment particles.

Pesticide Persistence

Pesticide persistence is a measure of how long a chemical stays in its original form in the soil and resists degradation. Typically, pesticides are not stable; degradation by soil microbial and chemical reactions eventually detoxifies a pesticide. This is a desirable process from the perspective of environmental safety because highly persistent pesticides pose the greatest risk of groundwater and surface water contamination. However, very fast degradation may render a pesticide ineffective for pest control, so a balance is desirable to nursery and greenhouse managers.

Persistence depends on the properties of the pesticide itself. Field dissipation half-life, DT_{50}, refers to the time required for half of a given quantity of a formulated pesticide to degrade or dissipate from the soil. Some pesticides are stable, and others are more susceptible to degradation. In general, pesticides that remain in the field for many weeks after treatment (that is, a half-life greater than 40 days) are more available to move in runoff because they last longer in the environment.

Water Solubility

Water solubility measures how easily a pesticide dissolves in water. As the solubility increases, K_{oc} usually decreases. However, there are exceptions to this general rule. For example, glyphosate (the active ingredient of Roundup) is highly water soluble but adsorbs strongly to soil and is not available to move in water. The pesticide formulation also affects solubility. In general, granules, water-dispersible granules, and emulsifiable concentrates tend to be more water soluble than wettable powders and microencapsulated formulations. Pesticides with high K_{oc} values are more likely to run off than leach.

Soil, Management, and Environmental Conditions

The actual runoff risk of pesticides at a given nursery closely depends on the soil, management, and environmental conditions at the site. Erodible soil, along with large impermeable surfaces (e.g., concrete pads) and slopes, contribute to significant transport of pesticide-laden organic matter and sediment in runoff water. Sites that are next to natural creeks are more vulnerable for discharging pesticides downstream. Management practices, especially irrigation practices, affect the actual pesticide runoff risk. Inefficient irrigation and overirrigation cause more surface runoff and should be replaced with precision irrigation methods such as drip irrigation. Because growth media are usually treated with certain pesticides, careless practices that cause widespread spills of potting mix increase pesticide runoff. In California, the weather pattern determines that the first few storms are likely the most important source of pesticide runoff. Preparation is therefore needed before the rainy season to curtail storm-related runoff.

Factors Affecting Pesticide Leaching

Three factors govern the possibility of groundwater contamination by pesticides passing through the soil: pesticide properties, soil properties, and water conditions.

Pesticide Properties

A pesticide's leaching potential is mostly a result of adsorption and persistence. Simply put, a pesticide that does not adsorb to soil readily but has a long persistence is a good candidate for leaching. The importance of adsorption and persistence can be illustrated through the groundwater ubiquity score (GUS) index. GUS is calculated using the following equation:

$$GUS = log(DT_{50}) \times (4 - log(K_{oc}))$$

If the GUS is greater than 2.8, the pesticide will likely be a "leacher." If the GUS is less than 1.8, the pesticide will be a "nonleacher." If the GUS is between 1.8 and 2.8, the pesticide is considered to be a marginal leacher. In California, pesticides with high leaching risk are generally certain preemergence herbicides, including those shown in table 6.1. These are examples only; not all of the pesticides listed are used in nurseries.

Soil Properties

Sensitive soils are those that allow rapid transmission of a pesticide to groundwater. Permeability and water table conditions control the leaching potential; organic matter and clay content control the adsorption potential. Adsorption of a given pesticide varies dramatically in different soils and generally increases with soil organic matter and clay content. Soils with low adsorption potentials are more sensitive to groundwater contamination than are soils with high adsorption potentials.

Permeability

Coarse-textured sandy and gravelly soils have the largest pores and the most rapid permeability. Fine-textured clay soils have very tiny pores and very slow permeability.

Water Table Conditions

Water table conditions include the height and persistence of water tables in the soil. Shallow water tables that persist for long periods increase the risk of groundwater contamination. Soil survey reports contain information on water table conditions in soil. Indications of shallow groundwater include riparian vegetation, persistently green unirrigated grass or herbaceous vegetation, springs, evidence of seasonal flooding, and low topographic position in relation to nearby surface water, springs, and riparian vegetation.

Soil Adsorption Potential

A soil's adsorption potential depends on its organic matter and clay content. Organic matter content is

Table 6.1. Pesticides with high leaching risk

Pesticide	Adsorption coefficient, K_{oc}	Field dissipation half-life, DT_{50} (days)	Groundwater ubiquity score, GUS
atrazine	100	60	3.6
bentazon	34	20	3.2
bromacil	32	60	4.4
diuron	480	90	2.6
norflurazon	600	90	2.4
prometon	150	500	4.9
simazine	130	90	3.7

the most important variable affecting adsorption of pesticides. The higher the organic matter and clay content, the higher the adsorption potential and the lower the leaching risk.

Water Conditions and Leaching

The total amount of water applied to the soil, or the hydraulic loading, is also important in determining the risk of groundwater contamination by pesticides. No matter how permeable the soil, the leaching risk remains low if there is insufficient water to move completely through the soil. Careful management of the amount and timing of irrigation water applications can be very effective in reducing leaching risk. The position of a soil in the landscape often influences its hydraulic loading. Soils near a hilltop often shed water, either by runoff over the surface or by subsurface lateral flow within the soil. Soils lower on the hillside and where the slope begins to flatten out often receive excess water from the highest positions. These soils are more susceptible to leaching from the added hydraulic loading.

Toxicity of Chemicals Used to Control Nursery Pests

Aquatic toxicity drives the concern and regulation of pesticide contamination of surface water, while human health consideration causes the concern for groundwater contamination by pesticides. Pesticides are specifically designed to kill different pests, such as weeds, insects, fungi, nematodes, and mites, among others. By design, pesticides differ greatly in their degree of toxicity. In general, insecticides tend to have high toxicity to fish and invertebrates, while certain herbicides have high toxicity to aquatic plants. Human toxicity is more pesticide-specific and may include acute toxicity (e.g., organophosphate insecticides) and chronic toxicities such as carcinogenicity (e.g., some herbicides). Information on the potential toxicity of a pesticide to nontarget organisms or humans can be found online at many Web sites (see the Resources at the end of this chapter).

Organophosphates, carbamates, and synthetic pyrethroids have runoff potential with a high associated risk for contaminating surface water and harming aquatic life. These include many commonly used pesticides for ornamental crops such as bifenthrin, carbaryl, chlorpyrifos, cyfluthrin, diazinon, malathion, fenpropathrin, permethrin, and many others. The pesticides that are of the most concern for nurseries in California are insecticides that include certain organophosphates, carbamates, and pyrethroids. Of the organophosphate compounds, diazinon and chlorpyrifos were the products of choice for insect management and are still used sporadically despite their restriction for nonagricultural and residential use. There are a few less used organophosphates and carbamates, such as malathion, dimethoate, and carbaryl. Pesticides that are currently drawing close scrutiny are the synthetic pyrethroids, which include active ingredients such as permethrin, bifenthrin, fenpropathrin, lambda-cyhalothrin, deltamethrin, esfenvalerate, cypermethrin, and cyfluthrin (these types of compounds typically end with "thrin"). Pyrethroids are problematic because they have high acute aquatic toxicity as well as high runoff potential.

Herbicides in Retention Ponds

Many large nurseries use on-site retention or recycling ponds to capture runoff and use the captured water for purposes such as crop irrigation. This practice sometimes leads to concerns about crop injury from the residual herbicides accumulated in the recycled water. Most herbicides are moderately hydrophobic and are effectively retained (adsorbed) by the planting media. Therefore, it may be expected that little herbicide can leach through containers. In addition, most herbicides are readily degraded in the retention pond through chemical, photochemical, and microbial transformations. These factors, when coupled with the fact that herbicide residues entering a retention pond are highly diluted, suggest that it is uncommon for the accumulation of herbicides in retention ponds to reach a level that can injure crops. However, certain practices that could lead to plant injury should be avoided. These are discussed in the "Mitigating Runoff and Leaching" section of this chapter.

Other Toxic Chemicals in Nursery Production

In addition to chemicals for controlling pests, other agricultural chemicals that are used in nursery production could potentially contaminate water. These include fertilizers, postharvest chemical treatments, growth regulators (which are classified as pesticides), and exterior shading compounds. For information on the toxicity and management of fertilizers, see chapter 4.

The ethylene blocker silver thiosulfate (STS) is a postharvest treatment agent used as a plant growth regulator. It is classified as a pesticide even though it is not used to control pests. STS was developed as a pretreatment for overcoming premature senescence and abscission due to ethylene gas in cut flowers and flowering plants. It was widely used in the cut flower industry until problems with registration and environmental concerns temporarily led to the lack of commercial STS-containing products in the United States. Recently, however, an STS-containing product (Chrysal AVB) was registered for use on cut flowers. Care should be exercised when using STS because silver is a heavy metal that persists in soil and water for long periods and may pollute drinking water. STS is very toxic to aquatic organisms, including fish and plankton in water bodies. When absorbed by the body, heavy metals accumulate and at toxic levels affect the nervous system.

Aside from pesticides and fertilizers, exterior shading compounds are the agricultural chemicals that have drawn the most fire in relation to nursery runoff. Beyond the safety issue, drainage ditches that are milky white following shade compound application have created a negative image of agriculture and have led to community and regulator entanglements. Most exterior shading compounds contain latex paint, which is toxic to marine life, and they may contain ethylene glycol, which can also be hazardous to humans. "Environmentally friendly" shading compounds may contain sodium hydroxide, which is strongly alkaline and must be disposed of properly because high pH water can be toxic to fish.

Mitigating Runoff and Leaching

By understanding the factors that affect pesticide transport in the environment, growers can have a better understanding of the risk associated with pesticide use. Armed with the knowledge of how soil, agricultural chemicals, and water factors interrelate, growers can design management programs to mitigate runoff and leaching. These include storm water, irrigation, and pesticide management practices as well as techniques to contain runoff and spilled contaminants such as planting mixes containing pesticides.

Consider the Site

Determine the susceptibility of the soil to leaching and runoff. Nurseries have many impervious or semi-impervious surface areas that are extremely conducive to runoff. In addition, permeable areas can be subject to leaching. Determine the depth of the water table and the relative permeability of the geologic layers between the soil surface and the groundwater. If sinkholes are present, surface water runoff can reach groundwater quickly with little natural soil filtering. A nursery located on a property with sandy soils, weak soil adsorption, and shallow groundwater tables has a high leaching risk, especially when using persistent pesticides. Slopes and other erodible land features enhance surface runoff. Insoluble pesticides and pesticides with high adsorption capacity can easily move with the eroding soil after irrigation or during a rain event.

Also evaluate the location of water bodies on the property and potential contamination, including wells. Pesticide contamination of groundwater is frequently associated with pesticide handling practices in the vicinity of wells. Pesticide mixing and loading activities should be kept at least 100 feet away from wells.

Select Pesticides Less Likely to Run Off and Leach

Pesticides should be selected for lower migration risk based on site conditions, pesticide labeling, and hazard warnings. Consider formulation, application timing, runoff potential, and leaching potential. Use online resources such as the University of California's PesticideWise Web site to obtain information on the product's potential for contaminating groundwater or surface water. In addition, the water-related risks of pesticide active ingredients can be compared at the UC IPM Pest Management Guidelines Web site and can be customized by application and site conditions by clicking the blue "Water Quality Compare Treatments" button at the top of the list of treatments.

To avoid hazards to aquatic life whenever possible, select pesticides that will not potentially contaminate surface water. These include organophosphate insecticides (e.g., chlorpyrifos, diazinon), carbamate insecticides (e.g., carbaryl), and synthetic pyrethroids (e.g., cyfluthrin, permethrin, bifenthrin). The strong adsorption of pyrethroids suggests that after application, pyrethroids are predominantly associated with the surface soil and organic materials. They move off-site only when the soil or potting media particles have eroded away under the force of storm runoff or irrigation-induced runoff. Effective steps to mitigate runoff of pyrethroids from nurseries always involve reducing off-site movement of potting mix and associated organic materials. Be especially careful if your property is adjacent to water bodies such as creeks, rivers, storm drains, or agricultural drainage areas. In runoff-sensitive areas, select pesticides with low aquatic toxicity and low mobility.

In areas with shallow water tables or where soils are permeable or have low organic matter content, avoid the use of groundwater-risk pesticides. Groundwater-risk pesticides include certain preemergence herbicides such as those listed in table 6.1 (chapter 6). Also be especially careful not to apply these types of pesticides in rainy weather.

Choose pesticides that are the most selective for the target pest species, avoiding broad-spectrum pesticides whenever possible. This enhances natural population control mechanisms and reduces the need for pesticides. Also, whenever possible, consider using nonchemical pest management practices, such as cultural or biological control.

Herbicide Management

Most herbicides used in nurseries are bound to organic matter and are not likely to cause problems with runoff. However, three to watch are simazine (Princep), metolachlor (Pennant), and isoxaben (Gallery; also a component of Snapshot). Anecdotal incidents of crop injury from herbicides in nurseries that use retention ponds may have been caused by one or more of the reasons below. Use caution to avoid these practices.

Container Spacing

When containers are closely arranged or "jammed" pot-to-pot, roughly 79 percent of the applied herbicide falls into containers. If pots are spaced just 3 inches apart, only 35 percent of the herbicide falls in the containers while 65 percent falls between them. Excessive herbicide contamination of a retention pond may be a result of treatment of a large area with loosely spaced containers.

Treatment Area and Timing

Most of the herbicide that accumulates in ponds is released during the first irrigation event following application. If a large area of nursery is treated at the same time and the retention is relatively small, there is a good chance for a peak in accumulation of that herbicide. To alleviate this risk, it is essential to divide the nursery into multiple sections and treat them over different days.

Soil Covers

Studies show that soil covers such as gravels are effective at trapping loose potting mix (which contain herbicides), while bare soil surfaces or concrete slabs enhance runoff of water and pesticides. Changing soil covers from impervious surfaces to porous surfaces may help prevent excessive contamination of a retention pond by herbicides.

Plant Sensitivity

Different plants have different sensitivities to the same herbicide. If crop injury persists, it is advisable to use the recycled water on less sensitive, more hardy crops. Information about plant sensitivities may be obtained from the pesticide manufacturer or by on-site small trials. Contact your UCCE Farm Advisor for help in setting up small site trials.

Management of Floral Preservatives Containing STS

When using STS for treatment of ethylene-sensitive cut flowers, do not allow the product to reach groundwater, surface waterways, or sewage systems. Residual product should be neutralized before disposal following the manufacturer's instructions.

An alternative to STS treatment is 1-methylcyclopropene (1-MCP, EthylBloc). Methylcyclopropene is a growth regulator registered for use on cut flowers, potted flowers, and bedding, nursery, and foliage plants. It is approved for use only in enclosed spaces, such as greenhouses, storerooms, coolers, enclosed truck trailers, and shipping containers. There are no expected risks to the environment because 1-MCP is approved for use only in indoor spaces and is quickly dissipated when released to open air. Toxicity tests show that methylcyclopropene is not expected to be harmful to living organisms or the environment. The effectiveness of 1-MCP or STS may vary with particular species or types of inflorescence. For some crops, STS may be more effective than 1-MCP, but there are no disposal issues associated with 1-MCP.

Management of Greenhouse Shading Compounds

Select relatively nontoxic exterior greenhouse shading compounds for temperature control or use interior shade fabric or reflective covers. When applying and removing exterior shading compounds, ensure that minimal runoff of the compound is produced and that the runoff is kept on the property and does not enter storm water, sewer, or agricultural drainage systems.

Practice Good Irrigation Techniques

Under dry weather conditions, irrigation is the single most important force driving pesticide runoff. Irrigation efficiency, irrigation uniformity, methods of irrigation, and timing of irrigation events can all play a role in pesticide runoff.

By maintaining irrigation systems with uniform distribution and by proper irrigation scheduling and timing, surface water and groundwater pollution can be reduced. Group crops with similar water needs together in the same production area. Replace defective sprinklers immediately. Replace hand-watering with precision irrigation methods such as drip irrigation. Do not apply pesticides before scheduled irrigations unless the product must be activated by moisture and is so indicated in the label instructions. Control the quantity of irrigation water to limit pesticide movement in irrigation water runoff and percolation. (For more information on irrigation practices, see chapter 3.)

Consider Weather

For crops located outside, delay pesticide applications if heavy or sustained rainfall is anticipated. The risk for pesticide runoff and leaching is enhanced by rainfall soon after applications. In order to avoid drift, do not spray when winds are in excess of 10 miles per hour.

Apply Pesticides Safely

Always apply pesticides according to the label and follow environmental hazard instructions. Know that your pesticide handling and application practices can impact groundwater and surface water. Know the exact location of the area to be treated and the potential hazard of spray drift or inadvertent pesticide movement to the surrounding areas.

Accurately measure pesticides to ensure that you are following the label rate and to eliminate disposal problems associated with excess spray solutions. Calibrate pesticide spraying equipment and replace worn nozzles to ensure the best coverage, effective pesticide applications, and accurate application rates. Also check equipment for leaks and malfunctions. Replace cracked hoses and faulty gauges.

Conduct pesticide mixing and loading operations on an impermeable surface such as a concrete floor to avoid saturating the soil with pesticide. Perform operations involving pesticides in areas where the potential for runoff is low and in areas over 100 feet downslope of a well or other water supply. Some pesticide labels may recommend greater distances.

Maintain records of the amount and type of pesticides applied. Use these records to plan future pest control measures and limit pesticide accumulation.

Whenever you are injecting pesticides into irrigation water, do not allow backflow into wells or other water sources. Prevent backflow during mixing operations by using a mechanical antisiphoning device or an air gap. Check backflow devices at least once a year and record the date and the result of this check.

Use check valves on application equipment. When applying pesticides from a tractor or rig in a field, shut off the nozzles during turns. Regularly verify that pesticide solution tanks are free of leaks.

Store Pesticides Safely

Store pesticides in a storage structure that complies with local, state, and federal guidelines. Lock or restrict access and locate the structure as far away as possible from water conveyances (streams, creeks, and storm drains), or at least 100 feet from wells. Inspect containers regularly for leaks and corrosion. Include a concrete pad and curb to contain spills and leaks in the pesticide storage facility. This pad area should be protected from rainfall and irrigation to prevent pesticide residues from washing into surface water bodies. Be sure that the area is fireproof. As soon as pesticides arrive, check the product labels for special storage instructions. Keep an up-to-date inventory of the pesticides in the storage area. Keep a spill kit

available at the storage facility. A spill kit should include detergent, hand cleaner, and water; absorbent materials, such as absorbent clay, sawdust, or paper to soak up spills; a shovel, broom, dustpan, and chemical resistant bags to collect contaminated materials; and a fire extinguisher.

Use Safe Disposal Methods

Triple rinse or pressure rinse empty pesticide containers and add the rinse to the spray tank. Do not contaminate nearby bodies of water when disposing of equipment wash water. Do not flush rinse water in potable water systems, storm drains, field drains, or other drains. Apply excess spray mix and rinsewater from pesticide application equipment to labeled crops; do not spray it on bare ground. This reduces pesticide contamination in nontarget areas during the cleanup process following application. Take empty, rinsed plastic pesticide containers to pesticide container recycling facilities or to sanitary landfills, or have them disposed of by licensed disposers of hazardous waste.

Consult the pesticide label for disposal instructions if you have leftover pesticide materials. Dispose of pesticides and pesticide containers according to label instructions and in an environmentally safe manner. Containers may require inspection by local agricultural commissioner offices before they can be offered for recycling or disposed of in a landfill.

Avoid Pesticide Spills and Leakage

When transporting pesticides, do not overfill trailers or tanks. Cover loads properly and display appropriate placards on vehicles. When transferring pesticides into on-farm storage or into pesticide application equipment, take care that you do not allow materials to spill. Always attach the pesticide label to secondary containers. Pesticides should be transported in the back of a truck, and all containers should be secured to prevent breaking or spilling. Never leave pesticides unattended in a vehicle unless they are in a locked container. If any pesticide is spilled in or from the vehicle, clean it up right away using the proper cleanup procedures. Refer to specific product labeling and the material safety data sheets (MSDS) for cleanup procedures.

Clean up any spilled potting media that contains pesticide residues. If pesticides are mixed into potting media before potting, use concrete curbs or sandbags to isolate these areas so the potting mix does not get washed away in the runoff.

Leaks or spills can occur during transporting, storing, or applying pesticides. Immediately clean up pesticide spills according to a predetermined protocol. All pesticide leaks or spills should be treated as emergencies. Concentrated pesticide spills are much more dangerous than spills of pesticides diluted with water, but both types should be treated seriously and immediately. Always refer to the pesticide product MSDS for information on cleaning up and decontaminating small spill sites. For leaks or spills that occur in the nursery, follow these general emergency procedures.

+ Minor spills or leaks of a few gallons or less can usually be cleaned up easily. Be sure to wear the personal protective equipment required for mixing and loading, including respiratory equipment if odor is persistent. Prevent further spillage by shutting off equipment, righting tipped containers, or catching the leak in a pan or other container.

+ Cordon off the area and flag it to keep people away from the spilled chemicals. Do not leave the spill area unless someone is there to confine the spill and warn of the danger. If the pesticide was spilled on anyone, immediately follow appropriate decontamination procedures. Do not let anyone enter the area until the spill is completely cleaned up.

+ Prevent the spill from spreading by building a dike of soil, sand, or other absorbent material, such as soil, kitty litter, sawdust, or absorbent clay, around the spill. Use absorbent material to soak up the spill. Shovel all contaminated material into a

leakproof container or chemical-resistant bag for disposal. Do not hose down the area because this spreads the chemical. Always work carefully, and do not hurry.

+ The disposal container must bear a label indicating its contents and the signal word of the pesticide. Dispose of material as you would excess pesticides at a hazardous waste disposal facility.

Keep Runoff and Sediment On-Site

Basins

Commonly used practices for managing pesticide runoff include capturing basins and recycling (tailwater recovery) systems. These systems keep soluble pesticides from running off the property. In addition, sediment basins are used to slow the movement of water entering the channel. They allow for the further settling of soil particles and serve as a temporary holding basin under low flow conditions. Pesticides such as pyrethroids that are attached to soil and potting mix particles usually settle out in a sediment basin.

Barriers, Traps, and Filters

When construction of a retention basin is not feasible, sandbags and berms can be used to curtail runoff and trap sediments. Vegetative buffers or filters remove pesticides by trapping sediment and providing a beneficial environment for decomposition. They are most effective when flow rate is slow, allowing for evapotranspiration to reduce overall flow. They may be used along drainage channels to trap sediment particles and stabilize the banks. Sediment traps are effective in slowing flow and allowing sediment to drop out. When using these sedimentation-based practices, the trapped sediment must be cleaned out before the rainy season, as large storms can sweep the sediment, along with the accumulated pesticides, into creeks and streams. Fiber filters or activated charcoal filters may be used along with the other practices for further removal of pesticides through physical filtration and adsorption.

Consider Using Polyacrylamide

Polyacrylamide (PAM) is a charged (anionic) linear chain polymer with a high molecular weight. PAM is available commercially in a granular, liquid, or tablet formulation. The University of California and other institutions have conducted many studies that have shown the effectiveness of PAM in settling suspended sediments and stabilizing surface soil in a field or along the banks of a drainage ditch. PAM causes suspended particles to flocculate, and the aggregated particles settle to the bottom under gravity. PAM is most effective when the flow is slow and the slope is less than 5 percent. PAM may be easily applied by dripping a concentrated PAM solution into the runoff ditch or by suspending a bag containing several PAM tablets. PAM granules can be applied onto soil surface by hand or with a fertilizer application device. If you decide to use PAM, keep in mind that the State Water Resources Control Board or other agencies may be regulating the use of PAM in the future. Use of the product must be such that it remains on-site. For more guidelines on using PAM, see chapter 7.

Consider Compacting Permeable Areas

Even though capturing and recycling water may prevent pesticide runoff, pesticides may still infiltrate outdoor ground areas with permeable surfaces. At sites with shallow groundwater and a sandy soil texture, the permeable surfaces can be compacted with grading equipment to prevent infiltration to the groundwater.

Provide Training for Personnel Handling Nursery Chemicals

Provide training to ensure that appropriate personnel understand how and when to use all pesticides applied in the nursery in a safe manner, including safe handling, transport, storage, and disposal practices. Ensure that all personnel know what to do in case of a pesticide spill and how to prevent environmental hazards such as drift and runoff.

Employees handling pesticides and field workers exposed to pesticides have different training requirements, as required in Title III of the California Code of Regulations Section 6724 and other regulations. Detailed requirements for applicators can be found in the DPR publication *Pesticide Safety Training for Employees Handling Pesticides*; detailed requirements for agricultural field workers can be found at the UC Agriculture and Natural Resources Environmental Health and Safety Web site (see the Resources below).

Training must be provided in a manner the employee understands, and training records should be kept at a central location at the workplace. Training should be refreshed every 5 years for field workers, and records should be kept for 5 years. Training should be refreshed every 2 years for employees who handle pesticides, and it should be continually updated to cover any new pesticides that are handled; records should be kept for 2 years.

Resources

California Department of Pesticide Regulation (DPR) Web site, http://www.cdpr.ca.gov/.

Extension Toxicology Network (EXTOXNET) Web site, http://extoxnet.orst.edu/index.html.

Natural Resources Conservation Service (NRCS) Pesticide Screening Tool (WIN-PST) Web site, http://www.wcc.nrcs.usda.gov/pestmgt/winpst.html.

Pesticide Action Network (PAN) Web site, http://www.pesticideinfo.org/Search_Chemicals.jsp.

Pesticide Safety Training for Employees Handling Pesticides, DPR Web site, http://www.cdpr.ca.gov/docs/enfcmpli/cmpliast/hndngpsts.pdf.

UC Agriculture and Natural Resources Environmental Health and Safety Web site, http://danrrec.ucdavis.edu/ehs/safety_notes/index.html.

UC IPM pest management guidelines for floriculture and nurseries, UC IPM Web site, http://www.ipm.ucdavis.edu/PMG/selectnewpest.floriculture.html.

UC PesticideWise Web site, http://www.pw.ucr.edu/.

Erosion Control and Runoff Management

Jianhang Lu, Assistant Project Scientist, Department of Environmental Sciences,
University of California, Riverside

Laosheng Wu, University of California Cooperative Extension Water Management Specialist,
Department of Environmental Sciences, University of California, Riverside

Ben Faber, University of California Cooperative Extension Farm Advisor, Ventura County

What is Erosion and Runoff?

Erosion is the process by which the surface of the soil is removed by water or wind. This chapter focuses mainly on water-induced erosion, with only a brief discussion on wind erosion.

Water-induced erosion begins when rain or irrigation water loosens soil or potting mix particles. When there is too much water to soak into the soil, the water fills surface depressions and begins to flow, creating runoff. With enough speed, this surface runoff carries away the loosened soil, which eventually becomes sediment. Sediment is a pollutant as well as a common pollution source because of its role as a carrier of nutrients, pesticides, and other pollutants.

Erosion in nursery operations can produce excess sediment that clogs pipes and ditches and causes flooding. Once discharged into the natural environment, sediment can interfere with the feeding and reproduction of fish and aquatic insects, disrupting the food chain. Phytoplankton (microscopic algae that form the base of the food chain) are also affected when water clarity is reduced. The presence of sediment (or suspended particles) above naturally occurring levels has serious implications to the health of the aquatic environment. To sustain environmentally friendly nursery production, it is important to implement appropriate management practices that can control soil erosion and reduce sediment runoff.

Why Control Runoff and Erosion?

+ Runoff can wash sediment, fertilizers, and pesticides into waterways.

+ Nitrogen and phosphorus from fertilizers carried by runoff into surface water have been associated with many environmental problems, including excessive algae growth, depletion of the water's oxygen supply, and suffocation of aquatic organisms.

+ Erosion removes valuable potting mix and topsoil and clogs waterways and reservoirs with sediments.

- Runoff can contribute to flooding problems inside and outside (downstream of) a nursery.

- Groundwater supplies much of California's water, and it must be recharged by infiltration through soil rather than runoff. Water that leaves a nursery as runoff can move quickly to ditches and rivers, reducing the groundwater recharge potential.

How is Runoff Water Quality Evaluated?

In order to comply with water regulations and determine options for reuse or treatment, it is necessary to monitor the water quality of irrigation and storm runoff. Monitoring efforts are usually conducted in order to estimate average concentration over time during a runoff event and to determine the total mass of sediment, nutrients, and pesticides leaving a field in storm runoff or irrigation tailwater. The first objective can usually be satisfied by sampling at the proper time, while the second objective requires a runoff volume measurement at the same time. Although sampling and analysis procedures should be designed according to a specific monitoring purpose, certain guidelines are generally applicable. For more information on sampling and other water quality issues, see Harter and Rollins 2008.

Sampling Location

Sampling locations should be specific to the field plot and the monitoring objectives. These locations may include but are not limited to outflow from individual houses, drain culverts, entry points of drainage into ditches, drainage ditches, larger drainage canals, and inlets and outlets of retention ponds or catchment basins. Sampling site locations should be chosen so that they are consistent with State Water Resource Control Board quality assurance objectives.

Sampling Methods

Grab sampling is appropriate for sampling concentrations at a single point at a specific time. To make grab samples more representative, try to

sample at the location where the entire runoff merges together, such as the inlet of a retention pond. Grab samples taken this way can be used to estimate the average concentrations of contaminants in the entire runoff. A more accurate sampling approach is time- or flow-volume-integrated sampling. This type of sampling, which is useful for evaluating average concentrations during extended runoff events, consists of taking composite samples periodically to yield an average concentration over the duration of sampling. Autosamplers are frequently used for time- and flow-volume-integrated sampling.

Flow Measurement

To determine the average runoff concentration or total mass load leaving a nursery product field, concurrent flow measurements during the sampling period are also required. Several methods are available to measure flow in watercourses, depending on the size of the water body and rate of flow. These include various configurations of flumes, weirs, and water flow meters. Flow measurements should be taken at the time of sampling.

Chain of Custody

A chain of custody form should be completed for each batch of samples. The following information should be recorded on the chain of custody: sample location (name of nursery, field, plot, or basin), sample number, date and time of sampling, and sampling personnel.

Sample container and preservation

This varies greatly with the chemicals needed to be analyzed. Follow commercial lab instructions for the requirements of sampling containers and preservation methods, as these greatly affect the results.

Sample analysis

Conduct analyses on runoff water samples to determine what is in them and at what levels. Parameters to be tested for include pH, electrical conductivity (EC), nitrate (NO_3^-), and phosphorus ($H_2PO_4^-$), which can be analyzed on-site with instruments and kits designed for use by growers. Alternatively, water samples can be sent to commercial labs. In addition, it is recommended to use a good commercial lab to test for other contaminants according to the products used, such as specific pesticides that you suspect may be present in runoff. The lab should use EPA standards and be certified for good laboratory practices (GLPs).

Chemicals used

Inventory chemicals used in your operation, especially those likely to be present in runoff, such as pesticides and fertilizers. Knowing what chemicals might be in the runoff water helps to determine the sampling procedure and to identify potential contaminants.

Water quality standard

Compare water analyses against local and state water quality standards and regulations.

Record keeping

Maintain runoff water quality records for at least 5 years. If the records are kept electronically, print a copy of the records and periodically back up the record files on external storage media (such as external hard drive, data CDs, or DVDs).

How Is Runoff and Erosion Reduced?

The best strategy for preventing sediment loss, water pollution, and damage to floriculture and nursery crops is to develop and implement a system of management practices. The goal for container plant production operators, particularly for new areas of production, is to allow no irrigation water to leave their property. To the extent possible, all irrigation runoff should be recirculated with no discharge to public waters. Considering the typical California soil, climate, and crop conditions, management practices include site selection, proper layout and construction, irrigation management, ground covers (plant or mulching), soil amendments, wetting agents, water retention ponds, grassed waterways, and use of polyacrylamide (PAM). Specific strategies may vary from site to site.

Site Selection

Besides economic and geographic reasons, appropriate consideration of hydrologic and topographic settings during initial nursery site selection has a long-term effect on reducing erosion. In California, water availability is the most important consideration for growing nursery crops in containers. Most container nurseries irrigate daily or every other day during the growing season. Having access to enough water for irrigating crops and expanding production in the future is essential. When selecting a site for starting or expanding nursery production, consider the following points to reduce the potential of runoff and erosion.

- High-quality irrigation water should be available. Water free of sediment and mineral deposits, such as iron and calcium bicarbonate, is necessary to avoid coating growing beds, irrigation equipment, pots, and plants or plugging drip, spray stake, or mist nozzles. Failure of irrigation equipment, even in a short period, can lead to overirrigation, causing severe erosion.

- The land should be level or slightly sloped (less than 3 percent slope). The plant-growing areas should have a very mild slope or be engineered (e.g, through contour plowing) to slow water velocity, increase filtration, and contain runoff. A variety of structures, storage facilities, and landscape features can direct and manage water movement around nurseries.

- Runoff from plant-growing areas should flow naturally to a low point where retention ponds can be built to capture and recycle irrigation water.

- The soils should be well drained with no seasonal high water table.

Layout and Construction

Field nurseries should be managed to avoid erosion (formation of rills, channels, or gullies). When arranging a site for a field nursery, consider the following management practices.

- Crop production areas should be across slopes and on contours. Take care to ensure that rows or gravel beds follow the proper contour to reduce soil loss during crop production. Avoid low spots within production rows where water will accumulate.

- Consider natural features of the land as well as the length, width, and turning radius required for sprayers, tractors, and wagons. Avoid cultivation or road construction on slopes greater than 25 percent.

- Plan for grassed waterways and field edge buffer strips to reduce erosion and sedimentation, especially on land too steep to use as a production area.

- Plan for sediment catch basins when erosive conditions are severe or irrigation runoff is constant.

- Plan for vegetative aisles between rows or production areas if topography creates erosive conditions.

- Plan for field filter strips to reduce the movement of sediment from the field.

- Plan for installation of a roof runoff system for large buildings so the runoff can be directed to an area that allows water to slowly percolate into the ground. Do not allow clean runoff from roofs to pass through nursery production areas.

- Plan for the installation of a drainage system for major roads. Do not allow road runoff to run through nursery production areas.

- Avoid large paved areas because they can contribute to erosion by directing a large amount of water in a short time to nearby areas that may be unable to absorb it quickly.

Irrigation Management

Since nursery production in Southern California depends heavily on irrigation, good irrigation management is essential there in reducing runoff and controlling erosion. Growers have the greatest control over their own irrigation practices, which may include metering the amount of irrigation water applied; accurately measuring the discharge from emitters, sprinklers, or watering nozzles; and controlling the time of application to meet plant water requirements. A good match of irrigation water application and plant evapotranspiration demand can reduce unnecessary runoff. Guidelines for good irrigation management are provided below, and detailed implementation methods can be found in chapter 3.

- Conduct an irrigation audit or use the services of a mobile irrigation laboratory and adjust the system accordingly. Use the catch-can method to determine the efficiency of a sprinkler or drip irrigation system.

- Avoid overirrigating. Irrigate according to the soil or substrate's water-holding capacity or adjust the substrate for high water-holding capacity.

- Avoid irrigating large open areas susceptible to erosion.

- Consolidate container plants and shut off irrigation in unused portions of production areas.

- Group container plants by container size, canopy architecture, and water requirements; place the containers close together.

- Match irrigation application rates with the infiltration or percolation rates of the soil or substrate.

- Use mulch to increase infiltration and prevent splashing.

- Use pulse or cyclic irrigation to apply irrigation water over short intervals, reducing the amount of water lost from containers and surrounding areas.

- Minimize the application of irrigation to saturated or nearly saturated soils or substrates; avoid irrigating just before or just after a significant rain.

- Convert overhead irrigation systems to drip, subirrigation, or hydroponic systems to reduce the impact of water droplets.

- Inject a flocculating agent such as PAM to increase infiltration rate and to reduce sediment.

Ground Covers (Plant Cover, Mulching, and Fiber Materials)

Ground covers provide one of the best erosion controls. They cover the soil surface to prevent soil from being exposed to rain or irrigation drop impact. Ground covers include inorganic materials (plastics, gravel, and concrete), cover crops, and mulching. All of these can have many benefits in improving soil and environmental qualities. When selecting a ground cover material, consider site factors such as slope steepness, soil type, weed control method, and anticipated foot traffic. When comparing erosion control options keep in mind the cost of the material, ease of installation, and how long the material will last.

As landscaping, plant cover not only adds beauty and value to your property but also helps control erosion by reducing the amount and speed of runoff. Grass strips can effectively slow runoff and trap sediment, reducing soil losses by 30 to 50 percent compared with bare soil. Organic mulching conserves moisture, adds organic matter to soils, improves soil structure, reduces soil erosion, provides weed control, improves root growth, and also improves the water-holding capacity of the soil. Beneficial arthropods and earthworms appear to be stimulated by ground cover.

Erosion control blankets, rolls, or mats made from natural or synthetic polymer fibers are another option for ground and slope stabilization. These products are composed of processed natural or polymer fibers that are structurally or chemically bound together to form a continuous matrix, providing erosion control and facilitating vegetation establishment. The most effective materials for erosion control appeared to be the coir and jute netting mats (or blankets and rolls). They are made of completely natural, biodegradable materials and are recommended for areas where little or no foot traffic is expected. They provide very effective erosion control on their own and as a protective mulch cover, as well as an environment good for seed germination and plant survival.

In nursery production, ground covers can be used in many ways to reduce erosion and runoff, and to control the direction of drainage.

- Concrete- or plastic-lined waterways or drainage channels reduce erosion adjacent to growing areas but can increase the velocity of runoff water. Where lined sections are not on steep slopes, use riprap or vegetation in channels to slow water movement, allowing sediment and dissolved substances to settle or be filtered out of returning water.

- Drainage channels can be established with permanent vegetation such as fescue grass or even aquatic plants. Permanent vegetation in drainage channels slows water velocity, reduces erosion, and reduces sediment and nutrients in runoff water.

- Permanent vegetation located at outlets of drainage channels also traps organic material, solids, soil, nutrients, and other dissolved pollutants before the water returns to irrigation supplies.

- Turfgrass is an important type of ground cover, but many other low-growing herbaceous and woody plants work well and, once established, require less fertilizer, pesticide, and other maintenance.

- Steep slopes can be easily eroded. Plant a vigorous ground cover to reduce erosion and increase water penetration into the soil on the slope. Turf is often impractical here because mowing is difficult and dangerous on steep terrain.

- Build terraces or retaining walls. These catch runoff, giving water time to soak into the ground, and also make attractive planting beds.

- In container nurseries, cover the surface of the potting media with mulch.

Soil Amendments

The quality of soil in a field nursery is prone to deteriorate due to soil losses as sod and balled and burlapped trees are harvested and sold, and also through runoff or wind erosion. Environmental conditions such as rainstorms and winds are responsible for major losses; however, soil compaction can also reduce the water penetration and moisture-holding characteristics of the soil.

Preventing further loss of soil and rebuilding soil in fields is essential for sustainable plant cultivation. Field nursery operators should implement growing practices that maintain and improve soil quality characteristics during uncropped fallow periods, as well as during field preparation for planting and even during the production cycle. Soil amendments are often added to soil or potting mix to improve soil quality and to reduce further soil loss.

A soil amendment is any material added to a soil to improve its physical or chemical properties, such as water retention, permeability, water infiltration, drainage, aeration, soil structure, salinity, or pH. Most soil amendments are used to improve the structure of the soil or substrate. These amendments increase the spacing among soil particles so that the soil can absorb and hold more moisture, which in turn reduces runoff and the damaging effects of excessive runoff on nursery production areas. Soil amendments can also improve other physical, chemical, and biological characteristics so that the soils become more effective in production while sustaining water quality.

Soil amendments can be classified as organic or inorganic. Organic amendments come from something that is or was alive; inorganic amendments, on the other hand, are mined or man-made. Organic amendments include sphagnum peat, wood chips, grass clippings, straw, compost, manure, biosolids, sawdust, and wood ash. Inorganic amendments include vermiculite, gypsum, perlite, tire chunks, pea gravel, and sand.

In most nursery production, organic amendments are recommended. Organic amendments increase soil organic matter content and offer many other benefits. Organic matter improves soil aeration, water infiltration, and water- and nutrient-holding capacity. Many organic amendments contain plant nutrients and act as organic fertilizers. In addition, organic matter is an important energy source for bacteria, fungi, and earthworms that live in the soil. Besides improving soil structure, water retention, drainage, aeration, and the quality of nursery stock grown, organic matter amendments also lessen the bulk density and make digging easier, especially in mineral soils. It has also been shown that some nursery species develop a more fibrous root system as the amount of organic matter is increased.

Animal wastes such as cattle manure or poultry litter can be applied to fields, but only in light applications (¼ to ½ inch) due to salinity concerns over surface areas. It is more efficient to incorporate them into the soil after application: if animal wastes are incorporated, 75 to 100 percent of the nitrogen in the waste may be plant-available in the first year. The rate of application should be based on nutrient analysis of animal manure. Particular attention should be given to the metal content of biosolids. Zinc and copper levels may be high enough to raise these elements to toxic levels if repeated applications are made year after year.

Wetting Agents

Organic materials such as peat moss and wood residues have a waxy outer coating that repels water. As these components dry they become increasingly difficult to wet again, and even though water is applied to dry media it may not penetrate the surface. Under these conditions water runs to the edge of the container, down the sides, and out of the bottom, without wetting the core of the root mass. If water cannot readily penetrate and wet the soil, the availability of moisture to plants is reduced, decreasing the germination rate of seeds, the emergence of seedlings, and the survival and productivity of crop plants. Lack of sufficient water in the soil also reduces the availability of essential nutrients to plants, further limiting growth and productivity. In addition, water that cannot penetrate the soil runs off the surface and increases soil erosion. Water repellency often occurs in localized areas. As a result, the soil wets nonuniformly, and dry spots occur.

Wetting agents help reduce surface tension and provide uniform water distribution throughout the medium. Before using a wetting agent, consider the following.

- Make sure water repellence is the problem. Wetting agents improve infiltration rates only in soils or potting mixes that have water-repellent properties, regardless of their texture, tilth, and aggregation. Several methods can be used to determine the extent to which a soil or mix is water repellent. The most precise methods require laboratory facilities, but several simple tests can be conducted in the field. The most useful one for preliminary tests is simply to place a drop of water on the soil surface and observe how long it takes to penetrate the soil. On a wettable soil, the water drop will flatten and move into the soil within a few seconds. On more water-repellent soils, the drop of water will stand more upright and will move more slowly into the soil.

- The extent of improvement in infiltration rate is affected by the type of wetting agent, its concentration, the history of wetting agent use on the soil, and the water content of the soil at the time water is applied. Try wetting agents with different active ingredients to find the most effective one for your soil or potting mix.

- Several commercial wetting agents are available, but a drop or two of dishwashing detergent in the irrigation water often does the trick.

- Do not overuse wetting agents, as they will end up in runoff. Several studies have shown that the infiltration rate of a hydrophobic soil, once it has been wetted, remains higher than before it was wetted, even if it is allowed to dry out again.

Water Retention Basins

Water retention basins (catchment basins or water recycling ponds) are permanent, constructed basins that detain irrigation and storm runoff, allowing particles and associated pollutants to settle out before discharging. Many nurseries recycle the captured water for irrigation purposes, and the practice is often mentioned as the primary method of eliminating potential problems that arise from container nursery runoff. In outdoor container nursery production, water collection ponds are increasingly used to capture and recycle runoff water and fertilizers and to reduce runoff water to downstream water bodies. During overhead irrigation, pesticides and nutrients are washed away from plants and potting mixes and move off-site with runoff water. By constructing water retention ponds, nutrients in the irrigation tailwater can be used again by plants, and pesticides can be retained in the ponds, where dissipation processes may take place. Guidelines for constructing and maintaining water retention basins are provided below; for further details on recycling water runoff, see chapter 8. When constructing and maintaining water retention basins or ponds, consider the following.

- Water retention basins should be designed by a licensed engineer. The engineer must consider many design specifications, such as length to width ratio, inlet and outlet location, depth to surface area, and the need for baffles. Design plans should facilitate regular maintenance such as dredging the pond.

- Construct the basins or ponds in the lowest spot so runoff can be directed to the ponds by gravity.

- Check for any legal stipulations regarding the holding capacity of the retention basin or pond. If there are no regulatory restrictions, design it to hold at least the volume of regular irrigation runoff. The capacity depends on the size of the area that drains into the structure, the irrigation method used, and the amount of water that needs to be recycled.

- In areas with sandy soils or a high groundwater table, line retention ponds with plastic to avoid groundwater contamination. In some areas of California, regulations require that all retention basins be lined. This type of regulation may be increasing in the future due to potential seepage from unlined basins into groundwater.

- After pond or basin construction, reestablish permanent native vegetation around the surrounding slopes.

- Maintain a 15- to 25-foot "chemical free" zone around the pond edge.

- Do not place production wastes such as leaves and grass clippings near retention ponds or dump them into the ponds.

- Inspect ponds annually for excess sediment accumulation. Dredge ponds when the sediment accumulation is more than 6 to 12 inches.

- Conduct routine inspections for trash or other debris that may be blocking the inlet or outlet pipes or the emergency spillway. Monthly and after rain events, remove all trash and debris from the basin. Inspect inlet and outlet pipes annually for structural integrity.

If captured water is continuously reused, persistent chemicals may build up in the pond, especially in the sediments. Our recent experiments investigated the persistence of four pesticides (diazinon, chlorpyrifos, chlorothalonil, and pendimethalin) under typical nursery recycling pond environments (Lu et al. 2006). These pesticides are among those widely used for outdoor container nursery production in California. Results showed that chlorothalonil and pendimethalin degraded very fast, with a half-life of less than 2.8 days in the sediments. The other two pesticides dissipated at a lower rate, but half of their amounts were degraded in 8 to 41 days, depending on the pond conditions. If not used excessively, it is unlikely that these pesticides will accumulate in a pond. To minimize the buildup possibility of other pesticides or toxic chemicals, consider the following suggestions.

- Use easily degradable (short half-life) pesticides.

- Alternate the use of pesticides with same or similar functions.

- Reduce the input of pesticides to the pond by following the practices and suggestions in chapter 6.

- Dredge the pond periodically.

- When buildup is suspected, have water and sediment samples from the pond tested for chemicals of concern.

Conservation Buffers

Conservation or vegetative buffers are areas or strips of land maintained in permanent vegetation to help control pollution. These buffers help manage soils, water, nutrients, and pesticides by preventing erosion and trapping pollutants. The vegetation captures nutrients by plant uptake and by holding soil particles that adsorb nutrients and pesticides in place as water flows through the buffer.

A buffer has three distinct layers: surface vegetation, root zone, and subsoil horizon. When water carrying sediments and other pollutants enters the buffer, surface flow is slowed and sediments drop out. When the inflow rate exceeds the buffer's infiltration rate, overland flow occurs, but if the buffer is well designed, it will still continue to remove sediments. In the root zone, some water infiltrates deeper into the subsoil, while the remainder becomes lateral subsurface flow. Pesticides in the root zone are more subject to degradation because of the high soil organic matter and because nutrients such as nitrate are more prone to denitrification. The effectiveness of buffers depends on their size, soil type, rainfall and irrigation intensity, topography, and plant height.

There are two principal forms of vegetative buffers: filter or buffer strips and grassed waterways. Further examples of conservation buffers can be found in "Conservation Buffers to Reduce Pesticide Losses" on the Natural Resources Conservation Service (NRCS) Web site (see the Resources at the end of this chapter).

Buffer Strips

Buffer strips can be within the nursery or field or on the edge of a field. They are areas of grass or other permanent vegetation that can reduce sediment, nutrients, pesticides, and other contaminants when runoff enters as sheet flow. Strips work best when concentrated flow is minimized so that maximum contact is made between sediments, pollutants, and the vegetation. Riparian buffer strips can be enhanced by including trees and shrubs along with perennial grasses. Deep roots may intercept nitrate entering streams or other bodies of water.

Grassed Waterways

Grassed waterways are channel-shaped or graded areas in which vegetation serves as a stable conveyance for runoff. They are designed to reduce the velocity of runoff water and intercept pollutants and soil sediments. The vegetation in the waterway serves as a filter and can effectively remove some of the sediment and nutrients contained in runoff. Grassed waterways have been shown to remove up to 50 percent or more of nutrients and pesticides and up to 75 percent or more of sediments carried in runoff (see the NRCS Web site "Buffer Strips"). In addition, grassed waterways often improve biodiversity on nursery farms and sometimes may act as a refuge for beneficial organisms. They not only help growers meet federal, state, or local pollution control requirements, they are also a visual demonstration of a commitment to land stewardship.

Grassed waterways should be planned, designed, and constructed to comply with all federal, state, and local laws and regulations. They should be designed so water enters and leaves in a sheet flow or so drainage channels contain adequate vegetation to decrease development of erosion channels. General principles for their planning and designing include the following.

+ They should be located between growing areas or between growing areas and catch basins.

+ They can be natural or constructed channels, but they must be shaped or graded to required dimensions and established with suitable vegetation.

+ The minimum capacity should be that required to convey the peak runoff expected from a storm of 10-year frequency, 24-hour duration.

+ The permissible water velocity for waterways lined with vegetation of good cover and with proper maintenance must not exceed 5 feet per second. For channels with poor cover and little maintenance, the velocity must not exceed 3 feet per second.

+ The bottom width of trapezoidal waterways should not exceed 100 feet unless multiple or divided waterways or other means are provided to control meandering of low flows.

+ The minimum depth of a waterway that receives water from terraces, diversions, or other tributary channels should be that required to keep the design water surface elevation at or below the design water surface elevation in the tributary channel, measured at their junction when both are flowing at design depth.

- The side slopes should not be steeper than a horizontal to vertical ratio of 2 to 1. They must be designed to accommodate the equipment anticipated for maintenance, tillage, or harvesting that will cross the waterway.

- They should have a stable outlet with adequate capacity to prevent ponding or flooding damages. The outlet can be another vegetated channel, an earthen ditch, grade stabilization structure, filter strip, or other suitable outlet.

- After construction, vegetation should be established as soon as conditions permit. Use mulch anchoring, a nurse crop, rock, straw or hay bale dikes, filter fences, or runoff diversion to protect the vegetation until it is established.

- Like filter strips, grassed waterways should not be used as travel lanes.

Constructed Wetlands

Constructed wetlands are artificial marshes or swamps created for treatment of wastewater before it is discharged into the natural environment. In nursery production, they can be built to further remove the pollutants in the effluent from the retention basin. In constructed wetlands, suspended solids are removed by physical filtration and settling within the gravel and root hair matrix. Organic matter may also be filtered by these physical processes, but it is ultimately removed through biodegradation.

Constructed wetlands usually have four parts: liner, distribution media, plants, and underdrain system. The liner keeps the runoff in and groundwater out of the system. Polyvinyl chloride (PVC) liner is recommended over clay liners because clay can crack if too thin, allowing untreated nursery runoff to move into the soil and contaminate groundwater. The distribution system spreads the nursery runoff evenly over the wetland. The underdrain system moves the treated effluent out of the wetland and keeps the water level high enough to sustain plant growth. Constructed wetland cells are usually planted with aquatic or riparian plants such as cattails, bulrushes, reeds, and sedges. The roots and stems of these plants form a dense mat where chemical, biological, and physical processes occur to treat the nursery runoff.

Constructed wetlands should be designed and built by licensed engineers and must be properly maintained and operated. For more information, see the NRCS *Conservation Practice Standard: Constructed Wetlands.*

Polyacrylamide (PAM)

Polyacrylamide (PAM) is a synthetic high-molecular-weight polymer that has been widely used in soil applications to reduce erosion, increase infiltration, and enhance excess nutrient removal (plant uptake). In nursery production, PAM can increase water infiltration rate, reduce sediments in runoff, and reduce wind erosion. Our preliminary work in a commercial production nursery in Irvine showed that PAM was very effective in reducing the transport of sediment, and consequently the attached phosphorus and pesticide, to surface water bodies. Note that the State Water Resources Control Board or other agencies may be regulating the use of PAM in the future. The product must remain on-site if used. Following are some essential considerations when using PAM.

Types of PAM

PAM used for erosion control must have a linear molecular structure and be water soluble; be negatively charged, with a charge density of 10 to 55 percent; have a molecular weight of 6 to 24 Mg/mole; and have a residual monomer (acrylamide) content of less than 0.05 percent. Two types of PAM are available: linear and crossed-linked. Cross-linked PAM, usually sold as granular crystals, is a modern garden product that absorbs water and releases it slowly to plant roots. Cross-linked PAM does not dissolve in water. Erosion control requires linear PAM, which is sold either as white granular powder or as a liquid solution. Linear PAM dissolves in water slowly, and a 1.0 percent PAM solution has the consistency of cold honey.

Application Rate

In nursery operations, PAM can be added to irrigation water, soils, or potting mix to reduce erosion and runoff. When used in an irrigation system, the concentration of PAM in the irrigation water should not exceed 10 mg/L of pure-form PAM (active ingredient). The total PAM applied per application event should not exceed 4 pounds (active ingredient) per acre of soil surface. If PAM is used to reduce wind erosion, spray a PAM solution of 20 to 50 mg/L.

Timing of PAM Application

PAM should be applied after major soil surface disturbance practices (plowing, planting, side-dressing, etc.), and before a storm. If PAM is applied with irrigation water through a sprinkler system, stop applying PAM after the first 20 millimeters of irrigation.

Application Method

PAM must be mixed and applied in accordance with all Occupational Safety and Health Administration (OSHA) Material Safety Data Sheet requirements and the manufacturer's recommendations for the specified use. An operation and maintenance plan should be prepared for and used by the persons responsible for PAM application. Granular PAM should be predissolved in an appropriate tank to obtain field stock solution (1 to 2.5% strength), then diluted to field application solution (0.1% strength) and finally injected into irrigation water (the final concentration of PAM in irrigation water should not exceed 0.001%, or 10 mg/L). Never add water to PAM; add PAM slowly to water. If water is added to PAM, the PAM tends to clot and form globs that can clog dispensers. The manufacturer or supplier should provide written application methods for PAM and PAM mixtures. The application method should ensure uniform coverage to the target area and avoid drift to nontarget areas, including surface water. The manufacturer or supplier should also provide written instructions to ensure proper safety, storage, and mixing of the product.

Related Practices

PAM works best when used in combination with other conservation and best management practices. Application of PAM typically increases infiltration of irrigation water. To compensate for this increase, adjustments in flow rates, irrigation time, and tillage practices should be considered.

Related Maintenance

PAM is a flocculating agent that may cause sediment deposition in downstream watercourses or other locations when it comes in contact with sediment-laden waters. Downstream deposition from the use of PAM may require periodic cleaning of channels to maintain normal functions.

Safety and Health

Use proper personal protective equipment such as gloves, dust masks, and other health and safety precautions in accordance with the label, industry, and other federal or state rules and guidelines. PAM solutions can cause surfaces, tools, and other items it contacts to become very slippery when wet. Caution signs should be posted in PAM application areas.

Toxicity of PAM

Anionic PAM when used at prescribed rates is nontoxic to humans, fish, animals, and plants. In soil, PAM degrades at a rate of at least 10 percent per year as a result of physical, chemical, and biological processes. Overexposure to the polymer PAM can lead to skin irritation and inflammation of mucous membranes. Users should read and follow label precautions, avoid exposure to eyes and other mucous membranes, and be careful not to breathe PAM dust. In addition, acrylamide, the monomer used in production of PAM, is a neurotoxin to human and aquatic organisms. When buying PAM, make sure the product contains less than 0.05 percent of the acrylamide monomer.

Wind Erosion Control

Dry, windy conditions are common in many areas of Southern California during autumn and early winter. Strong Santa Ana winds can cause significant loss of surface soils in nurseries. Wind erosion, the wearing away of topsoil by winds, physically removes the lighter, less-dense soil constituents such as organic matter, clays, and silts, which are the most fertile part of the soil; thus, it lowers soil productivity. Losing topsoil reduces the productivity of the nursery land and also contributes to air and water pollution.

Wind erosion can be controlled by maintaining good soil structure and by planting cover crops. Proper soil and land management is the key to reducing the effects of wind on the land. Methods that help reduce the effects of wind erosion include the following.

- Orient planting rows and containers at right angles to the prevailing wind.

- Plant trees, shrubs, or other vegetation as windbreaks along the upwind boundaries of a production field to reduce wind erosion and protect sensitive nursery stock from windburning and sandblasting. Windbreaks should be planted perpendicular, or nearly so, to the principal wind direction. Windbreaks reduce wind erosion by reducing the wind speed on the surface of the soil and the distance the wind travels across exposed soil surfaces.

- Apply a mulch cover or green manure to increase the organic content of the soil. The more organic material present in the soil, the greater the resistance of the soil to breaking into particles small enough to be carried away by wind or water, and the more moisture the soil will hold. A dense cover crop also reduces wind erosion. Maintaining a dense cover may require inputs such as irrigation and fertilization.

- In areas with light, sandy soil, which are particularly prone to wind erosion, plant cover crops such as sorghum, grain, or sudangrass or cover the soil with mulches. For container nurseries, apply mulches on pots. Establish the coverage before the windy seasons.

- Cover aisles, row ends, roads, and field border strips with gravel. Minimize the exposure of bare soil to the wind.

- Keep soil wet during strong wind events by irrigating regularly and using plant cover to retain moisture. Wind erosion occurs mainly when dry seedbeds in light sandy and peaty soils are unprotected by plant cover.

- During windy seasons (autumn and early winter in Southern California, spring and autumn in the Central Valley), minimizing or eliminating bare soil surfaces and reducing the frequency and speed of tillage reduce wind erosion, especially in light, sandy soils, as they are more prone to wind erosion.

- On areas where timely establishment of temporary erosion control is not possible, try chemical stabilization. A good choice is spraying a PAM solution onto the surface of the soil. Sprayed PAM binds the surface particles together to form a crust, which is not prone to wind erosion. For the application rate and method of PAM, follow the manufacturer's or supplier's suggestions.

Mosquito Control: An Important Consideration in Runoff Management Planning

Nursery runoff often contains high amounts of nutrients and organic matter. Runoff management practices such as plant filter strips, wetlands, grassed waterways, and recycling ponds can produce stagnant water if they are not properly designed and operated. Runoff water that is stagnant for over 72 hours can become suitable breeding sites for mosquitoes.

If you produce mosquitoes on your nursery property, you might be held financially liable. Mosquitoes can carry vector-borne diseases such as West Nile virus, malaria, and encephalitis. These diseases are transmitted to people through mosquito bites. Mosquitoes are also a nuisance, reducing the quality of life for nursery workers and local residents. They can be economically detrimental to nearby businesses.

Since public health and safety is a major component of all runoff management programs, mosquito management should be considered a high priority and must be integrated into the planning and operation of runoff management practices. Implementation of proper mosquito control methods could eliminate suitable mosquito habitats on nursery properties, and thus suppress their breeding, reduce health risks, and lessen legal liability.

Mosquito Control in Nursery Production

About 200 species of mosquitoes can be found in the United States, and all require water to complete their four-stage life cycle of egg, larva, pupa, and adult. Standing water is essential for all life stages of mosquitoes, except for the adults. Mosquito control is most effective when directed at immature stages in standing water and is best conducted using integrated pest management (IPM). An IPM program targets each life stage of the mosquito and attempts to eliminate as many mosquitoes as possible before they emerge as biting adults. A combination of biological, physical, and chemical control techniques is often used in an IPM program.

Biological mosquito control uses and enhances natural enemies of mosquitoes such as mosquitofish, large predatory fishes (e.g., perch and bass), dragonflies, diving beetles, birds, and bats. Mosquitofish, perch, and bass feed on immature mosquitoes, while dragonflies, beetles, birds, and bats eat adult mosquitoes. These natural mosquito predators can significantly reduce the mosquito population, though their effects are generally not sufficient to preclude chemical treatment. Common practices that promote biological control include periodical removal of emergent vegetation

from waterways and recycling basins, elimination of floating vegetation conducive to mosquito production, and maintaining the water level in a pond or wetland at depths in excess of 4 feet to limit the spread of invasive emergent vegetation.

Physical control makes habitats less suitable for mosquito production mainly by reducing standing water and blocking the egg-laying females from accessing the water. Practices include the following.

+ Keep water flowing; use pumps or aerators if necessary.

+ If you can't keep the water flowing, design runoff collection and management structures so they do not hold standing water for more than 72 hours.

+ Prevent and reduce the possibility of clogged discharge orifices (e.g., debris screens).

+ Avoid barriers, diversions, or flow spreaders that may retain standing water.

+ Completely seal, permanently or longer than 72 hours, structures that retain water to prevent entry of adult mosquitoes.

+ Design structures with pumping, piping, valves, or other equipment to allow for easy dewatering of the water retention structure if necessary.

Chemical control uses insecticides that target immature or adult mosquitoes. The insecticides available include larvicides (such as surface oils or films to suffocate the larvae), growth regulators to inhibit the development of the larvae, and adulticides to kill the adult mosquitoes. Chemical control is effective and may be easier to apply than biological approaches. However, the chemicals used are toxic and can be detrimental to the health of plants and microorganisms in wetland or grassed waterway environments. In addition, a permit may be required to apply the insecticides.

In most cases, a combination of the above approaches works best. Proper design of runoff management structures and ecological management that promotes biological and physical control methods are most effective, least expensive, and most environmentally friendly in controlling mosquitoes in nursery production sites.

Because of mosquitoes' propensity to breed, all existing runoff management treatments, regardless of their design, should be monitored periodically by vector control professionals with knowledge of the biology and ecology of local mosquito species. For future runoff management treatments, it is recommended that vector control professionals be included in preconstruction planning and that careful preventive design and maintenance plans for mosquito control be incorporated.

Additional Information

Additional information about mosquitoes and mosquito-transmitted diseases can be obtained by contacting your local mosquito and vector control agency, local health department, or by visiting the California West Nile Virus Web site (see the Resources, below). Additional information on mosquito control products and methods is available on the U.S. Environmental Protection Agency (EPA) Web site and also on the UC IPM Web site.

References

Harter, T., and L. Rollins, eds. 2008. Watersheds, groundwater, and drinking water: A practical guide. Oakland: University of California Agriculture and Natural Resources Publication 3497.

Lu, J., L. Wu, D. Merhaut, J. Gan, J. Newman, and B. Faber. 2006. Pesticides in nursery recycling ponds. CORF News 10(2): 1, 4. CORF Web site, http://www.corf.org/news.html.

Metzger, E. M. 2004. Managing mosquitoes in storm water treatment devices. Oakland: University of California Agriculture and Natural Resources Publication 8125. ANR CS Web site, http://anrcatalog.ucdavis.edu/pdf/8125.pdf.

Resources

California West Nile Virus Web site, http://westnile.ca.gov.

Natural Resources Conservation Service (NRCS). Buffer strips: Common sense conservation. NRCS Web site, http://www.nrcs.usda.gov/feature/buffers/#Anchor-WhatBuffer.

———. Conservation buffers to reduce pesticide losses. NRCS Web site, ftp://ftp.wcc.nrcs.usda.gov/downloads/pestmgt/newconbuf.pdf.

———. Conservation practice standard: Constructed wetland. NRCS Web site, http://efotg.nrcs.usda.gov/references/public/AL/al656.pdf.

UC IPM Web site, http://www.ipm.ucdavis.edu/.

U.S. Environmental Protection Agency (EPA) Mosquito Control Web site, http://www.epa.gov/pesticides/health/mosquitoes.

Water Recycling in Nurseries

DONALD J. MERHAUT, University of California Cooperative Extension Nursery and Floriculture Crops Specialist, Department of Botany and Plant Sciences, UC Riverside

Many areas of California now permit only storm water to run off from a nursery, forcing nurseries to recycle all runoff water from production sites during dry weather. Other regions of the state allow nurseries to release runoff water into storm drains; however, the regulations for the quality of the runoff water are so strict that most nurseries cannot comply, and therefore, opt to recycle the water. For example, many policies limit the concentration of nitrates in runoff to less than 10 parts per million (ppm) nitrate-nitrogen. This is a very low concentration, considering that many nurseries fertilize with 100 ppm or more of nitrogen. Other regulations apply to the concentrations of other nutrients, pesticides, and physical characteristics, such as odor, floating debris, and suspended particulate matter. For these reasons, more and more nurseries are capturing their runoff water and recycling it.

A nursery of any size can install a recycling system. In a recent evaluation of nurseries in Southern California, nurseries from 10 to 200 acres were found to be successfully recycling their runoff water. Regardless of whether irrigation water is applied through drip emitters, overhead sprinklers, or some form of hydroponics, used water can be recycled safely and efficiently. In fact, the cost of installing a recycling system is often recovered in the savings resulting from the use of less water and fertilizer.

In general, the cost of installing a recycling system is directly proportional to the size of the production facilities, with higher costs per acre for smaller operations. Larger nurseries that implement recycling systems tend to save the most water and recoup the most economic benefit. However, even small operations with little irrigation runoff may benefit from recycling storm runoff.

Major costs include basin construction, water sanitation processing, labor, equipment, and maintenance. Some of the primary considerations when recycling water are the cost of construction and maintenance, pathogen control, fertilizer requirements, and the residual nature of pesticides. Six basic steps must be performed when recycling water:

+ collection of runoff water

+ removal of floating debris and suspended particulate matter

+ sanitation (treatment for pathogen contamination)

- fertilizer injection

- blending of treated water with fresh water

- storage of blended water for application

For all of the collection and filtration systems described in this chapter, a small pilot system should be fabricated to test the feasibility and efficacy of use at a given nursery site.

Collection of Runoff Water

The factors that must be considered in designing runoff collection include the following.

- **Size of the collection basin.** The collection basin must accommodate all runoff water from the nursery site. This may include runoff not only from production sites but also from greenhouse roofs, driveways, parking lots, and other areas of the nursery. If a closed-hydroponics system is used for plant production, a collection and treatment system should be in place specifically for the hydroponic system, separate from collection systems for runoff from other areas of the nursery. Be sure to inquire about local regulations concerning what runoff must be collected. If regulations in your area specify collection and capture of runoff from the first storm event, an estimation of the volume of storm water runoff must also be known.

- **Location of the collection basins.** The topography of the nursery and space available must be taken into consideration. Also, if there are different types of production sites, such as propagation, plug production, field crops, and container crops, there may be multiple water sources and water recycling units. If the nursery is situated on a hill, the collection basin can often be located at the lowest elevation so that gravity can be used to collect runoff.

Filtration

Removal of Floating Debris

Most floating debris can easily be removed via baffles located at or near the collection basin or via separate sedimentation pits.

Removal of Suspended Material

Several methods may be implemented to remove suspended matter from runoff water. The technique to use will be determined by the degree of purification desired and the type of suspended residues in the water.

- **Sedimentation through gravity.** This is the most common and economical process used by nurseries. Most suspended material will settle out in the sedimentation pond or collection basin within a few hours. However, clay, being a very fine colloidal material, may require several days to settle out of the water. Sedimentation pits must be cleaned occasionally to remove the buildup of particulate matter on the bottom.

- **Flocculation.** This is the process whereby cations such as iron from ferric sulfate or aluminum from alum are added to the water to aggregate negatively charged particles such as clay and organic matter. When polymers are added to the water, these flocculated materials form larger particles, resulting in a rapid (5-minute) sedimentation of flocculated materials.

- **Sand or charcoal filtration.** This process is done to filter out any remaining suspended materials.

Sand Filtration Systems

Slow or rapid sand filtration systems can be used in nurseries. Rapid sand filtration systems are more common but do not provide pathogen control. Both types of filtration systems are described below.

Slow Sand Filtration

Slow sand filtration (SSF) is a method of filtering water through fine sand (0.15 to 0.35 mm). Unlike coarse sand (1.0 to 2.0 mm), fine sand traps some pathogens and also allows beneficial microorganisms to develop on the sand surface. These beneficial microorganisms kill pathogenic bacteria, fungi, and certain viruses, eliminating the need for chemical control methods such as chlorination.

Slow sand filtration for horticultural purposes has been used in Australia and Europe since the early 1990s and for the filtration of drinking water since the 1800s. Research has shown that this type of system, in addition to filtering organic matter and fine debris from the water, also reduces or eliminates pathogens. Filter efficiency is based on sand particle size and the beneficial microorganisms that develop on the sand surface (biofilm, or *schmutzdecke* in German), which actively break down pathogens via chemical, physical, and biological means.

Pathogen control

Pathogens can be physically trapped in the fine sand of the filter. The biological and chemical effect is created by the beneficial organisms that develop on the surface of the sand. This living matrix has been shown to eliminate pathogens such as *Phytophthora* and *Pythium* (Garibaldi et al. 2003; Wohanka 1995; Wohanka et al. 1999; Van Os et al. 1999; Van Os and Postma 2000) and *Legionella* (Calvo-Bado et al. 2003). Flow rates of 100 to 300 liters per hour per square meter (L/hr/m²) are recommended. The slower the flow rates, the more effective the system is in trapping and killing pathogens.

Advantages

+ Low operating costs since the system works through gravity.

+ No chemicals are required to kill most pathogens.

+ No technical components or control systems are needed.

+ Low maintenance requirements.

+ Adaptable to wide range of production systems.

+ Pathogen removal or breakdown when a biologically active film has formed on top of the sand.

+ Chemical control without altering the pH of the effluent water.

+ Herbicide and pesticide filtering or breakdown. A layer of granular-activated carbon (charcoal) can adsorb certain organic herbicides and pesticides.

Disadvantages

+ Slower filtration rate (0.05 to 0.55 gpm/ft²) than rapid sand filtration (2.0 to 20 gpm/ft²).

+ High installation costs due to installation of retention basins.

+ Occasional cleaning maintenance requires labor.

+ Requires approximately four times more surface area than rapid sand filtration.

+ Larger suspended debris should be removed before filtration, so that intervals between cleaning filters is extended.

+ Dissolved organic matter. Coloration due to dissolved organic matter and acids is not always removed through SSF.

Structural and operational considerations

Housing. The sand filter can be housed in cement tanks or in plastic or fiberglass drums or containers. The filter should have at least two smaller units rather than one large unit, so that one system can be shut off for cleaning, while still having the other unit operating.

Inlet. The inlet for untreated runoff water should be constructed so that the sand surface is not disturbed by incoming water.

Water. A constant depth of approximately 1 meter of water should be maintained above the top of the sand. The weight of the water allows percolation through the sand below.

+ The water level should not fluctuate; flow rates through the sand column should not change. Variable flow rates decrease filtering performance. A method to measure and control the flow rate through the sand bed is recommended.

+ The water level should never go below the level of the sand filter. Water protects the beneficial biologically active film that develops on the sand surface. High temperatures and drying kills or impedes the activity of the biological filter.

+ The flow rate should be steady. Biological filters die from oxygen starvation in stagnant water.

Organic film. The organic film is a layer of beneficial microorganisms and organic matter that naturally develop on top of the sand filter bed. This is the key component that filters or kills many pathogens.

Sand. A layer of sand 80 to 150 centimeters deep provides the bulk of the filtering.

+ A particle size of 0.15 to 0.35 millimeters is recommended.

+ The uniformity coefficient (UC) of the sand should be less than 5 and is recommended to be less than 2. UC equals d_{60}/d_{10}, where d_{60} is the sieve size (in mm), which allows passage through the sieve of 60 percent of the sand by weight, and d_{10} is the sieve size (in mm), which allows passage through the sieve of 10 percent of the sand by weight.

Granular activated charcoal (*optional*). This adsorbs most organic chemicals, such as pesticides and herbicides. A layer of granular activated charcoal can be placed between layers of sand, near the surface. The activated charcoal should be replaced when the top layer of sand is replaced.

Gravel bed. A layer of gravel prevents sand from blocking the outlet. In more sophisticated systems, three different graded layers of gravel are used: 2 to 8 mm, 8 to 16 mm, and 16 to 32 mm.

Drainpipe. A perforated drainage pipe should be placed in the bottom layer of gravel. Additional filtering can be accomplished with a fabric placed over or around the drainage pipe.

Flow meter and control valve. For optimal performance, flow rates should be consistently maintained with a control valve installed at the end of the drainpipe.

Operational settings

The filtration rate should be 10 to 30 cm/hr. Low flow rates (10 cm/hr) are recommended when control of pathogens such as *Fusarium* are required, while higher flow rates (30 cm/hr) are suitable for the control of pathogens such as *Phytophthora* and *Pythium* that are commonly found in nurseries producing containerized woody ornamentals.

A filter capacity of 100 to 300 $L/hr/m^2$ is recommended.

Maintenance

When flow rates diminish, the upper 1 to 4 centimeters of sand should be removed along with the biological *schmutzdecke* layer that developed on the surface. The frequency of this maintenance should be based on the cleanliness of the runoff water, the water temperature, and the amount of water being filtered in a given time. Cleaning frequency intervals may range from every several weeks to every several months. The frequency can be reduced by controlling algal blooms in the captured water.

Rapid Sand Filtration (RSF)

Rapid sand filtration is usually referred to as sand filtration, but for clarity of this section, it will be referred to as rapid sand filtration to differentiate it from the slow sand filtration process described above. Rapid sand filtration uses coarse sand and possibly other substrates such as activated charcoal to filter recycled irrigation water.

Rapid sand filtration filters water through coarse sand (usually > 1.0 mm). Unlike the finer sands used in slow sand filtration, it does not trap many pathogens; therefore, additional means of water sanitation, such as chlorination, may be needed. It is a relatively inexpensive system for filtering larger debris from runoff water. The operating principles are similar to slow sand filtration; filtration efficiency is based on sand particle size and the types of other substrates, such as activated charcoal, that may also be included in the filter profile.

Advantages

+ Low operational costs, since the system works by gravity.

+ Low installation costs, primarily for retention basins.

+ Rapid filtration time (15 to 25 gpm/ft^2) compared to that of slow sand filtration (0.05 to 0.55 gpm/ft^2).

+ No technical components or control systems.

+ Low maintenance requirements; routine backflushing requires minimal input.

+ Adaptable to many production systems.

+ Chemical control without altering the pH of the effluent water.

+ Requires less surface area than slow sand filtration.

Disadvantages

+ Chemicals such as chlorine may be required to kill pathogens.

+ Occasional cleaning maintenance requires labor.

+ No herbicide or pesticide breakdown or removal, although using a layer of granular-activated carbon (charcoal) can adsorb certain organic herbicides and pesticides.

+ Larger suspended debris should be removed before filtration so that intervals between cleaning filters is extended.

+ Coloration due to dissolved organic matter and acids is not always removed.

Structural and operational considerations

Housing. The sand filter can be housed in a cement tank or in completely enclosed steel tanks. It is recommended to have several smaller units rather than one large unit, so that one system can be shut off for backwashing using the water from the other sand filters.

Inlet. The inlet for untreated runoff water should be constructed so that the sand surface is not disturbed by incoming water.

Sand. A layer of sand, the thickness of which is variable, provides the bulk of the filtering.

+ A particle size of 1 millimeter and larger is recommended. As the coarseness of the sand increases, the speed of filtration increases but the quality of the filtered water decreases.

+ The uniformity coefficient (UC) has not been defined for rapid sand filtration. For more information on the uniformity coefficient, see the section on slow sand filtration, above.

Granular activated charcoal (*optional*). This adsorbs most organic chemicals, such as pesticides and herbicides. A layer of granular activated charcoal can be placed between layers of sand, near the surface. The activated charcoal should be replaced when the top layer of sand is replaced.

Gravel bed (*optional*). A layer of gravel prevents sand from blocking the treated water outlet. In more sophisticated systems, three graded layers of gravel are used: 2 to 8 mm, 8 to 16 mm, and 16 to 32 mm.

Drainpipe (*optional*). A perforated drainage pipe may be placed in the bottom layer of gravel. Additional filtering can be accomplished with fabric placed over or around the drainage pipe.

Flow meter and control valve. For optimal performance, flow rates should be consistently maintained with a control valve installed at the end of the drainpipe.

Operational settings

The filtration rate should be 15 to 25 gpm/ft². Unlike slow sand filtration, using a lower flow rate does not increase the control of pathogens since the sand is so coarse.

The filter capacity depends on the type and size of filtration system being used. The filtration rate of 15 to 25 gpm/ft² makes rapid sand filtration suitable for large-scale nurseries (>100 acres) using overhead irrigation.

Maintenance

Frequency of maintenance is dictated by the dirtiness of the water. Algal blooms in the captured water must be controlled since algae accelerate clogging. Daily backwashing is not uncommon. The debris from the backwash may be pumped back into the reservoir, pumped into fields, or drained and composted. Check with local agencies regarding regulations pertaining to the disposal of backwash debris.

Pathogen Control

Runoff water and irrigation water derived from surface water usually contain pathogens such as *Phytophthora*, *Pythium*, and other fungi and water molds (Ali-Shtayeh et al. 1991; Bush et al. 2003; MacDonald et al. 1994). Many nurseries in California have been using recycled water successfully without treatment for these pathogens. Before making any decisions on whether recycled water should be decontaminated, determine whether pathogens are present in the water and to what extent. Samples should be taken at the irrigation water source, at points of runoff, and at points where recycled water is delivered back to plants. This includes testing fresh water sources used in blending with recycled water. Groundwater drawn from properly constructed wells and water for human consumption should be pathogen free. However, water drawn from surface sources such as lakes and rivers may contain waterborne pathogens.

Samples can be analyzed by a diagnostic laboratory for pathogens such as *Pythium* and *Phytophthora*. Another practical way to sample irrigation water is to use leaves or fruit from specific plants to "bait" these pathogens out of the water. Check with your diagnostic laboratory for recommended protocol.

The risk in using recycled irrigation water can best be evaluated by looking for pathogens in the recycled water at the points of reuse. Even where pathogens are present in runoff water at relatively high concentrations, there may be few or no pathogens detectable at the points of reuse. This is because natural processes in the system such as microbial degradation or unfavorable water conditions reduce pathogens. Also, mixing recycled water with fresh water before reuse dilutes pathogens, reducing the risk of infection.

Crops that are highly susceptible to waterborne pathogens such as *Phytophthora* should be grouped together in the same part of the nursery. That way, pathogen-free fresh water can be reserved for these areas and for propagation. Where recycled water is used with no treatment other than settling, holding, and dilution, it should be used only for hardier or more mature plants that are relatively resistant to waterborne pathogens.

By following these strategies, nursery growers may elect not to decontaminate recycled water. However, although the chances for infection in these cases may be low, if an infection should spread in recycled water, the economic losses could be severe. If large parts of the nursery contain crops highly susceptible to waterborne pathogens, decontamination of recycled water is definitely advisable.

A number of options exist for treating pathogens in recycled water. First, filtration may eliminate plant pathogens, as described in the sections above. Modern sand filters remove most plant pathogens to a tolerable level, but they do not sterilize the water. This leaves many of the natural biological control organisms in place, which is an important advantage. More stringent filtration methods include reverse osmosis, nanofiltration, ultrafiltration, and microfiltration. These use smaller pore sizes to remove almost all plant pathogens.

Several other stringent methods of sanitation are available. The most common of these sanitation practices include chlorination, ultraviolet light, and ozonation. These decontamination methods have been adapted from purification methods for drinking water or swimming pool water. Copper ionization and heat treatments have also been used in nurseries to control pathogens in recycled water. These methods can be effective in eliminating plant pathogens and other microorganisms, but they require careful management to achieve the desired effect. The type of method to use will be determined by the cleanliness of the water, the degree of sanitation desired, the type or recycling system being used, and local regulations. Details of each method are described at right.

Membrane-Mediated Filtration Processes

The four types of membrane-mediated filtration processes are reverse osmosis, nanofiltration, ultrafiltration, and microfiltration. All of these involve passing dirty water through membranes that filter out unwanted substances. Energy is required to pump the water through the membranes. The smaller-pored membranes require more pressure to force water through the pores than do the larger-pored membranes. The major differences between these systems are the sizes of the pores. Their advantages and disadvantages are described in table 8.1, and the relative sizes and weights of chemicals and organisms found in irrigation water are described in table 8.2.

Reverse Osmosis

Reverse osmosis (RO), or hyperfiltration, uses membranes with the smallest pores of the four filter systems. Because of the relatively small pores, dissolved salts, charged particles, and compounds of molecular weight greater than about 200 daltons (1 dalton = 1 atomic mass unit [amu]), as well as most pathogens, are removed from the water. Nurseries that are forced to use low-quality (salty) water usually must use reverse osmosis to remove dissolved salts. Since this process removes fertilizer as well as other dissolved salts, it should not be used after fertilizer has been added to the irrigation system.

Table 8.1. Physical characteristics, cost of operation, and advantages and disadvantages of four types of membrane-mediated filtration systems

Membrane type	Approximate filtration pore size	Relative cost	Advantages	Disadvantages
reverse osmosis	0.1 nm	high	removes charged ions (salts) removes compounds ≥ 250 amu removes essentially all pathogens	removes dissolved fertilizer
nanofiltration	1.0 nm	moderate	removes some charged ions removes compounds ≥200–1000 amu removes essentially all pathogens	may remove some chelates
ultrafiltration	1–20 nm	low	removes bacteria removes fungal spores removes nematodes	viruses may not be removed
microfiltration	100–10,000 nm	lowest	requires least amount of energy	many pathogens will not be removed

Note: 1 dalton = 1 atomic mass unit (amu).

Nanofiltration

Nanofiltration uses membranes of a larger pore size than those used in reverse osmosis; however, pores are still small enough to filter out larger-sized molecules (about 200 to 1,000 daltons). These pores are usually large enough to allow chelated nutrients to pass through, since most chelates, such as iron-EDTA, have a molecular weight under 500 daltons. Also, some charged particles may not pass through these filters.

Ultrafiltration

Ultrafiltration uses membranes with pore sizes of approximately 1 to 20 nm, which are larger than pores of nanofiltration systems. This system does not remove dissolved salts (fertilizer). However, it does remove suspended clay and pathogens such as bacteria, nematodes, most fungal spores, and some viruses. Some smaller viruses are not removed; therefore, additional sanitation treatments to the water may be necessary.

Microfiltration

Microfiltration uses membranes with pore sizes of approximately 100 to 10,000 nm (0.0002 to 0.0100 mm). While this filtration system requires the least amount of energy to pass water through the membranes, it also does not screen out most pathogens; therefore, additional sanitation treatments will be required. This process is sometimes used before reverse osmosis.

Maintenance

+ All membrane systems require periodic flushing of membranes. The frequency of flushing depends on the cleanliness and the volume of water being treated during a given time.

+ The residues collected must be disposed of in a manner that follows local regulations.

+ Membranes must be replaced after a given period of usage.

Chlorination

Chlorination is a chemical method of treating water to kill plant and human pathogens. Through oxidation, chlorine disrupts cell membranes and uncouples electron transport in many enzymatic processes. Chlorine treatment of nursery irrigation systems is probably one of the most popular methods used for the control of pathogens. Effectiveness of chlorination depends on the following factors.

+ **Chlorine concentration:** the greater the chlorine concentration, the more quickly it disinfects. However, too much chlorine may also kill plants. Most plants are safe if residual chlorine concentrations are less than 100 parts per million (3 meq/L). Use chlorine with caution, as some floriculture crops are very sensitive to chlorine. If

Table 8.2. Relative sizes of water and fertilizer molecules and common pathogens sometimes found in irrigation water*

Organism/particle	Weight (daltons)†	Size (nm)
water molecule	18	0.20 nm
iron-EDTA chelate	526	—
virus	7,000,000	20–200 nm
E. coli	Over 3,000,000,000	2,000 nm
fungal spores	—	2,000–5,000 nm
nematodes	—	>300,000 nm

Notes:

* Sizes of pathogens are ranges, since there are many types of viruses, bacteria, and fungi. Note that there is no correlation between weight and size, since some organisms may be denser (heavier) than other organisms or chemicals of the same size.

† 1 dalton = 1 atomic mass unit (amu).

you are uncertain about a particular crop, check with your local UCCE Farm Advisor.

- **Duration of pathogen exposure to chlorine:** effective exposure times may range from 1 minute to 24 hours.

- **Initial cleanliness of water:** dirty water ties up chlorine, reducing disinfectant efficacy.

- **Water pH:** chlorine is more stable, and therefore more effective, when irrigation water has a neutral pH.

- **Pathogen type:** certain pathogens require higher chlorine concentration or longer exposure time for effective treatment.

- **Water temperature:** relatively high (>20°C, >68°F) or low (<10°C, <50°F) temperatures may decrease the effectiveness of chlorine.

When chlorine is added to the water supply, aside from killing pathogens it may also bind to organic matter or to chemicals such as ammoniacal nitrogen. If chlorine binds to organic or chemical components, the chlorine is considered unavailable for pathogen control. Therefore, the effective, or residual, chlorine concentration is reduced. This is why chlorination is more effective with water sources that are not heavily contaminated with organic matter. When most pathogens are exposed to high enough concentrations of chlorine for a sufficient period of time, they will be killed.

Pathogen populations and residual chlorine concentrations must be routinely monitored to ensure that disinfection is sufficient and that residual chlorine concentrations are not dangerously high for plant production.

Advantages

- Low operation costs, since chlorine injection requires limited energy.

- Low capital costs, since most of the costs are for chlorine.

- Most pathogens are killed within seconds to a few minutes of chlorine exposure.

- Few technical components are needed if sodium or calcium hypochlorite is used.

- Low maintenance requirements; if chlorine gas is used, the injection system must be inspected periodically.

- Adaptable to small or large production systems.

- Properly performed chlorination should not affect the chemical nature of the water.

- Aside from chlorine storage, no additional space is required.

- Low inputs of labor. Manual additions of liquid chlorine can be done. Some labor is required to routinely check equipment if chlorine gas is used.

Disadvantages

- Residual chlorine can kill plants. Some plants are more sensitive to chlorine than others. However, except in hydroponic systems, organic matter in water and media usually ties up excess chlorine before significant damage can occur on crops.

- Chlorine does not break down or remove most pesticides or herbicides.

- Larger suspended debris should be removed so that organic matter does not inactivate free chlorine.

- Coloration due to dissolved organic matter and acids is not eliminated.

Chlorination Methods

The three materials used to incorporate chlorine into irrigation water are sodium hypochlorite, calcium hypochlorite, and chlorine gas.

Chlorine as a disinfectant for water has been banned recently in some European countries due to the fact that chlorine reacts with humic compounds in water to form trihalomethanes, environmental pollutants that can be toxic to human health at high concentrations.

Sodium hypochlorite is commercial bleach with a chlorine concentration of 100,000 to 140,000 mg/L. This is often used in the nursery industry.

- **Caution:** Sodium may accumulate in closed recirculating production systems. In these cases, sodium levels should be monitored to prevent sodium toxicity.

- **Danger:** Sodium hypochlorite can be explosive. If sodium hypochlorite is stored in improperly sealed vessels and begins to break down, an explosion can result.

Calcium hypochlorite has a chlorine concentration of 350,000 mg/L. It is occasionally used in the nursery industry, especially if sodium buildup is a concern with the use of sodium hypochlorite.

Chlorine gas is the least expensive of the three products. However, chlorine gas is dangerous to work with, and many regulations dictate its storage and use. If chlorine gas is considered, check with local agencies for the necessary permits.

Ultraviolet Light

History

Using ultraviolet (UV) light to sanitize clear water sources is becoming more common, since it does not require the addition of any chemicals. In order to be effective, the water source must be clear enough for UV light to penetrate. Some hospitals, hotels, and nursing homes sanitize potable water sources with UV light to ensure that the water is free of human pathogens.

When properly used in some nursery facilities, it may help kill any organisms that may remain in the water after all clarification and filtering processes have been performed. The use of UV light treatment in nurseries is in the developmental stages. Studies have been conducted using it to control pathogens in closed recirculating systems (Runia 1994b). Since water sources and the degrees of water cleanliness vary among nurseries, small pilot systems should be installed and tested to ensure that UV treatment processes work for a given nursery.

Description and Mode of Action

UV light fits into the spectrum of wavelengths from 100 to 400 nanometers (nm). This is the same light wavelength that is known to cause skin cancer in humans. UV light disinfects by forming free radicals, which disrupt membranes and cellular processes. UV light, like chlorine treatments, kills pathogens (bacteria, fungi, and viruses) suspended in water. However, since it is a light source, the water must be clean of suspended clays and organic acids for the light to pass through the water. Because of this limitation, UV light treatment is more suitable for hydroponic systems rather than for production facilities that use organic media (such as peat or pine bark) or run water over soils that contain clays. The dissolved organic acids and clays reduce water clarity and the effectiveness of UV treatments.

UV Light Sources

UV light is produced by low-pressure mercury vapor lamps, xenon flashlamps, and excimer lasers. Low-pressure mercury lamps emit a wavelength of 254 nanometers. "High" pressure mercury lamps may also be used, but they emit wavelengths of 190 nanometers, which form ozone in the water. This ozone can also sanitize the water to a certain degree. Xenon flashlamps emit pulses of light that are higher in energy than that from low-pressure mercury vapor lamps. However, xenon lamps also emit wavelengths over a larger spectrum, some of which are not UV, making them less energy-efficient. The excimer laser emits pulses of light at 248 nanometers.

Use in Nursery and Floriculture Production

UV light treatments are used in water recycling systems after other water clarification processes such as sand or charcoal filtration or flocculation. This ensures that the water is clear enough for the most effective UV light penetration into the water. To ensure effective treatment, testing should be conducted to determine proper wattage and water flow rates.

Advantages

+ The cost of operation is low if the water source is already clarified. Cost of treatment increases with the degree of water cloudiness.

+ Relatively lower installation costs for cleaner water supplies such as those of hydroponic systems.

+ No chemicals are used, regardless of the light source.

+ Few technical components or control systems.

+ Kills pathogens such as bacteria, fungi, and viruses.

+ No effect on water pH.

+ Requires a relatively small space for the light source and power supply.

+ Kills algae suspended in the water.

+ Has no toxic effect on plants.

Disadvantages

+ The use of UV light in nursery systems is still being studied, and troubleshooting still needs to be conducted.

+ Light sources chemically denature chelates that may be used to keep micronutrients such as iron in a soluble form.

+ Since UV light must pass through the water, any dissolved or suspended substances such as organic acids or clay reduce its efficacy.

+ Does not remove other chemicals from the water but may break down light-sensitive herbicides and pesticides. Consult the system manufacturer for specifics.

+ Does not break down or remove floating debris.

+ Does not remove coloration due to dissolved organic matter and acids.

+ Does not remove clays and other soil particles.

+ May require an exposure time of 30 seconds or longer, depending on the clarity of the water. Lower flow rates are required than with other forms of treatment, but the lower flow rates also reduce water turbulence and the efficiency of UV light treatment.

Conclusions

When used properly, UV light treatment may effectively kill pathogens in some nursery systems. However, the most successful use of this technology is with cleaner water systems, such as those used in hydroponics. UV light may denature chelated micronutrients such as iron chelates used in fertilization.

Ozonation

Ozone, Free Radicals, and Oxidizing Agents

Ozone

Ozone is a chemically unstable gas molecule that consists of three oxygen atoms linked together. This molecule seeks two more electrons to become more stable. Since an ozone molecule must "take" electrons from another molecule, it is considered an oxidant.

Oxidants

An oxidant is a chemical that is capable of taking electrons away from another chemical. These types of chemical reactions were originally termed oxidation because it was believed that oxygen was the only element able to take electrons from another molecule. In the process, the oxygen bonded with the molecule from which it took electrons. However, materials other than oxygen are now known to be oxidants, but the term "oxidation" is still used. The ability of a specific chemical environment to cause oxidation is measured as redox potential (redox) or oxidation reduction potential (ORP). ORP values of 700 millivolts should provide complete disinfection. ORP values less than 300 millivolts are usually considered safe for most aquatic life.

Free radicals

A free radical is an atom or molecule (group of atoms) that has at least one unpaired electron but has an overall charge of 0 (neither positively nor negatively charged). Even though this free radical has a charge of 0, it still needs to have the unpaired electron teamed up with another electron. Most compounds are stable at an electrical charge of 0, and electrons are stable only as pairs. All free radicals are oxidants since they have the ability to take electrons from other molecules. Ozone is not a free radical because all of its electrons are paired together. However, when ozone breaks down during oxidation reactions, oxygen-free radicals $(O\cdot)$ and hydroxyl free radicals $(HO\cdot)$ can be produced.

Antioxidants

An antioxidant is a chemical that protects an organism from being oxidized or a chemical that inhibits the ability of oxidants to oxidize.

Mode of Operation

Ozone is used to disinfect water at hospitals (Blanc et al. 2005) and public drinking water supplies (Evans et al. 2003). In one hospital study, ozone was used with a water flow rate of 3 to 4 cubic meters per hour and a residual ozone concentration of 0.3 mg/L, with a contact time between water and the ozone of 18 minutes (Blanc et al. 2005). Ozonation is also used to treat water from closed recirculating production systems (Runia 1994). Ozone disinfects water by oxidizing (adding oxygen and removing electrons) the membranes and key physiological reactions in living organisms and in chemicals suspended or dissolved in the water. In addition, as ozone breaks down in water, it produces free radicals:

$$O_3 + H_2O \rightarrow O_2 + 2OH$$

Ozone + water → oxygen + 2 free radical hydroxyls

These free radicals also disrupt cell membranes and physiological processes by upsetting the electron balance of the cell wall structures and chemical pathways.

Procedures for Ozonation of Irrigation Water

- Provide a relatively pure oxygen source. Regular air does not work since it is only 21 percent oxygen.

- Electrically charge the oxygen (O_2), which forms ozone (O_3). This is often performed using corona discharge or plasma discharge units. Over 80 percent of the energy consumed is wasted in the form of heat, which must be removed from the ozone generator, since heat decomposes ozone.

- Bubble the ozone through the water source. An injection rate of 1 ounce per 1,000 gallons of water with a 1-hour exposure time is the target rate, but the actual rate may vary according to different water sources. Treated water should be maintained in a closed, pressurized system to prevent the ozone from being released.

+ Applying ultraviolet light during ozonation increases the rate that ozone breaks down, which rapidly increases the number of free radical hydroxyl (·OH) groups. This technique, known as advanced photo oxidation, is a better disinfectant than using ozone alone.

+ Deactivate excess ozone by venting it through an activated charcoal filter.

Advantages

+ Ozone breaks down to oxygen, so it leaves no chemical residues.

+ Proper ozonation requires no other chemical control.

+ No chemical storage, since ozone is made on-site.

+ The efficacy of the system can easily be monitored by measuring the ORP.

+ Low maintenance unless the oxygen source is not clean, in which case the electrodes must be cleaned.

+ Kills most pathogens.

+ Kills algae.

+ Oxidizes many pesticides.

Disadvantages

+ Depending on the amount of organic matter in water, ozone exposure may require up to 20 minutes to 1 hour to achieve 100 percent mortality of pathogens.

+ Since the efficacy of ozone is related to its concentration and exposure time, collection tanks for treated ozone water are needed so that ozonated water can be stored long enough for effective disinfection.

+ High operation cost for the electrical source.

+ Ozone increases water pH, so water acidification may be necessary.

+ Organic matter in the water reacts with ozone, decreasing the amount of ozone available to kill pathogens.

+ Does not break down or remove floating debris.

+ Does not easily kill the chlamydospores and microsclerotia of some pathogens.

+ Does not remove or break down clays and other soil particles.

+ May react with chelates if chelates for iron or other nutrients are used, precipitating the nutrient out of solution.

+ May oxidize and precipitate out of solution some essential nutrients such as iron, even if chelates are not being used.

Conclusions

When used properly, ozonation can be an effective method to disinfect irrigation water in some nursery systems. One of the main limitations to ozone use is the space required and cost of holding tanks for treated water. Since ozone is also dangerous to humans, proper safety procedures must be followed.

Copper Ionization

History

Copper and silver ionization is a popular method of treating drinking water for pathogens. This method of water treatment gained popularity after the outbreak of *Legionella pneumophila*, the bacteria responsible for Legionnaires' disease, which occurred at the fifty-eighth state convention of the American Legion in Philadelphia, Pennsylvania, in 1976. Since then, many hospitals and other public facilities have incorporated methods such as copper and silver ionization to kill pathogens in drinking water (Blanc et al. 2005). The concentration necessary for pathogen control is approximately 100 parts per billion (ppb) for drinking water and 20 ppb for pool water. In a hospital setting, treatments of 300 ppb have been used (Blanc et al. 2005). However, the use of copper ionization in the nursery industry is relatively new.

What Is Copper Ionization?

Copper ionization works by inserting copper-coated ceramic electrodes into the water system. An electric current passes through this electrode, releasing copper ions (Cu^{2+}). These positively charged copper ions are attracted to negatively charged particles, such as organic matter, silt, and clay particles, as well as to the membranes of bacteria, algae, and mold. When copper binds to the organic matter, silt, or clay, the copper becomes chemically inactive; however, if the copper binds to the membranes of the organisms, the organisms die.

Copper in Agriculture

Copper is a heavy metal that has been traditionally used in agriculture as a bactericide on crops through applications of copper sulfate, which has been used alone or with other pesticides. In addition, copper is an essential plant nutrient, which is required at relatively low concentrations (0.002 to 0.003%, 20 to 30 ppm plant dry weight). In most nutrient formulations, especially micronutrient blends, copper is mixed into media at a rate of approximately 0.01 to 0.40 grams per pot. For hydroponically grown crops, copper is supplied at concentrations of approximately 0.05 ppm. Because of such relatively low requirements, any additional copper that is added to a plant system, either as a pesticide or fertilizer, should be monitored for copper toxicity.

Copper Ionization in Nursery Production

Copper ionization has been successfully used in agricultural processes as a coolant pad water treatment to keep filters free of algae and for postharvest washing of fruits and vegetables. Information regarding copper ionization in irrigation water recycling systems is limited. In most copper ionization systems, recommendations are to maintain active copper ion concentrations at 0.50 to 1.5 ppm. Copper electrodes are inserted into the water system, preferably after the water has been filtered of debris, suspended clay, and organic matter. The number of copper electrodes required depends on the amount of water to be treated, the cleanliness of the water (presence of organic matter and suspended clay), and the size of the electrodes. Some of the models currently available treat about 200 gallons of water per minute. Additional electrodes are required for higher flow rates.

Advantages

+ Moderate operational costs consisting mainly of electrode replacement (up to $10,000) and the cost of electricity.

+ Low installation costs, primarily for installation of copper-coated electrodes and an electrical source.

+ Some system manufacturers claim that no additional chemicals are required for pathogen control. However, others indicate that oxidizers such as chlorine are needed, but at lower concentrations.

- Few technical components or control systems.

- Low maintenance (occasional replacement of copper electrodes).

- Kills pathogens such as bacteria and fungi.

- Does not alter the pH of the effluent water.

- Requires no additional land for the construction of large treatment facilities.

- Kills algae on water and on coolant pads.

Disadvantages

- Certain ornamental crops are sensitive to the copper concentrations (0.5 to 1.5 ppm) recommended to effectively treat water. No data is available on copper accumulation with long-term usage of copper ionization in a closed recycling irrigation system.

- Since copper ions are positively charged, they are attracted to and bind to negatively charged particles of organic matter and clay, making the copper ions inactive. Therefore, greater injection (release rates) of copper ions from electrodes are needed to keep the copper ions at concentrations effective to kill pathogens.

- Does not remove herbicides and pesticides from the water.

- Does not break down or remove floating debris.

- Does not remove coloration due to dissolved organic matter and acids.

- Does not effectively remove clays and other soil particles.

- Copper binds to organic matter and clay that settle out in reservoirs. Therefore, if this sludge is recycled back into the media, copper concentrations in the sludge could be toxic to certain crops. Tests should be performed to check copper concentrations of the sludge and media before use on crops.

Copper Toxicity Symptoms

The symptoms of copper toxicity in leaves are reddish brown lesions that coalesce in severe cases. In roots, it is seen as stunting and death of root tips and an increased production of lateral roots. Under severe toxicity, the entire root system will senesce.

Copper sensitivity tests should be conducted on new plants that are suspected of being sensitive to the copper concentrations used in the growing system.

Conclusions

When used properly, copper ionization can be used in certain nursery systems to control pathogens. However, the primary concern is that copper concentrations in closed recirculating systems, such as hydroponics, should not increase to toxic levels. In a recent study, copper toxicity was documented for chrysanthemum, miniature rose, and geranium at 0.32 ppm, 0.15 ppm, and 0.50 ppm, respectively, in hydroponic solutions.

Heat Disinfection

History

Heat sanitation has more commonly been used to sterilize substrates in the nursery industry than to treat water. However, it has long been used to sterilize water for nurseries in European countries. Since no chemicals are added in this process, there is no concern regarding chemical storage or chemical residues.

How Does Heat Treatment Work?

All living organisms have a certain heat tolerance, that is, the ability to withstand a certain maximum temperature for a specified period of time. Once this time or temperature is exceeded, the organism dies.

Viruses are killed at temperatures as low as 130°F if that temperature is maintained for a period of 1.5 hours. At higher temperatures, the time required to kill organisms decreases.

Procedures for Heat Treatment of Irrigation Water

To heat-treat irrigation water, metal heat exchangers are situated at one point along the water treatment system. The number and size of exchangers depends on the volume of water to be treated during a given time. Before passing over the heat exchanges, the water pH may be acidified to 4.5 to prevent calcium accumulation on the exchangers. If the water is particularly dirty, filtration may be recommended before heat treatment. After heating, the water must be cooled before use on plants.

Advantages

- No chemical residues since no chemicals are used.

- Proper heating procedures requires no chemical treatment.

- No maintenance, unless calcium builds up on exchangers.

- Kills all pathogens.

- Kills algae.

- If cooled sufficiently after heat treatment, water is not toxic to plants.

Disadvantages

- Water must be tested by laboratory procedures to ensure that all pathogens are killed.

- Water must be cooled before usage.

- Depending on the maximum temperature used, heating duration may take up to 1.5 hours to achieve 100 percent mortality of pathogens.

- Since the efficacy of heat treatment is related to exposure time at a certain temperature, tanks are needed to hold treatment water and cooling water.

- High operation cost for electricity, natural gas, or oil.

- Water requires acidification to approximately pH 4.5 before heating to prevent calcium buildup on heat exchangers, and must be neutralized to crop requirements after heat treatment.

- Does not break down or remove floating debris.

- Does not remove or break down clays and other soil particles.

- If chelates for iron or other nutrients are used, temperatures up to 150°F should not be a problem. However, accidental temperatures near boiling (212°F) denature chelates.

- Pesticide breakdown varies with pesticide; check pesticide labels for temperature stabilities in solutions.

Conclusions

When used properly, heat treatment can effectively disinfect irrigation water in certain nursery systems. Limitations to heat treatment include the space for holding tanks for heating and cooling water and the high cost of energy.

Fertilizer Injection and Blending

Fertilizer injection is usually the final step in the recycling process. This is done in conjunction with mixing fresh water with recycled water. Salinity of recycled water increases with each irrigation and recapturing cycle. However, if the runoff is blended with fresh water of lower conductivity, the salinity level increases at a slower rate and will reach an equilibrium, often within 6 to 10 cycles. The percentage of increase in salinity per cycle depends on evaporation rate, leaching fraction, and the degree of salt loading from soil mix components and fertilizer applications.

Growers should monitor salinity by determining the conductivity of the collected runoff and of the blended supply. In liquid feed programs, appropriate fertilizers are added either to achieve a target conductivity or a concentration of a specific nutrient. Since nutrients often account for a significant portion of the salinity, it is important to regularly analyze the recycled water for nutrient content. Liquid feed nutrient levels are usually maintained at levels similar to those in nurseries that do not recycle water, but there is significant reduction in fertilizer cost due to recycling.

Recycled water can have elevated levels of specific ions such as sodium, chloride, and boron. Plants exhibit a wide range of tolerance to salinity and specific ions. Where relatively high salinity is a problem, growers should group plant material in the nursery according to relative salinity tolerance. In addition, development of leaf burn due to sodium or chloride toxicity can be minimized by using drip irrigation or by irrigating at night to reduce foliar deposition of salts.

References

Ali-Shtayeh, M. S., J. D. MacDonald, and J. Kabashima. 1991. A method for using commercial ELISA tests to detect zoospores of *Phytophthora* and *Pythium* species in irrigation water. Plant Disease 75(3): 305–311.

Blanc, D. S., P. Carrara, G. Zanetti, and P. Francioli. 2005. Water disinfection with ozone, copper and silver ions, and temperature increase to control *Legionella*: Seven years of experience in a university teaching hospital. Journal of Hospital Infection 60:69–72.

Bush, E. A., C. Hong, and E. L. Stromberg. 2003. Fluctuations of *Phytophthora* and *Pythium* spp. in components of a recycling irrigation system. Plant Disease 87(12): 1500–1506.

Buyanovsky, G., J. Gale, and N. Degaqni. 1981. Ultraviolet radiation for the inactivation of microorganisms in hydroponics. Plant and Soil 60:131–136.

Calvo-Bado, L. A., J. A. W. Morgan, M. Sergeant, T. R. Pettitt, and J. M. Whipps. 2003. Molecular characterization of *Legionella* populations present within slow sand filters used for fungal plant pathogen suppression in horticultural crops. Applied and Environmental Microbiology 69(1): 533–541.

Evans, H., M. Bauer, N. Goodman, J. Hauge, and T. Ta. 2003. The role of ozone in improving drinking water quality in London and Oxford. Ozone Science and Engineering 25:409–416.

Evans, R. D. 1995. Control of microorganism in flowing nutrient solutions, In M. Bates, ed., Proceedings of the 16th annual conference on hydroponics. San Ramon, CA: Hydroponic Society of America. 31–43.

Garibaldi, A., A. Minuto, V. Grasso, and M. L. Gullino. 2003. Application of selected antagonistic strains against *Phytophthora cryptogea* on gerbera in closed soilless systems with disinfection by slow sand filtration. Crop Protection 22:1053–1061.

Jones, J. B., Jr. 2005. Hydroponics, a practical guide for the soilless grower. 2nd ed. Boca Raton, FL: CRC Press.

MacDonald, J. D., M. S. Ali-Shtayeh, J. Kabashima, and J. Stites. 1994. Occurrence of *Phytophthora* species in recirculated nursery irrigation effluents. Plant Disease 78(6): 607–611.

Runia, W. T. 1994. Disinfection of recirculation water from closed cultivation systems with ozone. Acta Horticulturae 361:388–396.

Runia, W. T., M. G. P. J. Michielsen, A. J. Van Kuik, and E. A. Van Os. 1997. Elimination of root infecting pathogens in recirculation water from closed cultivation system by ultraviolet radiation. Acta Horticulturae 316:361–372.

Wohanka, W. 1995. Disinfection of recirculating nutrient solutions by slow sand filtration. Acta Horticulturae 481:577–583.

Wohanka, W., H. Luedtke, H. Ahlers, and M. Luebke. 1999. Optimization of slow filtration as a means for disinfecting nutrient solutions. Acta Horticulturae 481:539–544.

Van Os, E. A., and J. Postma. 2000. Prevention of root diseases in closed soilless growing systems by microbialoptimisation and slow sand filtration. Acta Horticulturae 532:97–102.

Van Os, E. A., J. J. Amsing, A. J. Van Kuik, and H. Willers. 1999. Slow sand filtration: A potential method for the elimination of pathogens and nematodes in recirculating nutrient solutions from glasshouse-grown crops. Acta Horticulturae 481:519–526.

Von Broembsen, S. L. 1998. Capturing and recycling irrigation water to protect water supplies In Water quality handbook for nurseries. Stillwater: Oklahoma Cooperative Extension Service, Division of Agricultural Sciences and Natural Resources and Oklahoma State University, Circular E-95. pp 27–29. OSU CE Web site, http://osuextra.okstate.edu/pdfs/e-951.pdf.

Conducting an Environmental Audit

Julie Newman, University of California Cooperative Extension Farm Advisor, Ventura County
Valerie Mellano, University of California Cooperative Extension Farm Advisor, San Diego County
Karen Robb, University of California Cooperative Extension Farm Advisor, Mariposa County
Darren Haver, University of California Cooperative Extension Farm Advisor, Orange County

What Is an Environmental Audit?

An environmental audit is a way to evaluate current management practices that may impact the environment. This chapter provides an environmental audit for greenhouses and nurseries that focuses specifically on management practices that impact water quality. Reading through the sections of the checklists below and answering the questions with management personnel increases awareness of management practices that mitigate runoff and leaching. It also provides a convenient and easy way of conducting a self-assessment to identify areas that may require improvements.

The best time to complete this audit is after you have read and reviewed the list of management goals and management practices outlined in chapter 2 as well as the chapters in this manual that pertain to practices for

which you need further clarification. The audit should then be easy to complete. If you find that you do not understand some of the questions, go back to specific chapters to refresh your knowledge of the management practices and why they are recommended.

The first section concerns general information regarding your operation. The information in this section can be used to help complete documents required by regulatory agencies, such as conditional waiver and permit documents required by California regional water quality control boards. The nature of your operation and the types of crops that you grow can dictate some of the problems you may face in controlling runoff and leaching from your property. Explanatory notes are given below in the last column for appropriate questions. In the answers below, please circle whether your figures are in acres or square feet.

◟◞ General Operation

1. How large is the area in production?   total production _____ ac/ft$_2$

Larger operations that use greater volumes of water have a higher potential to create runoff. Operations that do not use all property space for production may have more options for managing runoff, such as reuse on landscaped areas or construction of collection ponds. Nonproduction areas must also be managed to avoid contributing contaminants to runoff or creating runoff.

2. How large is the entire commercial property?   total property _____ ac/ft$_2$

3. What types of plants are produced and how large is the area in production for each type?

Plant type may affect runoff potential based on moisture and leaching requirements. The amount or type of required chemical inputs for specific plants, such as fertilizers and pesticides, can affect contaminants that may be found in runoff.

bedding plants _____ ac/ft$_2$

cut flowers _____ ac/ft$_2$

potted plants for indoor use _____ ac/ft$_2$

outdoor container nursery _____ ac/ft$_2$

propagator (e.g., propagating plant material for use by other growers) _____ ac/ft$_2$

4. What types of operations are there and how large are they?

Indoor greenhouse operations may have different runoff issues than do outdoor nursery or shadehouse operations. Greenhouses must assess roof runoff management and the use of shading compounds. Outdoor nurseries may need to assess erosion. Container operations may have different runoff issues than do in-ground operations, depending on various factors. The use of small containers or propagation flats may have a higher runoff potential than the use of larger containers. Runoff from in-ground operations in the field may carry sediments containing contaminants such as pesticides and nitrates and will be significantly affected by property slope.

greenhouse _____ ac/ft$_2$

shadehouse or hoop house _____ ac/ft$_2$

no covering (field or nursery) _____ ac/ft$_2$

containers _____ ac/ft$_2$

in-ground _____ ac/ft$_2$

5. What types of floor surfaces are used in indoor production areas?

Permeable surfaces are less prone to runoff, though groundwater infiltration may be a problem.

☐ cement   ☐ gravel   ☐ plastic   ☐ weed cloth   ☐ other_____   ☐ none, bare soil

6. What types of ground surfaces are used in outdoor production areas?

☐ cement   ☐ gravel   ☐ plastic   ☐ weed cloth   ☐ other_____   ☐ none, bare soil

7. What types of irrigation systems are used? Estimate the percentage of each type.

overhead _____ %   low volume _____ %   capillary _____ %   hand water _____ %

8. Estimate the percentage of total production acreage on a water recycling system or systems (if any). _____ %

9. Does your operation drain into open surface water or any engineered or constructed drainage or flood control systems?

☐ yes   ☐ no

Many open surface waters are a part of a municipal storm water or sewer system. A higher potential to contaminate exists when naturally occurring or constructed wetlands, waterways, or surface waters are located on or adjacent to a growing operation. In addition, an operation's runoff may be subject to greater scrutiny by the state if it flows directly into impaired waters. Runoff discharges, including those emitted from greenhouse, nursery, and field operations, can be subject to one or more permits required by the state.

10. If yes, indicate the types of water bodies and drainage systems your property drains into.

☐ creek or river   ☐ wetland   ☐ pond   ☐ drainage ditch or flood control system

☐ other_____

The rest of the audit is divided into sections that focus on related management practices, such as irrigation management, nutrient management, and pest management. Management practices that are listed in each box in the table are discussed under the numbered section in chapter 2. Some sections or questions will not apply to all nurseries.

Fill out the audit as completely as possible. If a question is not applicable to your operation, check "NA." If you do not understand a question or require further information to complete the audit, review the chapters of this manual that provide background information on management practices. In addition, brief explanatory narratives are provided in the list of management goals and management practices in chapter 2.

When you complete the audit, go back to each question marked "No" and circle or highlight it. Answering "no" to any question indicates an issue that may need to be assessed. This does not necessarily imply a violation of water quality regulations or evidence of nonpoint source pollution. However, these are areas where you may be able to reduce potential runoff and groundwater contamination by implementing appropriate management practices and technologies in the coming year.

This audit should be completed each year and kept with your records for at least 5 years. It can be used to document to public and regulatory agencies your good stewardship.

A. Irrigation Management Goals and Management Practices

❧ **Management Goal A.1:** *Design or retrofit your irrigation system for improved irrigation uniformity and efficiency to reduce runoff and leaching.*

A.1.1. Do you conduct in-house irrigation audits or use professional services to determine the efficiency of the system and make appropriate adjustments based on these audits? ☐ Yes ☐ No ☐ NA

A.1.2. If irrigation uniformity remains low after all practical improvements have been made, have you considered converting to an irrigation system with the potential of high uniformity? ☐ Yes ☐ No ☐ NA

A.1.3. Do you use pressure regulators where appropriate? ☐ Yes ☐ No ☐ NA

A.1.4. Do you use emitters that minimize pressure differences or pressure compensating emitters? ☐ Yes ☐ No ☐ NA

A.1.5. When growing on slopes, do you compensate for pressure differences at the top and bottom of the slope by running the main line vertical to the slope with pressure controllers at each horizontal line junction, and running each subline horizontal to the slope, including a pressure control valve? ☐ Yes ☐ No ☐ NA

A.1.6. When using overhead or impact systems, do you use flow control nozzles when pressure is too high or variable? ☐ Yes ☐ No ☐ NA

A.1.7. Do you ensure that each watering zone has spray stake or emitters with similar flow rates and avoid combining emitters with different flow rates in the same watering zone? ☐ Yes ☐ No ☐ NA

A.1.8. Do you place plant types and pot sizes with similar water needs in the same watering zone? ☐ Yes ☐ No ☐ NA

A.1.9. Do you correlate emitter flow rates for spray stakes and drippers with plant types, media infiltration rates, and pot sizes in each watering zone? ☐ Yes ☐ No ☐ NA

A.1.10. Do you use appropriate and uniform nozzle sizes? ☐ Yes ☐ No ☐ NA

A.1.11. Do you use sprinkler heads with a high uniformity rating? ☐ Yes ☐ No ☐ NA

A.1.12. Do you use appropriate sprinkler spacing to assure proper overlap to attain optimal distribution uniformity? ☐ Yes ☐ No ☐ NA

Management Goal A.2: *Regularly maintain your irrigation system so that it continues to operate efficiently.*

A.2.1. Do you regularly inspect for leaks in mains and laterals, in irrigation connections, or at the ends of drip tape and feeder lines and repair any found leaks? ☐ Yes ☐ No ☐ NA

A.2.2. Do you regularly flush and unclog lines and emitters, keeping them free of mineral deposits and biological contaminants such as algae and bacterial slimes? ☐ Yes ☐ No ☐ NA

A.2.3. Do you ensure that appropriate filtration is used and regularly clean filters? ☐ Yes ☐ No ☐ NA

A.2.4. Do you maintain appropriate pressure throughout the system? ☐ Yes ☐ No ☐ NA

A.2.5. Do you regularly replace worn, outdated, or inefficient irrigation system components and equipment? ☐ Yes ☐ No ☐ NA

A.2.6. Do you keep maintenance records and update them regularly? ☐ Yes ☐ No ☐ NA

A.2.7. Do you have a schedule for regular audits? ☐ Yes ☐ No ☐ NA

Management Goal A.3: *Regularly manage crops, crop areas, and irrigation systems to avoid applying water to noncropped areas or applying irrigation when not needed.*

A.3.1. When spacing plants in areas irrigated with overhead or impact systems, do you regularly place plants as closely together as possible to avoid applying water to noncropped areas? ☐ Yes ☐ No ☐ NA

A.3.2. Do you manage spray stake and dripper systems to ensure that every emitter is located in a plant or pot? ☐ Yes ☐ No ☐ NA

A.3.3. Do you manage harvest operations and retail areas to avoid creating watering zones with emitters located outside of pots? ☐ Yes ☐ No ☐ NA

A.3.4. Do you consolidate plants and shut off irrigation in unused portions, including spray stakes and other emitters that can be "turned off" when not in use? ☐ Yes ☐ No ☐ NA

A.3.5. Do you use overhead emitters with check valves to prevent line drainage and drip damage? ☐ Yes ☐ No ☐ NA

A.3.6. Do you use an on/off valve in hand-watering systems to prevent runoff? ☐ Yes ☐ No ☐ NA

A.3.7. Do you check regularly to ensure that spray patterns of overhead irrigation systems uniformly deliver water only to plants, without creating overspray in walkways and edges? ☐ Yes ☐ No ☐ NA

Management Goal A.4: *Use appropriate irrigation rates and scheduling.*

A.4.1. Do you base irrigation scheduling and amount on environmental conditions and plant moisture needs? ☐ Yes ☐ No ☐ NA

A.4.2. Do you regularly adjust irrigation schedules to reflect changes in weather, plant needs, or measured soil moisture values? ☐ Yes ☐ No ☐ NA

A.4.3. Do you group pot sizes or plant types in watering zones according to moisture requirements? ☐ Yes ☐ No ☐ NA

A.4.4. Do you avoid irrigating outdoors in windy conditions unless using drip? ☐ Yes ☐ No ☐ NA

A.4.5. Do you use pulse irrigation to split irrigation into smaller increments that can more effectively be used by plants? ☐ Yes ☐ No ☐ NA

A.4.6. When automatic timers are used, do you check regularly for accuracy and adjust to correlate scheduling with changing environmental conditions and plant growth stage? ☐ Yes ☐ No ☐ NA

Management Goal A.5: *Provide appropriate training for personnel involved in irrigating in a language that personnel clearly understand, and maintain records documenting training.*

A.5.1. Do you provide training to ensure that irrigation duties are performed only by personnel who understand and practice appropriate irrigation scheduling, irrigation application practices, and crop management practices related to runoff management? ☐ Yes ☐ No ☐ NA

A.5.2. Do you ensure that appropriate personnel are trained in proper irrigation system maintenance procedures and recordkeeping? ☐ Yes ☐ No ☐ NA

A.5.3. If in-house irrigation audits are performed, do you ensure that personnel are trained to evaluate irrigation systems correctly and regularly? ☐ Yes ☐ No ☐ NA

A.5.4. Do you keep records of employee training and maintain them for at least 5 years? ☐ Yes ☐ No ☐ NA

B. Nutrient Management Goals and Management Practices

Management Goal B.1: *Evaluate irrigation water, soils, growing media, and plant tissue for nutrient constituents to optimize plant growth and avoid overfertilization.*

B.1.1. Do you monitor the quality of your irrigation source water seasonally or annually, analyzing for levels of constituents such as bicarbonates (HCO_3^-), sodium (Na), chloride (Cl^-), nitrate (NO_3^-), boron (B), soluble salts, and pH? ☐ Yes ☐ No ☐ NA

B.1.2. If well water is used on-site for human consumption, have you tested the well water regularly for contamination from fertilizers? ☐ Yes ☐ No ☐ NA

B.1.3. Do you maintain records of irrigation source water quality? ☐ Yes ☐ No ☐ NA

B.1.4. Do you consider nutrients already present in your irrigation water, recovered runoff, composts, manures, and previous fertilizer applications in fertilizer management decision making? ☐ Yes ☐ No ☐ NA

B.1.5. Do you regularly test soil or growing media for nutrients, soluble salts, and pH? ☐ Yes ☐ No ☐ NA

B.1.6. Do you test plant tissue to determine concentrations of macro- and micronutrients? ☐ Yes ☐ No ☐ NA

B.1.7. Do you use information and recommendations from soil, growing media, and plant tissue analyses in fertilization management? ☐ Yes ☐ No ☐ NA

B.1.8. When available, do you use nutrient recommendations for your specific crop? ☐ Yes ☐ No ☐ NA

B.1.9. Do you regularly test fertigation water to monitor fertilizer levels and ensure that injectors are operating properly? ☐ Yes ☐ No ☐ NA

B.1.10. Do you maintain records of fertilizer use? ☐ Yes ☐ No ☐ NA

Management Goal B.2: *Conduct efficient fertilizer and leaching practices.*

B.2.1. Do you incorporate solid fertilizers in a manner that optimizes nutrient availability to growing roots? ☐ Yes ☐ No ☐ NA

B.2.2. Do you use composts or manures that are thoroughly composted before application? ☐ Yes ☐ No ☐ NA

B.2.3. Do you carefully apply top-dressed fertilizers to keep granules in the pot or around the plants at the correct rate? ☐ Yes ☐ No ☐ NA

B.2.4. Do you ensure that injected fertilizers are carefully mixed and applied at the correct rate? ☐ Yes ☐ No ☐ NA

B.2.5. Do you calibrate fertilizer injectors to accurately deliver liquid fertilizer through the irrigation system? ☐ Yes ☐ No ☐ NA

B.2.6. Do you use slow-release or controlled-release fertilizers? ☐ Yes ☐ No ☐ NA

B.2.7. Do you time fertilizer applications with environmental parameters and the growth stage of the plants? ☐ Yes ☐ No ☐ NA

B.2.8. Do you flush excess salts from the root systems by using carefully managed leaching practices? ☐ Yes ☐ No ☐ NA

B.2.9. Do you use the electrical conductivity (EC) of root media or leachate water to determine leaching practices? ☐ Yes ☐ No ☐ NA

B.2.10. Do you set irrigation schedules to perform appropriate leaching by turning the fertilizer injectors off (using clear water) at set irrigation events or by applying the appropriate leaching fraction with fertilizer water at each irrigation? ☐ Yes ☐ No ☐ NA

B.2.11. Do you measure the amount of leaching that occurs and ensure that only 10 to 15 percent of the water applied runs through the container? ☐ Yes ☐ No ☐ NA

🌿 **Management Goal B.3:** *Avoid fertilizer material spills during all phases of transport, storage, and application.*

B.3.1. Do you have a plan for dealing with fertilizer spills? ☐ Yes ☐ No ☐ NA

B.3.2. Do you store fertilizers in a storage structure that complies with local, state, and federal guidelines? ☐ Yes ☐ No ☐ NA

B.3.3. Do you locate fertilizer storage and mixing areas as far away as possible from water conveyances (streams, creeks, and storm drains)? ☐ Yes ☐ No ☐ NA

B.3.4. In the fertilizer storage facility, do you include a concrete pad and curb to contain spills and leaks that is protected from rainfall and irrigation? ☐ Yes ☐ No ☐ NA

B.3.5. Do you equip fertilizer tanks with secondary containment to contain spills and leaks? ☐ Yes ☐ No ☐ NA

B.3.6. Do you conduct fertilizer mixing and loading operations on an impermeable surface such as a concrete floor in a covered area or where potential for runoff is low? ☐ Yes ☐ No ☐ NA

B.3.7. Do you perform fertilizer operations at least 100 feet downslope of a well or other water supply? □ Yes □ No □ NA

B.3.8. Do you regularly verify that fertigation equipment is properly calibrated and fertilizer solution tanks are free of leaks? □ Yes □ No □ NA

B.3.9. When transporting fertilizer, are you careful not to overfill trailers or tanks, being sure to cover loads properly and display appropriate placards on vehicles? □ Yes □ No □ NA

B.3.10. When transferring fertilizer into storage or into a fertilizer applicator, do you ensure that you do not allow materials to spill? □ Yes □ No □ NA

B.3.11. Do you immediately clean up fertilizer spills according to a predetermined protocol? □ Yes □ No □ NA

B.3.12. Do you use check valves on application equipment? □ Yes □ No □ NA

B.3.13. When applying fertilizer from a tractor or rig in a field, do you shut off the fertilizer applicators during turns? □ Yes □ No □ NA

B.3.14. Have you installed backflow prevention devices, and do you check them at least once a year, recording the date and result of this check? □ Yes □ No □ NA

B.3.15. Whenever you are injecting fertilizer into irrigation water, do you make sure that you do not allow backflow into wells or other water sources? □ Yes □ No □ NA

B.3.16. Do you dispose of fertilizer bags in trash bins with lids? □ Yes □ No □ NA

✒ **Management Goal B.4:** *Provide organized training sessions for personnel handling fertilizers in a language that personnel clearly understand and maintain records documenting training.*

B.4.1. Do you provide training to ensure that appropriate personnel understand how and when to use fertilizers? □ Yes □ No □ NA

B.4.2. Do you provide training to ensure that appropriate personnel understand how and when to leach? □ Yes □ No □ NA

B.4.3. Do you provide training to ensure that appropriate personnel understand safe fertilizer transport, storage, and disposal practices? □ Yes □ No □ NA

B.4.4. Do you provide training for all personnel on what to do in case of a fertilizer spill? □ Yes □ No □ NA

B.4.5. Do you keep records of personnel training provided and maintain them for at least 5 years? □ Yes □ No □ NA

C. Pest and Agricultural Chemicals Management Goals and Management Practices

Management Goal C.1: *Establish an integrated pest management (IPM) program to reduce pesticide use and the potential contamination of groundwater and surface water with pesticides.*

C.1.1.	Do you regularly monitor (scout) your crop for insects, mites, and other nursery pests such as snails and slugs, looking for pests and for pest damage?	☐ Yes	☐ No	☐ NA
C.1.2.	Do you regularly inspect crop and noncrop areas for weeds?	☐ Yes	☐ No	☐ NA
C.1.3.	Do you regularly inspect crop and noncrop areas for vertebrate pests?	☐ Yes	☐ No	☐ NA
C.1.4.	Do you ensure that all personnel who monitor pests and diseases are trained to identify disease symptoms and pests commonly found in your nursery and are familiar with pest and pathogen life cycles?	☐ Yes	☐ No	☐ NA
C.1.5.	Do you update training as new pests and diseases are introduced?	☐ Yes	☐ No	☐ NA
C.1.6.	Do you train other employees who handle or walk the crop, such as irrigators and flower harvesters, to recognize common pests and diseases so they can communicate problems they see to the scout?	☐ Yes	☐ No	☐ NA
C.1.7.	Do you use diagnostic lab services or other professional assistance to identify unknown pathogens, pests, or growth problems before implementing a control measure?	☐ Yes	☐ No	☐ NA
C.1.8.	Do you monitor environmental parameters to help predict growth of pest and pathogen populations?	☐ Yes	☐ No	☐ NA
C.1.9.	When applicable, do you use degree-days to predict insect development and timing of pesticide applications, or computer modeling programs for disease forecasting?	☐ Yes	☐ No	☐ NA
C.1.10.	Do you keep records of pest counts, degree of injury, and other data needed to determine pest pressure and pest population trends?	☐ Yes	☐ No	☐ NA
C.1.11.	Do you summarize monitoring data collected over time by graphing to illustrate pest population trends, or compare current data with the previous collection period?	☐ Yes	☐ No	☐ NA
C.1.12.	Do you base decisions on using pesticides and other control options on monitoring information?	☐ Yes	☐ No	☐ NA
C.1.13.	Do you use economic thresholds in deciding when and if chemical pesticides should be used?	☐ Yes	☐ No	☐ NA

C.1.14. Do you use monitoring and threshold data to select the most appropriate control strategies? ☐ Yes ☐ No ☐ NA

C.1.15. Do you use techniques to reduce pesticide use such as spot spraying, direct spraying, applying pesticides at the lowest recommended rate on the label, and using adjuvants? ☐ Yes ☐ No ☐ NA

C.1.16. Do you rotate classes of pesticides? ☐ Yes ☐ No ☐ NA

C.1.17. Do you use the most recent IPM recommendations for your crops? ☐ Yes ☐ No ☐ NA

Management Goal C.2: *Use good sanitation and other preventive control techniques to avoid pest problems and maintain a healthy production environment.*

C.2.1. Do you inspect plant material brought into the nursery to ensure that it is free of pests and diseases? ☐ Yes ☐ No ☐ NA

C.2.2. Do you treat or discard infected plant material promptly before introducing it into the growing area in a manner whereby other plants will not become infected by the discarded material? ☐ Yes ☐ No ☐ NA

C.2.3. Do you inspect propagation areas and treat or discard infected plants before they are introduced into the growing area? ☐ Yes ☐ No ☐ NA

C.2.4. Do you quarantine new plants before introducing them into growing areas? ☐ Yes ☐ No ☐ NA

C.2.5. Do you eliminate weeds in the growing environment and noncropped areas? ☐ Yes ☐ No ☐ NA

C.2.6. Do you fumigate, heat steam, or chemically treat planting areas and recycled media before establishing new crops to eliminate pests from previous crops? ☐ Yes ☐ No ☐ NA

C.2.7. Whenever possible, do you select plants that are tolerant or resistant to pests and diseases? ☐ Yes ☐ No ☐ NA

C.2.8. Do you use certified or culture-indexed stock where available and feasible? ☐ Yes ☐ No ☐ NA

C.2.9. Do you keep irrigation hose nozzles off the ground to avoid contaminating plants? ☐ Yes ☐ No ☐ NA

C.2.10. Do you avoid standing water in the growing environment? ☐ Yes ☐ No ☐ NA

C.2.11. Do you remove diseased plants, destroying them or treating them in an isolated area? ☐ Yes ☐ No ☐ NA

C.2.12. Do you use hand dispensers and foot baths at production house entrances and in propagation facilities to disinfest hands and shoes, ensuring that appropriate employees use them regularly? ☐ Yes ☐ No ☐ NA

Management Goal C.3: *Where feasible and appropriate, use nonchemical control tactics to reduce overall pesticide use.*

C.3.1. Do you incorporate cultural controls into your IPM program? ☐ Yes ☐ No ☐ NA

C.3.2. Do you incorporate mechanical controls into your IPM program? ☐ Yes ☐ No ☐ NA

C.3.3. Do you use environmental (physical) controls where feasible to reduce pests and prevent damage? ☐ Yes ☐ No ☐ NA

C.3.4. Are you familiar with the beneficial insects and mites that naturally occur in your growing area? ☐ Yes ☐ No ☐ NA

C.3.5. Do you monitor populations of beneficial insects and mites (natural or introduced)? ☐ Yes ☐ No ☐ NA

C.3.6. When beneficial insects are present, do you consider the effects of pesticides on them and use compatible pesticides whenever possible? ☐ Yes ☐ No ☐ NA

C.3.7. Do you use control strategies that conserve beneficial insects and mites, such as direct spraying, spot spraying, and reduced pesticide rates? ☐ Yes ☐ No ☐ NA

C.3.8. Have you incorporated commercially available beneficial organisms into your IPM program on crops where their use has been demonstrated to be effective? ☐ Yes ☐ No ☐ NA

C.3.9. Do you prevent ants from disrupting natural enemies? ☐ Yes ☐ No ☐ NA

Management Goal C.4: *When chemical pest control is necessary, select reduced-risk pesticides to prevent contamination of groundwater or surface water with toxic chemicals.*

C.4.1. Do you consider site conditions, pesticide labels, and hazard warnings of migration risk when selecting pesticides? ☐ Yes ☐ No ☐ NA

C.4.2. Whenever possible, do you select pesticides that do not potentially contaminate groundwater? ☐ Yes ☐ No ☐ NA

C.4.3. Do you avoid the use of groundwater-risk pesticides in rainy weather, in areas of shallow water tables, and where soils are sandy or have low organic matter content? ☐ Yes ☐ No ☐ NA

C.4.4. Whenever possible, do you select pesticides that will not potentially contaminate surface water? ☐ Yes ☐ No ☐ NA

C.4.5. Whenever possible, do you choose pesticides that are the most selective for the target pest species, avoiding the use of broad-spectrum pesticides? ☐ Yes ☐ No ☐ NA

Management Goal C.5: *Apply pesticides in a safe manner to reduce pesticide loads and potential runoff.*

C.5.1. Do you accurately measure pesticides to assure that you are within the label rate and to eliminate disposal problems associated with excess spray mix? ☐ Yes ☐ No ☐ NA

C.5.2. Do you know the exact location of the area to be treated, as well as the potential hazard of spray drift or subsequent pesticide movement to the surrounding areas? ☐ Yes ☐ No ☐ NA

C.5.3. Do you apply pesticides according to the label and follow environmental hazard instructions? ☐ Yes ☐ No ☐ NA

C.5.4. Do you calibrate pesticide spray equipment to ensure the best coverage and efficacy of pesticide applications and accurate application rates? ☐ Yes ☐ No ☐ NA

C.5.5. Do you check equipment for leaks and malfunctions and replace worn nozzles and screens, cracked hoses, and faulty gauges? ☐ Yes ☐ No ☐ NA

C.5.6. Do you avoid spraying pesticides when wind could move them off-target as drift? ☐ Yes ☐ No ☐ NA

C.5.7. Do you avoid applying pesticides when rain or scheduled irrigation will move pesticides in runoff and ground percolation? ☐ Yes ☐ No ☐ NA

C.5.8. Do you maintain records of the amount and type of pesticides applied? ☐ Yes ☐ No ☐ NA

C.5.9. Do you maintain uniform distribution in irrigation systems and use proper irrigation scheduling and timing to reduce surface water and groundwater pollution of pesticides? ☐ Yes ☐ No ☐ NA

Management Goal C.6: *Avoid pesticide spills and leakage during all phases of transport, storage, and application.*

C.6.1. Do you store pesticides in a storage structure that complies with local, state, and federal guidelines? ☐ Yes ☐ No ☐ NA

C.6.2. Do you locate pesticide storage and mixing areas as far away as possible from streams, creeks, and storm drains, and at least 100 feet from a well or other water supply? ☐ Yes ☐ No ☐ NA

C.6.3. Do you include a concrete pad and curb to contain spills and leaks in the pesticide storage facility that is protected from rainfall and irrigation? ☐ Yes ☐ No ☐ NA

C.6.4. Do you conduct pesticide mixing and loading operations on an impermeable surface such as a concrete floor in areas where potential for runoff is low? ☐ Yes ☐ No ☐ NA

C.6.5. Do you perform operations involving pesticides in areas at least 100 feet downslope of a well or other water supply? ☐ Yes ☐ No ☐ NA

C.6.6. Do you verify regularly that pesticide solution tanks are free of leaks? ☐ Yes ☐ No ☐ NA

C.6.7. When transporting pesticides, do you ensure that pesticides do not spill by not overfilling trailers or tanks and covering loads properly? ☐ Yes ☐ No ☐ NA

C.6.8. Do you ensure that pesticides are always transported in the back of a truck and that all containers are secured to prevent breaking or spilling? ☐ Yes ☐ No ☐ NA

C.6.9. Do you ensure that pesticides are never left unattended in a vehicle unless they are in a locked container? ☐ Yes ☐ No ☐ NA

C.6.10. When transferring pesticides into storage or into pesticide application equipment, do you take care to prevent materials from spilling? ☐ Yes ☐ No ☐ NA

C.6.11. Do you use check valves on application equipment, and when applying pesticides from a tractor or rig in a field, shutting off the nozzles during turns? ☐ Yes ☐ No ☐ NA

C.6.12. Whenever you are injecting pesticides into irrigation water, do you ensure that you do not allow backflow into wells or other water sources? ☐ Yes ☐ No ☐ NA

C.6.13. Have you installed backflow prevention devices, and do you check them at least once a year, recording the date and result of this check? ☐ Yes ☐ No ☐ NA

C.6.14. Do you clean up any spilled potting media that contains pesticide residues? ☐ Yes ☐ No ☐ NA

C.6.15. If pesticides are mixed into potting media before potting, are concrete curbs or sandbags used to isolate these areas so that the potting mix does not get washed away in the runoff? ☐ Yes ☐ No ☐ NA

C.6.16. Do you keep a spill kit available at the pesticide storage facility and any other appropriate sites where pesticides are used? ☐ Yes ☐ No ☐ NA

C.6.17. Do you immediately clean up pesticide spills according to a predetermined protocol, referring to the pesticide product material safety data sheet (MSDS) for information on cleaning up and decontaminating small spill sites? ☐ Yes ☐ No ☐ NA

C.6.18. Are you aware that all leaks or spills of pesticides must be reported to the local agricultural commissioner as soon as possible? ☐ Yes ☐ No ☐ NA

C.6.19. Do you distribute rinse water from pesticide application equipment evenly over the crop to reduce pesticide contamination in nontarget areas during the cleanup process following application? ☐ Yes ☐ No ☐ NA

C.6.20. Do you dispose of pesticides and pesticide containers according to label instructions and in an environmentally safe manner? ☐ Yes ☐ No ☐ NA

Management Goal C.7: *Ensure that the use of other agricultural chemicals potentially toxic to the environment (such as postharvest treatments containing STS and greenhouse shading compounds) and household cleaning and disinfectant products do not contribute to runoff.*

C.7.1. When using silver thiosulfate (STS, Chrysal AVB) for treatment of ethylene-sensitive cut flowers, do you ensure that the product does not reach groundwater, surface waterways, or sewage, and do you neutralize residuals before disposal following manufacturer instructions? ☐ Yes ☐ No ☐ NA

C.7.2. Where 1-methylcyclopropene (1-MCP, EthylBloc) is an effective treatment for ethylene-sensitive crops, do you select it as an alternative to STS? ☐ Yes ☐ No ☐ NA

C.7.3. Are you aware that plant growth regulators used for postharvest (e.g., 1-MCP and STS) and growth regulators used to control plant height are technically classified as pesticides, and do you treat them accordingly? ☐ Yes ☐ No ☐ NA

C.7.4. Do you select exterior greenhouse shading compounds that are relatively nontoxic, or select interior shade fabric or reflective covers? ☐ Yes ☐ No ☐ NA

C.7.5. Do you apply and remove exterior shading compounds so that they produce minimal runoff and remain on the property? ☐ Yes ☐ No ☐ NA

C.7.6. Do you exercise care when disposing of household products used in greenhouses and nurseries, such as cleaning products and disinfectants? ☐ Yes ☐ No ☐ NA

Management Goal C.8: *Ensure that runoff and sediment containing pesticide and other agricultural chemical residues remain on the nursery property and do not move off-site in water or by wind.*

C.8.1. If feasible and applicable, have you installed and maintained a capturing basin to collect runoff and sediment that may contain pesticides? ☐ Yes ☐ No ☐ NA

C.8.2. When construction of a basin is not feasible, do you use sandbags and berms to curtail runoff and trap sediments? ☐ Yes ☐ No ☐ NA

C.8.3. Do you use sediment traps and clean out the trapped sediment before the rain season? ☐ Yes ☐ No ☐ NA

C.8.4. If you use a recycling system, do you use fiber or activated charcoal filters to filter pollutants such as pesticides? ☐ Yes ☐ No ☐ NA

C.8.5. Have you established vegetation to filter sediment that may contain pesticides? ☐ Yes ☐ No ☐ NA

C.8.6. Have you considered using polyacrylamide (PAM) to hold adsorbed pesticides and reduce sediment runoff? ☐ Yes ☐ No ☐ NA

Management Goal C.9: *Provide organized training sessions for personnel handling pesticides in a language that personnel clearly understand, and maintain records documenting training.*

C.9.1. Do you provide training to ensure that appropriate personnel understand how and when to use pesticides in a safe manner? ☐ Yes ☐ No ☐ NA

C.9.2. Do you provide training to ensure that appropriate personnel understand safe pesticide transport, storage, and disposal practices? ☐ Yes ☐ No ☐ NA

C.9.3. Do you provide training for all personnel on what to do in case of a pesticide spill? ☐ Yes ☐ No ☐ NA

C.9.4. Do you keep records of personnel training provided and maintain them for at least 5 years? ☐ Yes ☐ No ☐ NA

D. Erosion and Runoff Management Goals and Management Practices

Management Goal D.1: *Evaluate the water quality of irrigation and storm runoff to comply with water regulations and determine options for reuse or treatment.*

D.1.1. Do you inventory chemicals used in your operation, especially those likely to be present in runoff? ☐ Yes ☐ No ☐ NA

D.1.2. Do you regularly sample runoff water, following commercial lab instructions for taking and handling samples? ☐ Yes ☐ No ☐ NA

D.1.3. Do you analyze (or have a lab analyze) runoff water samples to determine what is in it and at what levels, including pH, electrical conductivity (EC), nitrate (NO_3^-), and phosphate (PO_4^{3-})? ☐ Yes ☐ No ☐ NA

D.1.4. Do you compare water analyses against local and state water quality standards and regulations? ☐ Yes ☐ No ☐ NA

D.1.5. Do you maintain water quality runoff records for at least 5 years? ☐ Yes ☐ No ☐ NA

Management Goal D.2: *Use practices that improve soil/media infiltration and water-holding capacity to reduce soil erosion, runoff, and excessive leaching.*

D.2.1. Do you incorporate organic amendments on sandy soil to improve water-holding capacity and prevent excessive leaching? ☐ Yes ☐ No ☐ NA

D.2.2. Do you incorporate amendments on clay soil to improve infiltration and reduce runoff? ☐ Yes ☐ No ☐ NA

D.2.3. Do you use mulches or cover crops on bare soil to reduce runoff? ☐ Yes ☐ No ☐ NA

D.2.4. Do you test media used in containers and select media for high water-holding capacity as well as good drainage? ☐ Yes ☐ No ☐ NA

D.2.5. Do you use wetting agents to increase water absorption, allow quicker wetting, and reduce channeling down the sides of pots? ☐ Yes ☐ No ☐ NA

🌿 **Management Goal D.3:** *Use practices that retard movement of runoff water and sediment and keep it on the property.*

D.3.1. Do you determine where and how much erosion and runoff is generated and whether runoff exits the property? ☐ Yes ☐ No ☐ NA

D.3.2. Have you established engineered barriers or buffers between production areas and ditches, creeks, ponds, lakes, or wetlands? ☐ Yes ☐ No ☐ NA

D.3.3. Wherever possible, do you convert paved or bare soil areas to vegetation that retards runoff and takes up nutrients, pesticides, and other pollutants? ☐ Yes ☐ No ☐ NA

D.3.4. Have you considered using polyacrylamide (PAM) to remove sediment from runoff water? ☐ Yes ☐ No ☐ NA

D.3.5. Do you use windbreaks or shelterbelts in areas prone to wind erosion? ☐ Yes ☐ No ☐ NA

D.3.6. If your property is affected by discharge sediment or runoff from upslope or upstream properties, do you use practices to contain this sediment or runoff, such as diversions, filter strips, sediment basins, and underground outlets? ☐ Yes ☐ No ☐ NA

D.3.7. Have you implemented and maintained a record-keeping system for documenting management practices addressing runoff management? ☐ Yes ☐ No ☐ NA

🌿 **Management Goal D.4:** *Manage hilly, sloped areas to prevent soil erosion and increased runoff volume and velocity (including hilly production areas as well as sloped nonproduction areas).*

D.4.1. Do you use terraces where appropriate to control soil erosion and runoff? ☐ Yes ☐ No ☐ NA

D.4.2. Do you use mulches where appropriate to control soil erosion and runoff? ☐ Yes ☐ No ☐ NA

D.4.3. Do you use vegetation (cover crops, buffer strips, grassed swales, etc.) to control soil erosion and runoff? ☐ Yes ☐ No ☐ NA

D.4.4. Do you use berms to control soil erosion and runoff? ☐ Yes ☐ No ☐ NA

D.4.5. Do you use proper irrigation management in hilly production areas and in hilly landscaped nonproduction areas to avoid runoff and soil erosion? ☐ Yes ☐ No ☐ NA

D.4.6. Do you use proper pest and nutrition management practices in hilly production areas and in hilly landscaped nonproduction areas to avoid pesticide and fertilizer runoff? ☐ Yes ☐ No ☐ NA

Management Goal D.5: *Design and manage nursery roads to prevent erosion and contaminated runoff.*

D.5.1.	Do you ensure that all new roads are properly designed and permitted to avoid erosion?	☐ Yes	☐ No	☐ NA
D.5.2.	Do you use waterbreaks (waterbars) on nursery roads with gradients exceeding 8 percent, ensuring that the waterbreaks are properly sized and placed?	☐ Yes	☐ No	☐ NA
D.5.3.	Do you use filter strips between roads and waterways to absorb runoff from roads and trap toxic sediment?	☐ Yes	☐ No	☐ NA
D.5.4.	Do you inspect culverts and clean them out during winter rains so that water drains freely?	☐ Yes	☐ No	☐ NA
D.5.5.	Do you prevent contaminant-laden dust from traffic and wind erosion by sealing or watering unpaved roads, ensuring that dust control with applied water does not create runoff?	☐ Yes	☐ No	☐ NA

Management Goal D.6: *Collect excess irrigation and storm water runoff and sediment.*

D.6.1.	Do you use retention basins to store excess irrigation runoff and storm water?	☐ Yes	☐ No	☐ NA
D.6.2.	Do you use captured water to irrigate noncrop areas, preventing overflow?	☐ Yes	☐ No	☐ NA
D.6.3.	Do you use captured water and then recycle it onto crops, treating or blending with fresh water as necessary, avoiding basin overflow during both dry and wet weather?	☐ Yes	☐ No	☐ NA

Management Goal D.7: *Manage greenhouse roof runoff from storms to reduce pollution and erosion, prevent flooding, and improve drainage.*

D.7.1.	Do you direct roof runoff to avoid flow across areas where contaminants could be washed into a municipal storm water system, sewer system, or agricultural drainage system?	☐ Yes	☐ No	☐ NA
D.7.2.	Do you direct roof runoff into pervious areas such as gravel, vegetation, paving material, self-contained tailwater system, or retention ponds?	☐ Yes	☐ No	☐ NA
D.7.3.	Do you reuse collected roof runoff to irrigate noncrop or crop areas?	☐ Yes	☐ No	☐ NA

Management Goal D.8: *Provide organized training sessions for personnel in runoff management in a language that personnel clearly understand, and maintain records documenting training.*

D.8.1.	Do you ensure that all appropriate employees receive training in runoff management and all applicable regulations?	☐ Yes	☐ No	☐ NA
D.8.2.	Do you train staff so that they become aware of all drainage conduits and ditches on the property and know where they drain?	☐ Yes	☐ No	☐ NA
D.8.3.	Do you ensure that all municipal storm water or sewer system conduits and ditches are stenciled or designated with signs, and that there are no illicit connections to the municipal storm water or sewer system?	☐ Yes	☐ No	☐ NA
D.8.4.	Do you keep documentation and records of employee training for at least 5 years?	☐ Yes	☐ No	☐ NA

E. Management Goals and Management Practices for Nonproduction Areas

Management Goal E.1: *Ensure that all nonproduction areas where nursery-related activities occur do not contribute to dry– or wet–weather runoff, including walkways, driveways, packing areas, loading areas, and parking areas.*

E.1.1.	Do you clean indoor walkways, loading areas, and packing areas using only dry methods (such as sweeping or dry absorbents)?	☐ Yes	☐ No	☐ NA
E.1.2.	Do you periodically clean outdoor driveways, walkways, parking areas, loading areas, and packing areas to remove debris, vehicle residues, and other contaminants and prevent them from washing off during wet weather, using only dry methods?	☐ Yes	☐ No	☐ NA

Management Goal E.2: *Maintain vehicles, trucks, and tractors and their storage areas so that they do not leak fluids into groundwater or surface water.*

E.2.1.	Do you regularly maintain vehicles, trucks, and tractors used in the nursery to detect and prevent fluid leaks?	☐ Yes	☐ No	☐ NA
E.2.2.	Do you ensure that wash runoff from vehicles, trucks, and tractors remains on the property and does not drain into a municipal storm water or sewer system, or leach into groundwater?	☐ Yes	☐ No	☐ NA
E.2.3.	Do you properly dispose of collected fluids?	☐ Yes	☐ No	☐ NA

E.2.4. When there are vehicles, equipment, and storage tanks that are no longer used on the property, do you drain fluids and properly dispose of them? ☐ Yes ☐ No ☐ NA

E.2.5. Do you locate maintenance and storage areas for vehicles, trucks, and tractors where wet weather will not wash fluids into surface water or cause them to percolate into groundwater? ☐ Yes ☐ No ☐ NA

E.2.6. Do you clean maintenance and storage areas to avoid oil and grease buildup? ☐ Yes ☐ No ☐ NA

E.2.7. Do you immediately and properly clean up spills from vehicles, trucks, and tractors? ☐ Yes ☐ No ☐ NA

❧ **Management Goal E.3:** *Locate and maintain fuel tanks so that they do not leak, spill, overflow, or leach into groundwater or surface water.*

E.3.1. Do you locate fuel tanks where wet weather will not wash fluids into surface water or cause them to percolate into groundwater? ☐ Yes ☐ No ☐ NA

E.3.2. Do you check and maintain fuel tanks to prevent leaks? ☐ Yes ☐ No ☐ NA

E.3.3. Do you perform fueling activities carefully to avoid overflow and spills? ☐ Yes ☐ No ☐ NA

E.3.4. Do you immediately and properly clean up fuel spills? ☐ Yes ☐ No ☐ NA

❧ **Management Goal E.4:** *Keep the nursery property free of debris and trash so that it does not clog storm drains and litter or pollute waterways and beaches.*

E.4.1. Do you regularly maintain the entire nursery property to keep it clean and free of debris? ☐ Yes ☐ No ☐ NA

E.4.2. Do you ensure that an adequate number of waste containers are available where needed and that they are regularly collected to avoid overflow? ☐ Yes ☐ No ☐ NA

E.4.3. Do you ensure that waste containers are kept in good condition and kept closed? ☐ Yes ☐ No ☐ NA

E.4.4. Do you ensure that waste containers, collection areas, storage areas, and stockpile areas are located indoors or covered when outdoors? ☐ Yes ☐ No ☐ NA

Management Goal E.5: *Maintain restrooms to avoid spills and leakage of fecal coliform from human waste into the municipal storm water system.*

E.5.1. Do you ensure that adequate restrooms and portable toilets are available where needed? ☐ Yes ☐ No ☐ NA

E.5.2. Do you ensure that toilets and floor and sink drains in restrooms are properly hooked up to the sanitary sewer system? ☐ Yes ☐ No ☐ NA

E.5.3. Do you ensure that portable toilets are located where wet weather will not wash waste into a municipal storm water system? ☐ Yes ☐ No ☐ NA

E.5.4. Do you ensure that restrooms and portable toilets are regularly maintained to prevent sewage and human waste from entering a municipal storm water system? ☐ Yes ☐ No ☐ NA

Management Goal E.6: *Provide organized training sessions in waste, sanitation, and spill management for all personnel in a language that they clearly understand, and maintain records documenting training.*

E.6.1. Do you ensure that all employees receive training in proper waste disposal and use of restrooms and mobile toilets? ☐ Yes ☐ No ☐ NA

E.6.2. Are all employees trained on what to do in the event of a spill? ☐ Yes ☐ No ☐ NA

E.6.3. Do you educate and require your employees to recycle all the waste that you can from your nursery operation, such as metal, oil, paper, and plastic? ☐ Yes ☐ No ☐ NA

E.6.4. Do you educate employees in the proper disposal of batteries, paints, and other potentially hazardous materials used in the nursery? ☐ Yes ☐ No ☐ NA

E.6.5. Do you document and maintain records of employee training for a minimum of 5 years? ☐ Yes ☐ No ☐ NA

English–Metric Conversions

English	Conversion factor for English to metric	Conversion factor for metric to English	Metric
Length			
inch (in)	2.54	0.394	centimeter (cm)
foot (ft)	0.3048	3.28	meter (m)
yard (yd)	0.914	1.09	meter (m)
Area			
acre (ac)	0.4047	2.47	hectare (ha)
square inch (in^2)	6.45	0.15	square centimeter (cm^2)
square foot (ft^2)	0.0929	10.764	square meter (m^2)
square mile (mi^2)	2.59	0.386	square kilometer (km^2)
Volume			
fluid ounce	29.57	0.338	milliliter (mL)
gallon (gal)	3.785	0.26	liter (L)
acre-inch (ac-in)	102.8	0.0097	cubic meter (m^3)
acre-foot (ac-ft)	1,233	0.000811	cubic meter (m^3)
cubic foot (ft^3)	28.317	0.353	liter (L)
cubic yard (yd^3)	0.765	1.307	cubic meter (m^3)
gallon per acre	9.36	0.106	liter per hectare (l/ha)
Mass			
ounce (oz)	28.35	0.035	gram (g)
pound (lb)	0.454	2.205	kilogram (kg)
ton (T)	0.907	1.1	metric ton (t)
Pressure			
pound per square inch (psi)	6.89	0.145	kilopascal (kPa)
Temperature			
Fahrenheit (°F)	°C = (°F − 32) ÷ 1.8	°F = (°C x 1.8) + 32	Celsius (°C)

⟪◯⟫ INDEX

erosion

    pollution effects, 3, 4–5, 83

    from wind, 94, 155

    See also runoff

ethylene glycol, 4, 22, 77

evapotranspiration, estimating, 13, 30–31

federal laws, water quality, 2

fertigation, 50, 51–53

fertilizers, pollution effects, 3

    See also nutrient management

field dissipation half-life, defined, 74

filters, runoff, 81–82

filtration, emitter devices, 41, 44

filtration methods, water recycling, 98–102

flocculation, 98

flow measurement, runoff evaluation, 84–85

flushing, emitter devices, 44

foliar analysis, 48, 49*t*

free radicals, 108

fuel tanks, 26, 134, 157

fungus gnats, monitoring, 62

general operations, audit checklist, 116–117

grab sampling, runoff evaluation, 84

grassed waterways, 86, 87, 91–92, 154

gravel beds, sand filtration systems, 100, 101

greenhouse practices. *See specific topics, e.g.,* irrigation practices;

    monitoring programs; runoff

ground covers, 87–88

    See also mulches; vegetative buffers

groundwater ubiquity score (GUS) index, 75

growth regulators

    insects, 69–70

    plant, 4, 21, 77, 79

GUS index (groundwater ubiquity score), 75

heat treatments

    pest management, 18, 66, 68, 150

    water pathogens, 111–112

herbicides, 3, 76–77, 78–79

    See also pesticides

housings, sand filtration systems, 99, 101

hydraulic loading, pesticide leaching, 76

hyperfiltration, 103

identification of pests, 17, 56–57

indicator plants, pest monitoring, 62–63

infiltration, 1, 88–89, 90–91

injection practices, nutrient management, 51–53

inlets, sand filtration systems, 99, 101

insecticides, pollution effects, 3, 5, 20

    See also pesticides

integrated pest management (IPM)

    overview, 6–7, 17–22, 56–57

    audit checklist, 124–125

    control techniques, 65–71, 95–96

    monitoring programs, 57–65, 149

    treatment thresholds, 60–61

ionization, copper, 110–111

IPM. *See* integrated pest management (IPM)

irrigation practices

    overview, 86–87

    audits, 12, 33, 36, 42, 118–120

    backflow prevention, 53

    challenges summarized, 4–5

    efficiency techniques, 36, 39–40

    management goals and practices, 6, 7–8, 12–14

    microirrigation system operations, 29–30, 41–44, 144–147

    performance measures, 30

    for pest control, 67

    photographs, 144–148

    scheduling factors, 13–14, 30–36

    sprinkler system operations, 29, 37–40

    system types, 29–30

    water quality monitoring, 45–46, 152

    See also leaching management; runoff

leaching management

    checklists, 121–122, 130–131

    fertilizers, 5, 15, 48, 50, 51, 148

    irrigation scheduling, 32–33

    pesticides, 75–76, 77–78

leaks. *See* spills, chemical

lime clogging, emitter devices, 44

magnesium, 46

maintenance

    checklists, 118

    filtration systems, 100, 101, 102, 104

    pesticide equipment, 20

    retention ponds, 89, 90

    sprinkler systems, 12–13, 40, 79, 145

    vehicles, 25–26

management goals and practices, overviews

    irrigation, 6, 12–14, 118–120

    nonproduction areas, 8

    nutrients, 6, 14–16

    pesticides, 6–7, 16–22

    runoff and erosion, 7–8, 22–25

COLOR PLATES

Plate 1. MP A.1.1.
The distribution uniformity of this impact sprinkler system is being evaluated using a "catch can" method. *Photo:* A. Ellis.

Plate 2. MP A.1.2.
The impact sprinkler irrigation system originally used in these roses (A) generated too much runoff. The grower converted to a drip system (B) that produces a more uniform distribution of water and less runoff. *Photos:* D. Zurawski.

Plate 3. MP A.1.3.
Pressure regulators deliver water to the system at the appropriate pressure for the system to work efficiently. *Photo:* J. K. Clark.

Plate 4. MP A.1.4.
These pressure compensating emitters deliver a more uniform amount of water to the plants when pressure fluctuates. They also stop drainage from emitters positioned below the system. *Photo:* D. Zurawski.

Plate 5. MP A.2.1.
Irrigation systems should have a regularly scheduled audit to ensure that they are not leaking, as shown above, or clogged. *Photo:* D. Zurawski.

Plate 6. MP A.2.4.
Regular system maintenance includes checking to ensure that appropriate pressure throughout the system is maintained. *Photo:* K. Gilbert.

Plate 7. MP A.3.3.
Emitters outside the pots cause unwanted standing water or runoff.
Photo: D. Zurawski.

Plate 8. MP A.3.4.
Stakes are available that can be "turned off" when not in use (A). These emitters, when properly installed, avoid applying water to noncropped areas (B).
Photos: D. Zurawski.

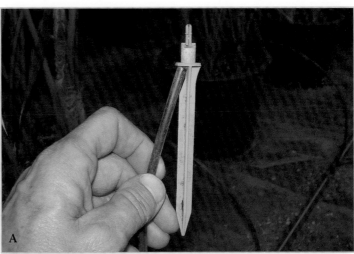

Plate 9. MP A.3.4.
Shut off irrigation in unused crop areas to avoid applying water when not needed. In this photo the overhead irrigation system is watering large areas with no plants.
Photo: D. Zurawski.

Plate 10. MP A.3.5.
Use overhead emitters with check valves to prevent line drainage and drip damage.
Photo: D. Zurawski.

Plate 11. MP A.3.6.
Using an on/off valve in hand-watering helps prevent runoff.
Photo: D. Zurawski.

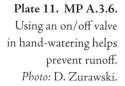

Plate 12. MP A.3.7.
Spray patterns of overhead irrigation systems should not create overspray in walkways and edges, as illustrated here.
Photo: D. Zurawski.

Plate 13. MP A.4.1.
Even a drip system with the potential for high uniformity needs an irrigation schedule based on plant requirements to prevent over-irrigation. *Photo:* D. Zurawski.

Plate 14. MP B.1.1.
Water sampling allows irrigation water to be evaluated for undesirable constituents that can affect crop growth. *Photo:* K. Gilbert.

Plate 15. MP B.2.3.
Top-dressed fertilizers should be applied to keep granules in the pot. When pots are filled to the brim as in this photo, fertilizer runoff and leaching can occur. Spilt substrate on the ground can also be a source of groundwater and surface water contamination. *Photo:* D. Zurawski.

Plate 16. MP B.3.7.
Fertilizer mixing operations should be located on an impermeable surface far away from water sources. *Photo:* D. Zurawski.

Plate 17. MP B.4.1.
Training sessions ensure
that appropriate personnel
understand fertilizer application
techniques and safe handling.
Photo: D. Zurawski.

Plate 18. MP C.1.1.
Ornamental crops are typically
monitored by inspecting plants and
plant parts for pests and damage
(A) and by setting out sticky traps
in the crop. A scout (B) identifies
and counts the number of trapped
insects captured on the yellow sticky
traps and records the information.
Photos: J. K. Clark.

Plate 19. MP C.1.15.
Reducing pesticide use by spraying at the lowest recommended application rate can minimize pesticide loads to the environment. *Photo:* J. K. Clark.

Plate 20. MP C.2.4.
Isolating incoming or new plants from the rest of the production area until they have been thoroughly inspected can prevent the spread of pests. *Photo:* J. K. Clark.

Plate 21. MP C.2.6.
Growing media can be a major source of pathogens unless it is properly treated. In photo A, potting mix in the cart is being pasteurized by piping steam into the bottom of the cart. In photo B, a tarp-covered planting bed is being pasteurized by applying steam through porous pipes laid on top of the bed. Steam is being introduced through the high-pressure hoses in the foreground. *Photos:* J. K. Clark.

Plate 22. MP C.2.9.
Keeping hoses off the ground reduces the spread of pathogens. *Photo:* J. K. Clark.

Plate 23. MP C.5.4.
Calibration of spray equipment helps ensure that pesticides are applied at the desired rate. *Photo:* J. K. Clark.

Example of Water Sampling Results

Constituent	Units	Irrigation 19 Jul 05	Irrigation 13 Sept 05	Storm 17 Oct 05	Storm 4 Apr 06	Irrigation 27 Jun 06	Irrigation 15 Aug 06
Temperature	°C	30.1	22.5	16.1	14.6	21.3	28.9
Dissolved Oxygen	mg/L	7.00	8.36	9.5	9.4	8.11	8.73
Turbidity	NTU	22	38	120	85	18	6
pH		8.14	7.65	7.3	6.41	8.10	8.04
EC	uS/cm	0.76	0.65	0.66	0.66	0.79	1.01
ammonium-N (NH4-N)	mg/L	0.00	0.22	0.27	0.27	0.08	1.44
Nitrate-Nitrite (NO3-N + NO2-N)	mg/L	11.17	4.69	12.64	4.83	10.20	4.33
Nitrite (NO2-N)	mg/L	0.15	0.13	0.22	0.00	0.07	0.14
Nitrate (NO3-N)	mg/L	11.02	4.56	12.42	4.83	10.13	4.19
Ortho-P	mg/L	1.72	2.77	3.05	1.90	0.65	2.45
Total P	mg/L	29.75	44.23	19.56	20.36	66.70	61.25
TSS	mg/L	14.00	85.00	197	44	161	85.0
Pyrethroid Pesticides							
bifenthrin	ng/L	n/d	n/d	n/d	n/d	11	n/d
fenopropathrin	ng/L	n/d	n/d	n/d	n/d	n/d	n/d
cis-pennethrin	ng/L	n/d	n/d	n/d	n/d	n/d	n/d
trans-permethrin	ng/L	n/d	n/d	n/d	n/d	n/d	n/d
cyfluthrin	ng/L	n/d	n/d	n/d	n/d	n/d	n/d
cyfenvalerate	ng/L	n/d	n/d	n/d	n/d	n/d	n/d
deltamethrin	ng/L	n/d	n/d	n/d	n/d	n/d	n/d
Organophosphate Pesticides							
diazinon	ng/L	n/d	n/d	n/d	n/d	811.0	n/d
chlorpyrifos	ng/L	n/d	n/d	n/d	n/d	9.3	n/d
Carbamate Pesticides							
carbaryl	ng/L	n/d	n/d	n/d	n/d	n/d	n/d
Organochlorine Pesticides							
a-BCH	ng/L	n/d	n/d	n/d	n/d	n/d	n/d
g-BCH	ng/L	n/d	n/d	n/d	1.2	n/d	n/d
heptachlor	ng/L	n/d	n/d	n/d	n/d	2.7	n/d
trans-chloradane	ng/L	n/d	n/d	n/d	n/d	n/d	21
p.p. DDE	ng/L	n/d	n/d	n/d	91.4	n/d	n/d
dieldrin	ng/L	n/d	n/d	n/d	n/d	n/d	n/d
p.p. DDD	ng/L	n/d	n/d	n/d	n/d	n/d	n/d
endosulfan sulfate	ng/L	n/d	n/d	n/d	n/d	n/d	n/d
p.p. DDT	ng/L	n/d	n/d	n/d	n/d	n/d	n/d

Plate 24. MP D.1.2 and D.1.3: Water sampling results taken over a year. Samples include both irrigation and storm water runoff to account for seasonal variation. *Source:* A. Ellis.

Example of Water Quality Objectives or Benchmarks

Constituent	Units	Concentration	Notes
Flow	CFS (ft³/sec)		
pH	pH units	6.5-8.5*	
Temperature	°C		The temperature of receiving waters shall not be changed more than 2.7°C (5°F) due to discharge*
Dissolved Oxygen	mg/L	>7.0*	
Turbidity	NTU		Turbidity shall not be increased by more than 20% in receiving waters with 0-50 NTU or by more than 10% in waters with turbidity greater than 50 NTU*
Total Dissolved Solids	mg/L		Waters shall not contain suspended or settable materials in concentrations that cause nuisance or adversely affect beneficial uses.
Chloride	mg/L	~50-150*	Value dependant upon reach of river
Ammonia	mg/L	0.133-35.0*	Value is pH and temperature dependant, and is dependant upon reach of receiving waters. See tables 3.1 to 4.4 in LA Basin Plan
Nitrate-Nitrogen	mg/L	10*^	
Aldrin	ng/L		
Chlordane	ng/L	0.59	
4.4*-DDT	ng/L	0.59	
4.4*-DDD	ng/L	0.84	
DDE	ng/L	0.59	
Dieldrin	ng/L	0.14	
Toxaphene	ng/L	0.75	
Chlorpyrifos	ng/L	25	
Pyrethroids	ng/L		
Diazinon	ng/L	100	
Toxicity, chronic	TU$_c$	1	
Phosphate	mg/L		
Sulfate	mg/L	~250-650	Value dependant upon reach of river
Organophosphate Suite	mg/L		
Organochlorines Suite	mg/L		

These values are as lised in the LARWQCB Ag Waiver. Values denoted with an (*) were obtained in the Basin Plan for the Coastal Watersheds of Los Angeles and Ventura Counties, available online at http://www.swrcb.ca.gov/rwqcb4/html/meetings/tmdl/Basin_plan/basin_plan_doc.html

*^ = The primary drinking water standard for the concentration of nitrogen in the form of nitrate (NO_3^{-1}) is 10ppm, the primary drinking water standard for nitrogen in the form of nitrite (NO_2^{-1}), the std is 1ppm if you were to measure the whole nitrate molecule (including the oxygen) the standard is 45ppm.

Plate 25. MP D.1.4: Runoff sampling results from your property should be compared to the water quality objectives set by your local regional water quality control board. If objectives are not met, investigate and implement appropriate MPs to attain compliance.
Source: Los Angeles Regional Water Quality Board.

Plate 26. MP D.2.3.
Mulches used to cover bare soil can reduce soil runoff and promote infiltration. *Photo:* A. Ellis.

Plate 27. MP D.3.1.
Although runoff is being monitored and measured in this photo, it should not be allowed to flow off the property and into the street. *Photo:* K. Gilbert.

Plate 28. MP D.3.2.
Plants in runoff channels can slow runoff while using some of the conveyed water and nutrients. Photo A is an example of a grass-lined channel. In photo B, runoff drainage channels are used as growing areas for water-loving plants that are also marketed. These plants take up excess water and nutrients that would otherwise be wasted or discharged. *Photos:* D. Zurawski (A); K. Gilbert (B).

Plate 29. MP D.3.2.
Unlined detention basins capture irrigation and storm water runoff, allowing it to evaporate and percolate slowly into the ground. *Photo:* A. Ellis.

Plate 30. MP D.3.3.
Vegetation is a better option than pavement or bare soil for open areas because it can absorb water and prevent the movement of runoff, nutrients, and pesticides. *Photo:* D. Zurawski.

Plate 31. MP D.3.4.
Polyacrylamide (PAM), held in the anchored bag, removes sediment from runoff entering a retention basin. *Photo:* A. Ellis.

Plate 32. MP D.3.5.
A row of trees can be a windbreak to protect crop areas and bare soil from wind erosion. *Photo:* D. Zurawski.

Plate 33. MP D.4.1. and D.4.2.
Terraces and mulch slow water that runs down the hill and also provide erosion control. *Photo:* A. Ellis.

Plate 34. MP D.6.1.
Retention basins. Captured water in a large retention basin (A) is blended with fresh water and reused to irrigate the property. The mid-sized retention basin in photo B has been relined and the sides stabilized with rock riprap. *Photos:* D. Zurawski.

Plate 35. MP D.6.3.
Captured runoff is pumped,
blended with fresh water,
and reused to irrigate crops.
Photo: D. Zurawski.

Plate 36. MG D.7.
Roof runoff is collected and piped
underground to a retention basin,
where it is recycled in the nursery.
Capturing the rainwater from the
roofs prevents contamination that
could occur during overland flow.
Photo: D. Zurawski.

Plate 37. MP E.1.1.
Indoor storage areas are
best cleaned using only "dry"
methods such as sweeping.
Photo: D. Zurawski.

Plate 38. MP E.3.1.
Fuel tanks should be located
where they will not leak into
groundwater or surface water.
Photo: D. Zurawski.

Plate 39. MP E.4.1.
It is important to regularly maintain the entire nursery property to keep it clean and free of debris. Solid waste in channels can be transported to marine areas (A). Debris can cause fatalities for marine life through strangulation or ingestion (B).
Photos: D. Zurawski.